Network Fundamentals, CCNA Exploration Labs and Study Guide

Antoon W. Rufi
Priscilla Oppenheimer
Belle Woodward
Gerlinde Brady

Cisco Press

800 East 96th Street

Indianapolis, Indiana 46240 USA

Network Fundamentals, CCNA Exploration Labs and Study Guide

Antoon W. Rufi, Priscilla Oppenheimer,
Belle Woodward, and Gerlinde Brady

Copyright© 2008 Cisco Systems, Inc.

Published by:
Cisco Press
800 East 96th Street
Indianapolis, IN 46240 USA

Printed in the United States of America

Seventh Printing   July 2011

Library of Congress Cataloging-in-Publication Data:

Library of Congress Cataloging-in-Publication Data

Network fundamentals : CCNA exploration labs and study guide / Antoon W.

Rufi ... [et al.].

   p. cm.

 ISBN 978-1-58713-203-2 (pbk.)

 1. Computer networks--Examinations--Study guides. 2. Electronic data

processing personnel--Certification--Study guides. I. Rufi, Antoon W.

II. Title: CCNA exploration labs and study guide.

 TK5105.5.N46555 2008

 004.6076--dc22

                            2007050396

ISBN-13: 978-1-58713-203-2

ISBN-10: 1-58713-203-6

Publisher
Paul Boger

Associate Publisher
Dave Dusthimer

Cisco Representative
Anthony Wolfenden

Cisco Press Program Manager
Jeff Brady

Executive Editor
Mary Beth Ray

Production Manager
Patrick Kanouse

Development Editor
Dayna Isley

Project Editors
Patrick Kanouse
Jennifer Gallant

Copy Editors
Gayle Johnson
Keith Cline

Technical Editors
Cindy G. Layman
Michael Duane Taylor
Tony Chen

Editorial Assistant
Vanessa Evans

Book and Cover Designer
Louisa Adair

Composition
Mark Shirar

Proofreader
Leslie Joseph

Warning and Disclaimer

This book is designed to provide information about the Network Fundamentals course of the Cisco Network Academy CCNA Exploration curriculum. Every effort has been made to make this book as complete and as accurate as possible, but no warranty or fitness is implied.

The information is provided on an "as is" basis. The authors, Cisco Press, and Cisco Systems, Inc. shall have neither liability nor responsibility to any person or entity with respect to any loss or damages arising from the information contained in this book or from the use of the discs or programs that may accompany it.

The opinions expressed in this book belong to the author and are not necessarily those of Cisco Systems, Inc.

Trademark Acknowledgments

All terms mentioned in this book that are known to be trademarks or service marks have been appropriately capitalized. Cisco Press or Cisco Systems, Inc. cannot attest to the accuracy of this information. Use of a term in this book should not be regarded as affecting the validity of any trademark or service mark.

Corporate and Government Sales

The publisher offers excellent discounts on this book when ordered in quantity for bulk purchases or special sales, which may include electronic versions and/or custom covers and content particular to your business, training goals, marketing focus, and branding interests. For more information, please contact: **U.S. Corporate and Government Sales**   1-800-382-3419 corpsales@pearsontechgroup.com

For sales outside the United States please contact: **International Sales** international@pearsoned.com

Feedback Information

At Cisco Press, our goal is to create in-depth technical books of the highest quality and value. Each book is crafted with care and precision, undergoing rigorous development that involves the unique expertise of members from the professional technical community.

Readers' feedback is a natural continuation of this process. If you have any comments regarding how we could improve the quality of this book, or otherwise alter it to better suit your needs, you can contact us through e-mail at feedback@ciscopress.com. Please make sure to include the book title and ISBN in your message.

We greatly appreciate your assistance.

Americas Headquarters	Asia Pacific Headquarters	Europe Headquarters
Cisco Systems, Inc.	Cisco Systems, Inc.	Cisco Systems International BV
170 West Tasman Drive	168 Robinson Road	Haarlerbergpark
San Jose, CA 95134-1706	#28-01 Capital Tower	Haarlerbergweg 13-19
USA	Singapore 068912	1101 CH Amsterdam
www.cisco.com	www.cisco.com	The Netherlands
Tel: 408 526-4000	Tel: +65 6317 7777	www-europe.cisco.com
800 553-NETS (6387)	Fax: +65 6317 7799	Tel: +31 0 800 020 0791
Fax: 408 527-0883		Fax: +31 0 20 357 1100

Cisco has more than 200 offices worldwide. Addresses, phone numbers, and fax numbers are listed on the Cisco Website at **www.cisco.com/go/offices.**

About the Authors

Antoon "Tony" W. Rufi currently is the associate dean of computer and information science for all the ECPI College of Technology campuses. He also teaches the Cisco Networking Academy CCNA, CCNP, Network Security, Fundamentals of Wireless LAN, and IP Telephony curricula. Before becoming an instructor for ECPI, he spent almost 30 years in the U.S. Air Force, working on numerous electronic projects and computer programs. Tony has a master's degree in information science from the University of Maryland and a bachelor's degree in industrial technology from Southern Illinois University.

Priscilla Oppenheimer is an author and network consultant with more than 25 years of experience in the computer industry. Priscilla has a master's degree in information science from the University of Michigan and has worked at such big-name companies as Apple Computer and Cisco Systems. She currently teaches at Southern Oregon University and provides network consulting to companies in her hometown of Ashland, Oregon, and elsewhere.

Belle Woodward, CCNA, CCAI, CCNP, is an assistant professor in the School of Information Systems and Applied Technologies in the College of Applied Sciences and Arts at Southern Illinois University (SIU) in Carbondale, Illinois. She has more than nine years experience in the networking and network security field. Belle teaches network security, advanced networking, and telecommunications. After redesigning the networking and network security undergraduate curriculum, her students took first place at the 2006 Regional Midwestern Collegiate Cyber Defense Competition (CCDC) and fourth place at the national CCDC. In addition to publishing several journal articles in the network security discipline, Belle has also contributed several chapters included in published network security and networking books.

Gerlinde Brady has been teaching Cisco CCNA and CCNP courses at Cabrillo College, a Cisco Regional Networking Academy, since 1999. She holds a master's degree in education from the University of Hannover, Germany, and a master's degree in translation (English/German) from the Monterey Institute of International Studies. Her IT industry experience includes LAN design, network administration, technical support, and training.

About the Technical Reviewers

Cindy G. Layman has been an instructor at Itawamba Community College in Tupelo, Mississippi, for more than 10 years. She has been teaching programming, computer servicing, and networking courses, including the full CCNA curriculum in the Cisco Networking Academy. Cindy has a bachelor of science degree in mathematics and a bachelor of science degree in computer science, both from Mississippi State University. Before teaching at ICC, she was a programmer analyst for nine years.

Michael Duane Taylor is department head of computer information sciences at the Raleigh Campus of ECPI College of Technology. He has more than seven years of experience teaching introductory networking and CCNA-level curriculum and was awarded the Instructor of the Year Award. Previously, Michael was a lab supervisor with Global Knowledge working with router hardware configuration and repair. He holds a bachelor's degree in business administration from the University of North Carolina at Chapel Hill and a master of science degree in industrial technology/computer network management from East Carolina University. His certifications include CCNA, CCNP-router, and MCSE.

Dedications

I would like to dedicate this book to my wife, Linda, who is instrumental in getting me to apply myself. Always supportive, she has been the catalyst that has kept me going. —*Tony Rufi*

This book is dedicated to my hard-working students who have inspired me to be a better teacher. —*Priscilla Oppenheimer*

This book is dedicated to my husband, Jeff, and son, Alan, whose tireless support helped see me through another project. —*Belle Woodward*

To my wonderful husband, Paddy, and my daughters Fiona, Teresita, and Ejay, who let me take time away from them to be a part of this project. —*Gerlinde Brady*

Acknowledgments

From Tony Rufi:

I'd like to give special recognition to Mike Taylor for his diligent approach to tech editing. He has provided a tremendous amount of input to get the technical aspects of this endeavor correct. I have enjoyed working with him.

I also want to thank Mary Beth Ray; she has been instrumental in allowing me to pursue the dream of authoring a book.

A special thank you to ECPI College of Technology, specifically President Mark Dreyfus, Vice President of Academic Affairs John Olson, and Director of Operations Barbara Larar. Without their support, I would not have been able to write this book.

From Priscilla Oppenheimer:

I'd like to thank Cisco Press for giving me the opportunity to work on this project. I especially want to thank Mary Beth Ray and Dayna Isley for turning this complex project into a success. Thanks also go to our technical reviewers for their persistence and attention to detail. Finally, I'd like to thank the Cisco Networking Academy for developing courses that inspire students to do amazing things with networks.

From Belle Woodward:

It has been a great pleasure to be part of such an outstanding group of professionals, and to these people and everyone on the team I extend my heartfelt thanks. Dayna Isley, thanks for all your help and patience. Cindy and Michael, thanks for providing your expert technical knowledge in editing the book.

I want to give special recognition to Susanne Ashby, a great friend, who has always been willing to read and edit my work.

From Gerlinde Brady:

I would like to thank Dayna Isley and Mary Beth Ray for their unending patience. A special thanks goes to the technical editors, Cindy Layman, Mike Taylor, and Tony Chen, for their diligence and expertise.

Contents at a Glance

Contents

Icons Used in This Book

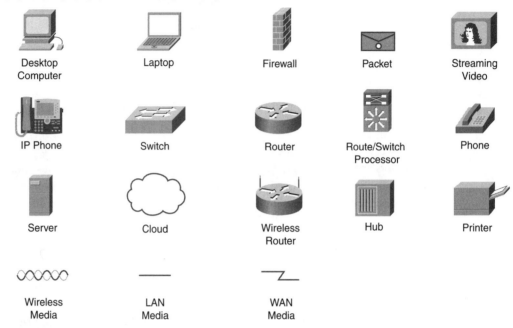

Desktop Computer

Laptop

Firewall

Packet

Streaming Video

IP Phone

Switch

Router

Route/Switch Processor

Phone

Server

Cloud

Wireless Router

Hub

Printer

Wireless Media

LAN Media

WAN Media

Command Syntax Conventions

The conventions used to present command syntax in this book are the same conventions used in the IOS Command Reference. The Command Reference describes these conventions as follows:

- **Boldface** indicates commands and keywords that are entered literally as shown. In actual configuration examples and output (not general command syntax), boldface indicates commands that are manually input by the user (such as a **show** command).

- *Italics* indicate arguments for which you supply actual values.

- Vertical bars (|) separate alternative, mutually exclusive elements.

- Square brackets [ ] indicate optional elements.

- Braces { } indicate a required choice.

- Braces within brackets [{ }] indicate a required choice within an optional element.

Introduction

The Cisco Networking Academy is a comprehensive e-learning program that provides students with Internet technology skills. A Networking Academy delivers web-based content, online assessment, student performance tracking, and hands-on labs to prepare students for industry-standard certifications. The CCNA Exploration curriculum includes four courses oriented around the topics of the Cisco Certified Network Associate (CCNA) certification.

Network Fundamentals, CCNA Exploration Labs and Study Guide is a supplement to your classroom and laboratory experience with the Cisco Networking Academy. To be successful on the exam and achieve your CCNA certification, you should do everything in your power to arm yourself with a variety of tools and training materials to support your learning efforts. This Labs and Study Guide is just such a collection of tools. Used to its fullest extent, it will help you gain knowledge and practice the skills associated with the content areas of the CCNA Exploration Network Fundamentals course.

Goals and Methods

First and foremost, this book is designed to help you learn all the required materials of the first course in the Networking Academy CCNA Exploration curriculum. By establishing a firm foundation in the fundamental topics taught in this course, you will be better prepared to move on to the rest of the CCNA Exploration curriculum and ultimately to pass the CCNA certification exam (640-802). Passing this foundation exam means that you not only have the required knowledge of the technologies covered by the exam, but also that you can plan, design, implement, operate, and troubleshoot these technologies. In other words, these exams are rigorously application based. You can view the exam topics any time at http://www.cisco.com/go/certifications.

The Study Guide sections of this book offer dozens of exercises to help you learn the concepts crucial to your success as a CCNA exam candidate. Each chapter is slightly different and includes multiple-choice, fill-in-the-blank, matching, and open-ended questions designed to help you

- Review vocabulary
- Strengthen troubleshooting skills
- Boost networking skills
- Reinforce concepts
- Research topics

Each chapter also includes a Labs and Activities section that includes the online curriculum labs and a Packet Tracer Skills Integration Challenge activity.

Many of the hands-on labs include Packet Tracer companion activities, where you can use Packet Tracer to complete a simulation of the lab.

Each chapter also includes a culminating activity called the Packet Tracer Skills Integration Challenge. These activities require you to pull together several skills learned from the chapter—and previous chapters and courses—to successfully complete one comprehensive exercise.

A Word About Packet Tracer

Packet Tracer is a self-paced, visual, interactive teaching and learning tool developed by Cisco. Lab activities are an important part of networking education. However, lab equipment can be a scarce resource. Packet Tracer provides a visual simulation of equipment and network processes to offset the challenge of limited equipment. Students can spend as much time as they like completing standard lab exercises through Packet Tracer, and have the option to work from home. Although Packet Tracer is not a substitute for real equipment, it allows students to practice using a command-line interface. This "e-doing" capability is a fundamental component of learning how to configure routers and switches from the command line.

Packet Tracer version 4.x is available only to Cisco Networking Academies through the Academy Connection website.

A Word About Eagle Server

The CCNA Exploration courses are designed to provide a hands-on learning approach to networking. The top-down approach adopted in the Network Fundamentals course enables students to set up and implement application layer services in a network lab environment.

Many of the hands-on labs in Network Fundamentals are based on an Internet model that uses a local server to provide a range of network services and applications that students can experiment with in the lab environment. The Eagle Server is developed by the Cisco Networking Academy to provide network services and applications that are typically accessed over the Internet in an isolated lab environment.

The Eagle Server provides the following network services:

- DNS
- Web server
- FTP
- TFTP
- SSH
- Instant messaging
- Wiki server
- E-mail

The Eagle Server is required to complete most of the labs in CCNA Exploration. The Eagle Server software and complete FAQ documentation can be downloaded by your instructor from the Tools section of Academy Connection. Your instructor needs to follow those instructions to set up the labs for you accordingly.

Audience for This Book

This book's main audience is anyone taking the CCNA Exploration Network Fundamentals course of the Cisco Networking Academy curriculum. Many academies use this textbook as a required tool in the course, while other academies recommend the Companion Guides as an additional source of study and practice materials.

How This Book Is Organized

Because the content of *Network Fundamentals, CCNA Exploration Companion Guide* and the online curriculum is sequential, you should work through this Lab Study Guide in order, beginning with Chapter 1.

The book covers the major topic headings in the same sequence as the online curriculum for the CCNA Exploration Network Fundamentals course. This book has 11 chapters, with the same numbers and similar names as the online course chapters.

Chapters and Topics

The book has 11 chapters, as follows:

- **Chapter 1, "Living in a Network-Centric World,"** provides exercises and labs to supplement your study of the basics of communication and how networks support the way we live. The questions in the chapter focus on network architectures, network components, scalability, quality of service (QoS), security issues, and network collaboration tools. Activities and labs let you practice your skills using and configuring network applications such as Google Earth, Internet Relay Chat, blogs, wikis, and Packet Tracer.

- **Chapter 2, "Communicating over the Network,"** introduces the devices, media, and protocols that enable network communication. The Study Guide portion of this chapter uses different types of questions to test your knowledge of how devices communicate over the network. The Lab Exercises portion of this chapter includes all the online curriculum labs to further reinforce that you have mastered the practical, hands-on skills needed to use some critical tools, such as Wireshark, to help evaluate network communications.

- **Chapter 3, "Application Layer Functionality and Protocols,"** introduces you to the top network model layer, the application layer. Work through the different types of questions to test your knowledge of the TCP/IP application and OSI application, presentation, and session layer. The labs further reinforce that you have mastered the skills needed to work with the application layer of the OSI model.

- **Chapter 4, "OSI Transport Layer,"** provides exercises and labs that focus on the role of the transport layer as it provides the end-to-end transfer of data between applications. You learn how TCP and UDP apply to common applications.

- **Chapter 5, "OSI Network Layer,"** introduces the concepts of routing packets from a device on one network to a device on a different network. The questions and labs help you reinforce important concepts related to addressing, path determination, data packets, and IP.

- **Chapter 6, "Addressing the Network: IPv4,"** focuses on network addressing in detail and tests your knowledge of how to use the address mask, or prefix length, to determine the number of subnetworks and hosts in a network. This chapter also includes questions and labs related to Internet Control Message Protocol (ICMP) tools, such as ping and trace.

- **Chapter 7, "OSI Data Link Layer,"** supplements your study of how the OSI data link layer prepares network layer packets for transmission. This chapter tests your ability to describe the encapsulation processes that occur as data travels across a LAN and a WAN. The chapter also helps you study Media Access Control (MAC) and MAC addressing. A hands-on lab lets you practice your skills using Wireshark to capture and analyze Ethernet frames. A Packet Tracer skills integration lab provides an opportunity to practice IP subnetting, and building and configuring a complex network.

- **Chapter 8, "OSI Physical Layer,"** provides questions and labs that explore the functions, standards, and protocols associated with the physical layer (Layer 1). Use this chapter to reinforce that you have mastered the practical, hands-on skills needed to understand and work with the OSI physical layer.

- **Chapter 9, "Ethernet,"** examines the technologies and operation of Ethernet. Topics include the evolution of Ethernet technologies, MAC, and Address Resolution Protocol (ARP). This chapter continues the examination of Ethernet frames that you started in Chapter 7, with a focus on ARP frames. The chapter also helps you develop skills related to examining Cisco switch MAC address tables. A Packet Tracer skills integration lab lets you simulate the steps of installing an Ethernet card in a PC, connecting it to a switch, and setting speed and duplex settings.

- **Chapter 10, "Planning and Cabling Networks,"** focuses on designing and cabling a network. You will apply the knowledge and skills developed in the previous chapters to determine the appropriate cables to use, how to connect devices, and how to develop an addressing and testing scheme.

- **Chapter 11, "Configuring and Testing Your Network,"** provides questions and extensive, challenging labs that ask you to connect and configure a small network using basic Cisco IOS commands for routers and switches. You will configure Cisco routers and switches for basic network operations.

About the CD-ROM

The CD-ROM included with this book has all the Packet Tracer Activity, Packet Tracer Companion, and Packet Tracer Challenge files that are referenced throughout the book as indicated by the Packet Tracer Activity, Packet Tracer Companion, and Packet Tracer Challenge icons.

You can obtain updates to these files from the website for this book, http://www.ciscopress.com/title/1587132036. The files will be updated to cover any subsequent releases of Packet Tracer.

About the Cisco Press Website for This Book

Cisco Press may provide additional content that can be accessed by registering your individual book at the Ciscopress.com website. Becoming a member and registering is free, and you then gain access to exclusive deals on other resources from Cisco Press.

To register this book, go to http://www.ciscopress.com/bookstore/register.asp and enter the book's ISBN, which is located on its back cover. You'll then be prompted to log in or join Ciscopress.com to continue registration.

After you register the book, a link to any supplemental content will be listed on your My Registered Books page.

Living in a Network-Centric World

The Study Guide portion of this chapter uses a combination of matching, fill-in-the-blank, multiple-choice, and open-ended questions to test your knowledge of the importance of data networks and the major components and characteristics of network architectures.

The Labs and Activities portion of this chapter includes all the online curriculum activities and labs to ensure that you have mastered the practical, hands-on skills needed to understand the opportunities and challenges associated with modern networks.

As you work through this chapter, use Chapter 1 in the Network Fundamentals CCNA Exploration online curriculum or the corresponding Chapter 1 in *Network Fundamentals, CCNA Exploration Companion Guide* for assistance.

Study Guide

Communicating in a Network-Centric World

Humans are social animals who need to communicate with each other. Communication was once limited to face-to-face conversations, but it has evolved over the years to encompass many types of media, ranging from paper to fiber-optic cabling. High-speed data networks that span the globe with cabling and networking devices have had a profound effect on human communication and will continue to revolutionize how humans interact with each other.

Concept Questions

1. In addition to data networks, what other breakthroughs in communication media have extended the reach of human interactions?

   _____

   _____

2. How has data networking changed your community (your family, school, city, or country?)

   _____

3. Early data networks carried character-based messages between computer systems. What types of network traffic do modern networks carry, and how has this changed human interactions?

   _____

   _____

   _____

   _____

Vocabulary Exercise: Completion

Fill in the blanks in the following questions.

1. _____ is a form of online real-time communication between two or more people based on entered text.

2. A _____ is a web page that is easy to update and edit by someone who wants to publish a record of his or her thoughts on a subject.

3. A _____ is a web page that groups of people can edit and view together.

4. _____ is an audio-based medium that lets people record audio and publish it on a website.

5. _____ is a Cisco collaborative learning tool that provides a way to build virtual representations of networks that behave much like actual networks.

Communication: An Essential Part of Our Lives

Communication helps us work, play, and learn. Because communication is so important, communication networks include rules (or protocols) that help ensure reliable delivery of messages. Rules help data networks function despite the many factors that can degrade communication. Factors that are external to the message can affect reliability, as can internal factors that are related to aspects of the message itself.

Concept Questions

1. List four external factors that affect data networks.

   _____

   _____

   _____

   _____

2. List three internal factors that affect data networks.

   _____

   _____

   _____

The Network as a Platform

Data networks provide a platform for humans to communicate and thus play an increasingly important role in the business and personal lives of humans. Modern networks support fast and reliable message transfer among millions of users across the globe. To achieve the scale, speed, and reliability that are required, network experts have standardized many elements and components of a data network.

Vocabulary Exercise: Define

Table 1-1 lists the four fundamental elements of a network. Fill in the definition for each element.

Table 1-1   Network Element Definitions

Element	Definition
Rule	
Medium	
Message	
Device	

Vocabulary Exercise: Identify

Networks consist of many elements. Network engineers often include these elements in network topology drawings. Engineers use a set of standard icons to refer to the elements. Figure 1-1 shows some of these icons. The figure shows a network topology for a typical small company.

Figure 1-1   Network Topology Icons

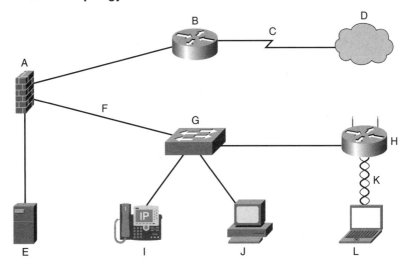

Provide the name of each element in the network topology shown in Figure 1-1.

A _____

B _____

C _____

D _____

E _____

F _____

G _____

H _____

I _____

J _____

K _____

L _____

Vocabulary Exercise: Matching

In Table 1-2, match the term on the left with its definition on the right.

Table 1-2   Network Devices

Device	Definition
a. Switch	__ One form of a wide-area network (WAN) connection
b. Firewall	__ Interconnects computers and cabling to form a local-area network (LAN)
c. Router	__ Summarizes a group of network elements in topology drawings
d. Wireless router	__ A device often found in home and small networks that lets laptop computers connect to a network without cabling
e. Cloud	__ Connects two or more networks and directs messages as they travel across a set of networks
f. Serial link	__ Provides network security

Vocabulary Exercise: Completion

Fill in the blanks in the following questions.

1. In wired connections, the medium is either _____, which carries data in the form of electrical signals, or _____, which carries data in the form of light signals.

2. Wireless media include the wireless connection between a _____ and a computer in a home network, the _____ wireless connection between two ground stations, or the communication between devices on Earth and _____ in orbit.

3. Network _____ such as web browsing, e-mail, and instant messaging require a network to provide _____.

4. _____ are the rules that network devices use to communicate.

5. _____ is a set of standard protocols that is widely used in home and business networks as well as on the Internet.

6. Messages must be converted to _____ (binary coded digital signals) before they are sent to their destination.

Concept Questions

1. List the steps that take place on a network when you send an instant message.

_____

_____

_____

_____

_____

_____

2. What is meant by the term *converged network*, and why are converged networks becoming so common? What advantages do converged networks offer?

_____

_____

_____

_____

_____

_____

The Architecture of the Internet

A network architecture describes a network's physical infrastructure and the high-level services and protocols that move messages across that infrastructure. The Internet's architecture shares many of the same characteristics of any large network that supports numerous users. Business networks, education networks, and the Internet must provide fault tolerance, scalability, quality of service, and security. Many large networks, including the Internet, are also hierarchical, with different tiers offering different levels of service.

Vocabulary Exercise: Define

Table 1-3 lists four fundamental characteristics of network architectures. Fill in the definition for each characteristic.

Table 1-3   Network Architecture Characteristics

Characteristic	Definition
Fault tolerance	
Scalability	
Quality of service	
Security	

Concept Questions

1. Why was fault tolerance a major focus of the initial design for the Internet?

2. Compare and contrast circuit switching and packet switching. Why did the Internet designers choose packet switching instead of circuit switching?

3. How does the Internet benefit from using a hierarchical architecture?

4. List some applications that are time-sensitive and the negative consequences of their packets getting dropped or delayed.

— Telephone — in case of emergency
— check in process at airline — delay could offline & plane will get delayed
— Bank getting info, ↳ need info quickly.
— email.

5. List some consequences of a network security breach.

— N/W outrage
— Loss of personal or business fund
— Identity theft
— Exposure of confidential customer data
— attacks scams virus.
maintain entigrity

Vocabulary Exercise: Completion

Fill in the blanks in the following questions.

1. The two types of network security concerns are network _____ security, which protects devices and cabling, and _____ security, which protects the information carried in packets and stored on network-attached devices.

2. Tools to provide security for individual messages must be implemented on top of the underlying _____, which are the rules that govern how packets are formatted, addressed, and delivered.

3. Three fundamental security measures include ensuring _____ so that only intended and authorized recipients can read data, maintaining _____ to ensure that information is not altered in transmission, and ensuring _____ so that timely and reliable access to services is not disrupted by security breaches.

4. Network _____ can help ensure system reliability by detecting, repelling, and coping with network attacks.

Trends in Networking

Data networks continue to evolve quickly. Modern networks need to be ready to support increasing numbers of users who will make innovative use of the networks to enhance human communication. Networks will need to be scalable, fault-tolerant, and flexible as users continue to depend on their networks to help them live, learn, work, and play.

Multiple-Choice Questions

Choose the best answer for each of the following questions.

1. Which of the following are major trends that are contributing to the current evolution of networks? (Choose two.)

   a. The increasing number of mobile users

   b. Fewer services as networks converge

   c. Fewer applications as networks converge

   d. Increasing use of simplified network devices

   e. The need to protect networks from unauthorized access

   f. The need to support circuit switching

2. Which of the following is most associated with the concept of converged networks?

   a. More users wanting to access web pages in character mode

   b. More voice and video transmissions that require a level of consistent quality and uninterrupted delivery

   c. More networks that are locked down so that new applications and services cannot be added

   d. More networks that are open and unconcerned with protection from unauthorized access

3. Which of the following is a relatively new information technology (IT) job title?

   a. Programmer

   b. Information security officer

   c. Network technician

   d. Software engineer

4. Which of the following best defines a fault-tolerant network?

   a. A fault-tolerant network supports users who have different viewpoints.

   b. A fault-tolerant network limits the impact of hardware or software failures and recovers quickly when a failure occurs.

   c. A fault-tolerant network can expand quickly to support new users and applications without causing errors for existing users.

   d. A fault-tolerant network is built to withstand earthquakes.

5. Which of the following best defines a scalable network?

   a. A scalable network is built to support high-altitude environments, including skyscrapers and satellite dishes on mountains.

   b. A scalable network supports redundant connections so that alternative paths are available when a device or link fails.

   c. A scalable network can expand quickly to support new users and applications without impacting the performance of the service being offered to existing users.

   d. A scalable network ensures that priorities are matched with the type of communication and its importance to an organization.

Labs and Activities

 ## Activity 1-1: Using Google Earth to View the World (1.1.1.4)

Upon completion of this activity, you will be able to

- Explain the purpose of Google Earth.
- Explain the different versions of Google Earth.
- Explain the hardware and software requirements needed to use Google Earth (free edition).
- Experiment with Google Earth features such as Help and Tutorial.
- Experiment with Google Earth to explore continents, countries, and places of interest.

Background

Google Earth is a popular application that executes on the desktop of most operating systems; it requires a broadband connection to the Internet. Google Earth displays the Earth as a manipulated 2D or 3D image. The popular world news channel CNN regularly uses Google Earth to show where a news story has occurred.

Currently, three versions of Google Earth exist. The version that fits most needs is the free version, Google Earth. The Google Earth Plus version includes GPS support, a spreadsheet importer, and other support features. The Google Earth Pro version is for professional and commercial use. The URL http://earth.google.com/product_comparison.html contains a description of the versions. Use this link to answer the following questions:

1. Which versions support Tilt and 3D rotation?

   _____

2. Which Google Earth version supports the highest resolution?

   _____

To use Google Earth, version 4, the following minimum computer hardware requirements must be met:

- **Operating system:** Microsoft Windows 2000 or Windows XP
- **CPU:** Pentium 3 with 500 MHz
- **System memory (RAM):** 128 MB
- **Hard disk:** 400 MB of free space
- **Network speed:** 128 kbps
- **Graphics card:** 3D-capable with 16 MB of video RAM (VRAM)
- **Screen:** 1024×768 pixels, 16-bit high-color screen

Scenario

This activity is to be performed on a computer that has Internet access and on which you can install software.

Estimated completion time, depending on network speed, is 30 minutes.

Task 1: Install Google Earth

If Google Earth is not installed on the computer, you can download the free application from http://earth.google.com/download-earth.html. Follow the installation instructions, and the Google Earth download should start automatically. Remember, you may have to disable any popup blockers on your browser. Figure 1-2 shows the opening screen for Google Earth.

Figure 1-2   Google Earth Opening Screen

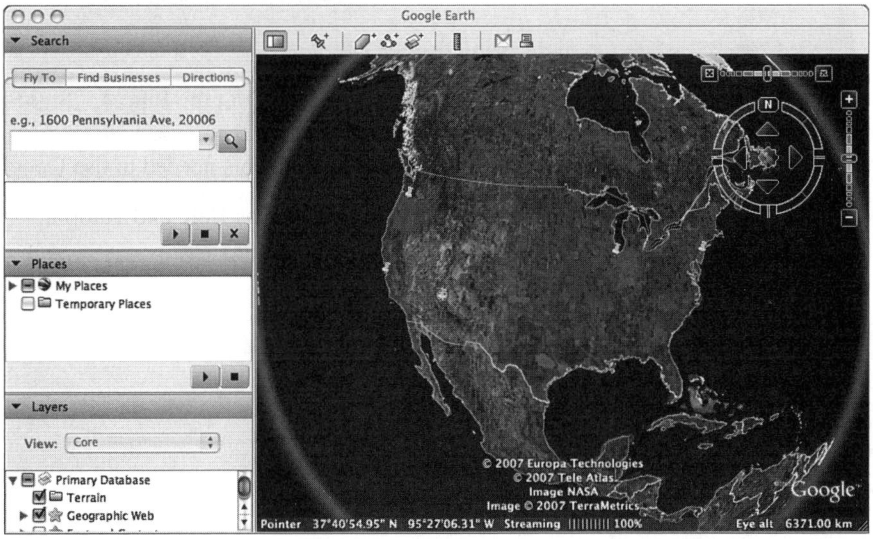

Task 2: Run Google Earth

Refer to Figure 1-2, the opening screen. The Menu bar is located in the upper-left corner. On the Help menu, choose **User Guide** to launch a default web browser and bring up the Google Earth User's Guide (http://earth.google.com/userguide/v4/). Take a few minutes to browse the User's Guide. Before leaving the User's Guide website, answer the following questions:

1. List the three ways to move the image.

   _____

2. Which mouse control zooms in and out?

   _____

3. What is the purpose of the left mouse button?

   _____

Task 3: Navigate the Google Earth Interface

Step 1:   Use the Overview Map feature.

Choose **View > Overview Map**. This handy feature provides a relative global position of the magnified image.

Step 2:   Review the navigation controls.

The navigation controls, shown in Figure 1-3, are located in the upper-right quadrant. They control the image magnification and position. The mouse pointer must be moved close to the controls; otherwise, only a compass is displayed.

Figure 1-3   Google Earth Screen Navigation Tools

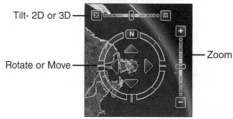

Step 3:   Use the Sightseeing feature.

On the left navigation bar, experiment with the **Places > Sightseeing** folder. Expand Sightseeing, choose a location that you want to see, and double-click that location. The image takes you to that site. When the location has been reached, an image streaming indicator reports when the image resolution is complete.

Step 4:   Experiment with the **Search > Fly To** folder.

Enter 95134, a U.S. zip code.

What U.S. state and city are displayed?

_____

What if you would like to "Fly To" London, UK? What data would you need to enter?

_____

Step 5:   Use the Fly To feature.

Some locations have better resolution than others, and some location images are older than others. For example, one user commented that he found his home, but the new house next door had not yet been built. Try to find your home using the **Search > Fly To** folder.

Is the resolution for your home the same quality as the Sightseeing location in Step 3?

_____

If the resolution for your neighborhood is sufficient, browse the surrounding area to see if you can determine approximately how old the image is.

Step 6:   View geographic coordinates.

Geographic coordinates are displayed in the lower-left quadrant of the image. The first number is called the *latitude*; it's the angle between a point and the equator. For example, the equator is an imaginary line dividing the globe into a Northern and Southern Hemisphere. The equator has a 0° latitude. The second number is called the *longitude*; it's the angle east or west of an arbitrary earth point. The Royal Observatory, United Kingdom, is the international zero-longitude point. The combined longitude and latitude are called the *common graticule*. Common graticule is the grid created by the longitude and latitude lines as depicted on a globe. The coordinate measurements are in degrees, minutes, seconds, and tenths. For latitude, the reference is North (N) or South (S) of the equator. For longitude, the reference is East (E) or West (W) of the Royal Observatory.

Choose **View > Grid** to display Google Earth Gridlines.

Using the pointer and coordinates shown in the lower-left quadrant of the image, what are the coordinates of your home?

_____

Task 4: Reflection

Google Earth can bring the world into your home or office. While enjoying the images, consider what digital communication resources were used. For example, satellite communication with an Earth station transmitted the image of your home to a ground location. Some type of database was used to store the image. A LAN sent your image request across the Internet, probably through several WANs and then to another LAN with a computer that returned the image to you. The delay in retrieving the image may have been short or long, depending on the slowest speed of all network connections in the path between the database repository and your computer.

Could the image be displayed faster if data compression techniques were used?

Consider network security. Could someone eavesdrop on your network connection?

Task 5: Challenge

Google Earth displays image coordinates in the lower-left quadrant of the image. Use the following URL to learn about different coordinate systems: http://www.colorado.edu/geography/gcraft/notes/coordsys/coordsys.html. Wikipedia also contains a useful definition of common geographic terms.

Use the geographic coordinate system to describe your home with as much accuracy and detail as possible.

Task 6: Clean Up

You may be required to remove Google Earth from the computer. If so, follow these steps:

Step 1.   Choose **Start > Settings > Control Panel**.

Step 2.   Double-click **Add or Remove Programs**.

Step 3.   Locate and click **Google Earth**.

Step 4.   Click **Remove** and follow the prompts.

Additional removal information is available at http://earth.google.com/support/bin/answer.py?answer=20738&ctx=sibling.

Unless instructed otherwise, turn off the computer.

Activity 1-2: Identifying Top Security Vulnerabilities (1.4.5.3)

Upon completion of this activity, you will be able to

- Use the SANS site to quickly identify Internet security threats.

- Explain how threats are organized.

- List several recent security vulnerabilities.

- Use the SANS links to access other security-related information.

Background

One of the most popular and trusted sites related to defending against computer and network security threats is SANS. SANS stands for SysAdmin, Audit, Network, Security. SANS contains several components, each a major contributor to information security. For additional information about the SANS site, go to http://www.sans.org/ and select items from the Resources menu.

How can a corporate security administrator quickly identify security threats? SANS and the FBI have compiled their list of the top 20 Internet Security Attack Targets at http://www.sans.org/top20/. The list is regularly updated with information related to the following:

- **Operating systems:** Windows, UNIX/Linux, Mac

- **Applications:** Cross-platform, including web, database, peer-to-peer, instant messaging, media players, DNS servers, backup software, and management servers

- **Network devices:** Network infrastructure devices (routers, switches, and so on), VoIP devices

- **Human elements:** Security policies, human behavior, personnel issues

- **Special section:** Security issues not related to any of the preceding categories

Scenario

This activity introduces you to computer security vulnerabilities. You will use the SANS website as a tool for threat vulnerability identification, understanding, and defense. You must complete this lab outside of the Cisco lab from a computer with Internet access.

Estimated completion time is one hour.

Task 1: Locate the SANS Resources

Step 1.   Open the SANS Top 20 List.

Using a web browser, go to http://www.sans.org. On the **resources** menu, choose **top 20 list**, as shown in Figure 1-4.

Figure 1-4   SANS Menu

The SANS Top-20 Internet Security Attack Targets list is organized by category. A letter indicates the category type, and numbers separate category topics. Router and switch topics fall under the Network Devices category, **N**. There are two major hyperlink topics:

- N1. VoIP Servers and Phones

- N2. Network and Other Devices Common Configuration Weaknesses

Step 2:   Click hyperlink N2. Network and Other Devices Common Configuration Weaknesses to jump to this topic.

Task 2: Review the SANS Resources

Step 1.   Review the contents of N2.2 Common Default Configuration Issues.

For example, N2.2.2 (as of this writing) contains information about threats associated with default accounts and values. Open Google and search on **wireless router passwords** to return links to multiple sites that publish a list of wireless router default administrator account names and passwords. Failure to change the default password on these devices can lead to compromise and vulnerability by attackers.

Step 2.   Note the CVE references.

The last line under several topics' references is Common Vulnerability Exposure (CVE). The CVE name is linked to the National Institute of Standards and Technology (NIST) National Vulnerability Database (NVD), sponsored by the Department of Homeland Security (DHS) National Cyber Security Division and US-CERT, which contains information about the vulnerability.

Task 3: Collect Data

The remainder of this lab walks you through a vulnerability investigation and solution.

Step 1:   Choose a topic to investigate, and click a sample CVE hyperlink.

Note: Because the CVE list changes, the current list may not contain the same vulnerabilities as those that were present at the time of this writing.

The link should open a new web browser connected to http://nvd.nist.gov/ and the vulnerability summary page for the CVE.

Fill in the following information about the vulnerability:

Original release date: _____

Last revised: _____

Source: _____

Overview: _____

Step 2.   Under the Impact heading are several values. The Common Vulnerability Scoring System (CVSS) severity is displayed. It contains a value between 1 and 10.

Fill in information about the vulnerability impact:

CVSS Severity: _____

Range: _____

Authentication: _____

Impact Type: _____

Step 3.   The next heading, References to Advisories, Solutions, and Tools, contains links with information about the vulnerability and possible solutions. Using the hyperlinks, write a brief description of the solution as found on those pages.

_____

_____

Task 4: Reflection

The number of vulnerabilities for computers, networks, and data continues to increase. Governments have dedicated significant resources to coordinating and disseminating information about the vulnerability and possible solutions. It remains the responsibility of the end user to implement the solution. Think of ways that users can help strengthen security. Think about user habits that create security risks.

Task 5: Challenge

Try to identify an organization that will meet with you to explain how vulnerabilities are tracked and solutions are applied. Finding an organization willing to do this may be difficult, for security reasons, but this will provide beneficial information about how vulnerability mitigation is accomplished in the world. It will also give representatives of the organization an opportunity to meet the class and conduct informal intern interviews.

Lab 1-1: Using Collaboration Tools: IRC and IM (1.6.1.1)

Upon completion of this lab, you will be able to

- Define Internet Relay Chat (IRC) and Instant Messaging (IM).

- List several collaborative uses of IM.

- List several misuses of and data security issues involving IM.

- Use IRC to demonstrate collaboration.

Background

E-mail permits multiple users to collaborate, share ideas, and transfer files. However, unless the user constantly monitors the e-mail account, unread e-mail may go unnoticed for a long period of time. When people have wanted immediate contact, the telephone has been the technology of choice. Unfortunately, the telephone cannot be used to transfer files. What collaborators need for communication in the human network is a tool that has the flexibility of e-mail with the responsiveness of the telephone. IRC and IM fit nicely into these requirements. Using the Internet or a private corporate network, users can easily exchange ideas and files. IMing and chatting are both methods of real-time communication; however, they are implemented differently.

IM provides one-on-one communication with "accepted" individuals. To initiate an instant message, one person needs to "invite" another. The recipient of the invitation knows about—and accepts—the IM session based on the other user's screen name. IM clients allow you to have an approved list of users, often called a Buddy List. If you want to communicate with more than one person at a time, you can open additional IM windows. Each of these windows represents a two-person communication.

IRC, on the other hand, allows multiple people to interact. Chat also provides a degree of anonymity. To start chatting, you establish a connection to a Chat server and join a discussion on a particular topic. When you join, you are said to "join a room." In the chat room, you typically create your own identity and can give as little information about yourself as you choose.

Although the following discussion focuses primarily on IM, a brief hands-on lab will demonstrate the ease of IRC.

IM requires a device providing services that allows users to communicate. This device is called the *Instant Messenger Server*. The users on the end devices, such as a computer, use a piece of software called the *Instant Messenger Client*. This arrangement is called a client/server relationship. IM clients connect to an IM server, and the server joins clients. This relationship is called an IM network. Many different IM networks are available, each with a dedicated following of users. Popular IM networks include America OnLine (AOL) Instant Messenger (AIM), Windows Live Messenger (MSN), Yahoo! Messenger, and ICQ (I Seek You). Figure 1-5 shows the AIM client application connected to the AIM network.

Figure 1-5   AIM Client

Features

IM services have several common features:

- When an IM client connects to the IM network, any existing connections can be alerted through a contact list—a list of other people that you communicate with through the IM client.

- File sharing between IM clients enables work collaboration.

- Text messaging between clients is possible and can be logged.

- Some IM networks offer audio services.

- Newer services that some IM networks are beginning to provide include videoconferencing, Voice over IP (VoIP), web conferencing, desktop sharing, and even IP radio and IPTV.

Protocols

Each IM network uses an agreed-upon method of communication, called a protocol. Many of the IM networks use proprietary protocols. AIM and ICQ (purchased by AOL) use the proprietary Open System for Communication in Real Time (OSCAR) protocol. Both Microsoft and Yahoo! have proprietary protocols but have partnered services for joint connectivity.

Throughout this course we will learn about many different protocols. The Internet Engineering Task Force (IETF) has attempted to standardize IM protocols, notably with Session Initiation Protocol (SIP). SIPv2 was originally defined in RFC 2543 and was made obsolete by RFC 3261. As with proprietary IM protocols, numerous open-source protocols exist.

Some IM client applications, such as Gaim and Trillian, can differentiate between the various IM network protocols; IM servers can also incorporate this support. The IETF formalized an open standard, Jabber, based on the Extensible Messaging and Presence Protocol (EMPP). Applicable IETF references are RFC 3920 and RFC 3921. Encrypted communication is supported.

Social misuse of IM has been a concern for parents, and many IM networks encourage parental control. Child restrictions include limiting IM contacts and providing supervision while online. AIM and

Yahoo! Messenger provide free supervision software tools. Some parental supervision tools include background logging, online time limits, chat room blocking, blocking specific users, and disabling certain functions of the client.

Security

Multiple security issues have been identified with IM. As a result, many organizations either limit or block IM from entering the corporate network. Computer worms, viruses, and Trojan horses, categorized as malware, have been transferred to IM client computers. Without strong security methods, information exchanged between users can be captured and disclosed. IM clients and IM servers have experienced application vulnerabilities, which have resulted in vulnerable computers. Even legitimate users can congest network throughput by transferring large files.

The SANS Institute recommends several countermeasures that system administrators can use to protect their networks from IM vulnerabilities and misuse. The following list is from the SANS website at http://www.sans.org/top20/#c4:

C4.4 How to Protect Against IM Vulnerabilities and Unauthorized IM Usage

- Establish policies for acceptable use of IM. Ensure that all users are aware of those policies and clearly understand the potential risks.

- Standard users should not be permitted to install software. Restrict Administrative and Power User level privileges to support personnel acting in their support capacity. If a user must have Administrative or Power User privileges, create a separate account to be used for his or her daily office functions, Internet surfing, and online communication.

- Ensure that vendor patches are promptly applied to IM software, interrelated applications, and the underlying operating system.

- Employ antivirus and antispyware products.

- Do not rely on external IM servers for internal use of IM; provide a commercial-grade IM proxy or internal IM server.

- Create secure communication paths when using IM with trusted business partners.

- Appropriately configure intrusion detection and prevention systems. Understand that many IM applications can enable associated communications to masquerade as otherwise legitimate traffic (for example, HTTP).

- Consider deploying products specifically designed for IM security.

- Filter all HTTP traffic through an authenticating proxy server to provide additional capabilities of filtering and monitoring IM traffic.

- Block access to known public IM servers that have not been explicitly authorized. (Note: This offers only partial protection because of the number of potential external servers.)

- Block popular IM ports. (Note: This offers only partial protection because of the number of potential protocols and associated ports and the ability of applications to bypass port restrictions.)

- Monitor using an Intrusion Detection/Prevention system for users creating tunnels for IM or bypassing proxies.

The Future of IM

The future of IM is promising, enabling users to adapt new technologies for collaboration. For example, mobile IM supports mobile users, providing IM services to handheld cellular phones. Most popular cellular phone manufacturers have their own form of mobile IM. Another popular handheld appliance is the BlackBerry. The BlackBerry supports common IM tools, such as text messaging, as well as push e-mail, telephony, and web browsing.

Scenario

Figure 1-6 shows two computers connected to a "cloud." In networking, a cloud is often used to symbolize a more complex network, such as the Internet, which is not the current focus of this discussion. In this lab, the cloud represents the network and networking devices between an IRC client and a server called *eagle-server*. In subsequent chapters you will study in great detail the devices and protocols that are inside the cloud. This lab uses Gaim as the IRC client, but any IRC client may be used if available. An IRC client is available for download from eagle-server at http://eagle-server.example.com/pub.

Note: Eagle Server is a component of the Cisco Networking Academy. Some of the labs in this book, including this one, assume that a Cisco Networking Academy instructor has already set up Eagle Server and named it eagle-server.example.com.

Figure 1-6   Topology for Lab 1-1

Estimated completion time is 45 minutes.

Task 1: Configure the Chat Client

The IRC protocol is an open standard, originally described in RFC 1459, for communicating across plain-text links.

Step 1:   Verify that an IRC client is on the lab computer.

If not, download and install gaim-1.5.0.exe (a Windows executable) from ftp://eagle-server.example.com/pub/eagle_labs/eagle1/chapter1. Accept the default settings during the installation. After verifying that the Gaim chat client is installed, follow the next steps to configure Gaim.

Step 2:   Open the Accounts window.

Open Gaim and select the Login window, icon **Accounts**. The Accounts window is shown in Figure 1-7.

Figure 1-7   Gaim Accounts Window

In the Accounts window, click **Add.**

Step 3:   Add a new account.

In the Add Account window, expand the **Show more options** option. Fill in required information, as shown in Figure 1-8:

- **Protocol:** IRC

- **Screen Name:** (how others will know you)

- **Server:** eagle-server.example.com

- **Proxy type:** No Proxy

Figure 1-8   Gaim Add Account Window

When you're finished, click **Save**.

Close the Accounts window.

Task 2: Connect to the Chat Server

Step 1:   Sign on.

Return to the Login window, where the new account to eagle-server should be visible. Click **Sign-on**. Two windows should open. Figure 1-9 shows the IRC Connect Status window. Figure 1-10 shows the main Gaim IM client window, used for chatting or IM.

Figure 1-9   IRC Connect Status Window

Figure 1-10   Gaim IRC Client Window

Step 2:   Join the chat.

When the IRC client connects to the IRC server, the status window closes, and a Buddy List window appears. Click **Chat**, as shown in Figure 1-11.

Figure 1-11   Joining a Chat

Note: For you to join a chat channel, the Channel name *must* start with #. If the Channel name is incorrect, you will be in a chat room alone (unless other students made a similar error).

Task 3: Consider the Chat Session

Figure 1-12 shows a brief chat between users *root* and *student2*. Multiple students can join and interact with each other.

Figure 1-12   Participating in a Chat

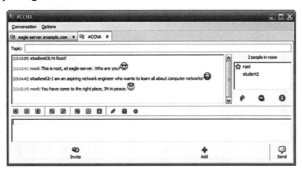

During the chat, consider how you—as a parent or network administrator—would manage this type of connection.

Task 4: Reflection

On a network with an Internet connection, the Gaim IM client can be used to connect to several different IM providers. Most teenagers and young adults today are familiar with IMing between friends and sharing files, but you might not understand the communication between the client and server. As a future network engineer, you should understand the social and security issues with IM and IRC.

Task 5: Challenge

While you are connected in chat, transfer files between partners. Use a continuous ping from the host to Eagle Server to monitor network throughput. Observe the response time before and during the file transfer. Write a brief description of the network response time—during file transfers and without file transfers.

Task 6: Clean Up

Check with your instructor before removing Gaim and shutting down the computer.

Lab 1-2: Using Collaboration Tools: Wikis and Web Logs (1.6.2.1)

Upon completion of this lab, you will be able to

- Define the terms wiki and blog.

- Explore wiki features.

Background

The lab topology shown in Figure 1-13 should be configured and ready for use. If there are connectivity issues with the lab computer connecting to Eagle Server, ask the instructor for assistance.

Figure 1-13   Topology for Lab 1-2

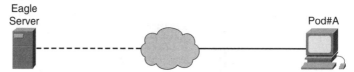

Figure 1-13 shows two computers connected to a "cloud." In networking, a cloud is often used to symbolize a more complex network that is not the current focus of discussion. In this lab, you will use a host computer that connects across the cloud to access the TWiki wiki server. In subsequent chapters you will study in great detail the devices and protocols that are inside the cloud.

Scenario

In this lab, you have the opportunity to learn about the different parts of a wiki. If you have ever used Wikipedia, you are probably familiar with the look and feel of a wiki.

To gain experience with a wiki, you explore the TWiki wiki server installed on Eagle Server in this lab.

Task 1: Define the Terms Wiki and Blog

Wiki is a Hawaiian-language word that means *fast*. In networking terms, a wiki is a web-based collaboration tool that permits almost anyone to immediately post information, files, or graphics to a common site for other users to read and modify. A wiki lets you access a home page (first page) that provides a search tool to assist you in locating the articles that interest you. A wiki can be installed for the Internet community or behind a corporate firewall for employee use. The user not only reads wiki contents but also participates by creating content within a web browser.

Although many different wiki servers are available, the following common features have been formalized into every wiki:

- Any web browser can be used to edit pages or create new content.

- Edit and auto links are available to edit a page and automatically link pages. Text formatting is similar to creating an e-mail.

- A search engine is used for quick content location.

- Access control can be set by the topic creator, defining who is permitted to edit content.

- A wiki web is a grouping of pages with different collaboration groups.

For more information on wikis, visit the following URLs outside of class:

http://www.wiki.org/wiki.cgi?WhatIsWiki

http://www.wikispaces.com/

A web log, called a blog, is similar to a wiki in that users create and post content for others to read. Blogs are normally the creation of a single person, and the blog owner controls blog content. Some blogs permit users to leave comments and provide feedback to the author, but others are more restrictive. Free Internet blog hosting is available, similar to a free website or e-mail account, from such providers as www.blogger.com.

Task 2: Explore Wiki Features with the TWiki Tutorial

The TWiki tutorial explores some of the more common features of a wiki. It covers the following major topics:

1. Get set...

2. Take a quick tour.

3. Open a private account.

4. Check out TWiki users, groups.

5. Test the page controls.

6. Change a page and create a new one.

7. Use your browser to upload files as page attachments.

8. Get e-mail alerts whenever pages are changed.

As you investigate each topic in the tutorial, complete the questions in this task. Note that you won't be able to carry out the instructions in the "3. Open a private account" topic. TWiki requires e-mail verification for new accounts, and e-mail has not been configured on the lab host computers. Instead, users have already been created for steps that require login privileges.

The power of a wiki is in the rich hyperlink content. Following hyperlinks can present continuity problems. It is recommended that you open two browsers. Point one browser at the TWiki URL, and use the other browser for "working" pages. Adjust the browser window sizes so that instructions can be viewed in one browser and actions can be performed in the other. Any external links that are selected will result in an error.

Step 1:   Establish a web client connection to the Eagle Server wiki.

Open a web browser and connect to the TWiki Sandbox at http://eagle-server.example.com/twiki/bin/view/Sandbox/WebHome. The URL name is case-sensitive, so enter it exactly as shown. The Sandbox, shown in Figure 1-14, is a web topic designed to test wiki features.

Figure 1-14   TWiki Sandbox Web

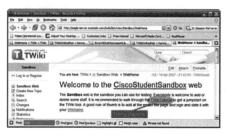

Step 2:   Open the TWiki Tutorial.

Click the TWiki Tutorial link, highlighted in Figure 1-14, to open the wiki tutorial page.

Step 3:   Complete the TWiki tutorial.

Refer to the tutorial, topic 1, "Get set..." and topic 2, "Take a quick tour." After completing the first two tutorial sections, answer the following questions:

What is a WikiWord?

_____

_____

How many results are returned from a search of WebSearch?

_____

Refer to the tutorial, topic 3, "Open a private account." E-mail is not possible at this time; therefore, you will not be able to register. Instead, user IDs have been created for you to use later in this lab.

The key point to understand about this step is that registration is a two-part process. First, users fill in registration information and submit the form to TWiki.

List the mandatory information required for registration:

_____

_____

_____

_____

_____

_____

TWiki responds to a registration request by sending an e-mail to the user that contains a unique activation code.

The second part of the registration process is when the user either enters the code in the activation window or responds with e-mail by clicking the TWiki response link. At this time, the user account is added to the TWiki database.

Refer to the tutorial, topic 4, "Check out TWiki users, groups." A list of TWiki users and groups is displayed. After completing this tutorial section, answer the following questions related to user and group issues:

How is a user's password reset?

_____

_____

_____

How can inappropriate changes be fixed in a wiki topic?

_____

Tutorial topic 5, "Test the page controls," makes you familiar with page-editing commands. After completing this tutorial section, answer the following question:

What is the latest revision number?

_____

In Table 1-4, place the correct action link next to the descriptions of page controls. Place the following action links: Attach, Backlinks, Edit, History, More, Printable, r3 > r2 > r1, and Raw View.

Table 1-4   Action Links

Description	Action Link
Add to or edit the topic	
Show the source text without editing the topic	
Attach files to a topic	
Find out what other topics link to this topic (reverse link)	
Additional controls, such as rename/move, version control, and setting the topic's parent	
Topics are under revision control—shows the topic's complete change history, such as who changed what and when	
View a previous version of the topic or the difference between two versions	
Goes to a stripped-down version of the page; good for printing	

Tutorial topic 6, "Change a page and create a new one," is an opportunity for you to add content to the wiki. Complete this tutorial, using Table 1-5 to log in to the wiki server.

On Eagle Server, a group with private accounts has been created to allow participation in a private TWiki topic. These accounts are **StudentCcna1** through **StudentCcna22.** All accounts have the same password, **cisco.** You should use the account that reflects your pod and host computer number. Refer to Table 1-5.

Table 1-5   Account Logins

Lab pod#host#	Account Login ID (Case-Sensitive)
Pod1host1	StudentCcna1
Pod1host2	StudentCcna2
Pod2host1	StudentCcna3
Pod2host2	StudentCcna4
Pod3host1	StudentCcna5
Pod3host2	StudentCcna6
Pod4host1	StudentCcna7
Pod4host2	StudentCcna8
Pod5host1	StudentCcna9
Pod5host2	StudentCcna10
Pod6host1	StudentCcna11
Pod6host2	StudentCcna12
Pod7host1	StudentCcna13
Pod7host2	StudentCcna14
Pod8host1	StudentCcna15
Pod8host2	StudentCcna16
Pod9host1	StudentCcna17
Pod9host2	StudentCcna18
Pod10host1	StudentCcna19
Pod10host2	StudentCcna20
Pod11host1	StudentCcna21
Pod11host2	StudentCcna22

From the lab Wiki Welcome Screen, click the **Log In** link, located in the upper-left corner of the page. See Figure 1-15.

Figure 1-15   Log In Link

A login box similar to the one shown in Figure 1-16 should appear. Enter the applicable TWiki user-name and password **cisco**. Both the username and password are case-sensitive.

Figure 1-16   Login Box

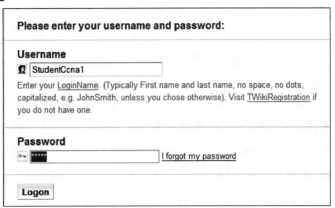

This should bring up your wiki topic page, similar to the one shown in Figure 1-17.

Figure 1-17   Wiki Topic Page

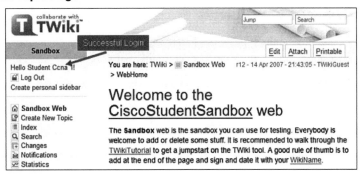

Tutorial topic 7, "Use your browser to upload files as page attachments," describes the process of uploading files into the wiki. To complete this tutorial, create a document using Notepad, and upload it to the wiki server.

What is the default maximum file size that can be transferred?

Tutorial topic 8, "Get e-mail alerts whenever pages are changed," details how to receive e-mail alerts whenever a particular page has been updated. Sometimes it is not convenient to return regularly to a wiki simply to check for updates to postings. Because e-mail is not configured on the host computer, alerts are not sent.

Describe how you could receive e-mail notifications whenever a topic changes.

_____

Edit the WebNotify page, and add the web name and your e-mail address.

Here's a possible format:

```
three spaces * [ webname . ] wikiName - SMTP mail address
three spaces * [ webName . ] wikiName
three spaces * SMTP mail address
three spaces * SMTP mail address : topics
three spaces * [ webname . ] wikiName : topics
°   ccna1@example.com: CiscoStudentsStuff
```

Task 3: Reflection

This lab presented the mechanics of a wiki. Usefulness and collaboration will not be realized until you actually join a wiki. Here are some wikis of possible interest:

- **CCNA:** http://en.wikibooks.org/wiki/CCNA_Certification

- **Cisco Systems corporate history:** http://en.wikipedia.org/wiki/Cisco_Systems

- **Wiki web about Cisco equipment and technology:** http://www.nyetwork.org/wiki/Cisco

- **Network+:** http://en.wikibooks.org/wiki/Network_Plus_Certification/Study_Guide

- **Network Dictionary:** http://wiki.networkdictionary.com/index.php/Main_Page

- **Wireshark network protocol analyzer:** http://wiki.wireshark.org/

Task 4: Challenge

Depending on the type of Eagle Server installation, the class may be able use the TWiki wiki server to post interesting topics related to computer network theory and class progress.

Create a personal blog of your network education experience. Internet access is required.

Task 5: Clean Up

Close all web browsers and shut down the computer unless instructed otherwise.

Skills Integration Challenge: Introduction to Packet Tracer (1.7.1.3)

Figure 1-18 shows the topology for this challenge, and Table 1-6 reflects the addressing information.

Figure 1-18   Topology for Skills Integration Challenge

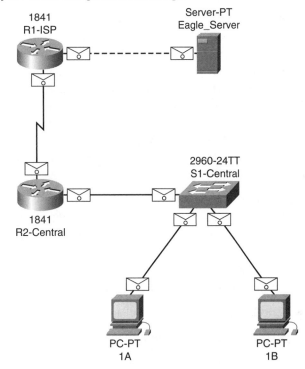

Table 1-6   Addressing Table

Device	Interface	IP Address	Subnet Mask	Default Gateway
R1-ISP	Fa0/0	192.168.254.253	255.255.255.0	—
	S0/0/0	10.10.10.6	255.255.255.252	—
R2-Central	Fa0/0	172.16.255.254	255.255.0.0	10.10.10.6
	S0/0/0	10.10.10.5	255.255.255.252	10.10.10.6
S1-Central	VLAN 1	172.16.254.1	255.255.0.0	172.16.255.254
PC 1A	NIC	172.16.1.1	255.255.0.0	172.16.255.254
PC 1B	NIC	172.16.1.2	255.255.0.0	172.16.255.254
Eagle Server	NIC	192.168.254.254	255.255.255.0	192.168.254.253

Upon completion of this activity, you will be able to

- Explore Packet Tracer Real-time mode.

- Explore the Logical Workplace.

- Explore Packet Tracer operation.

- Connect devices.

- Examine a device configuration.

- Review the standard lab setup.

- Describe the devices.

Background

Throughout the course you will use a standard lab setup created from actual PCs, servers, routers, and switches to learn networking concepts. This method provides the widest range of features and the most realistic experience. Because equipment and time are limited, this experience can be supplemented by a simulated environment. The simulator that is used in this course is Packet Tracer. Packet Tracer provides a set of protocols, equipment, and features but only a fraction of what is possible with real equipment. Packet Tracer is a supplement and not a replacement for experience with real equipment. You are encouraged to compare the results obtained from Packet Tracer network models with the behavior of real equipment. You are also encouraged to examine the Help files built into Packet Tracer, which include an extensive "My First PT Lab," tutorials, and information on the strengths and limitations of using Packet Tracer to model networks.

This activity gives you an opportunity to explore the standard lab setup using the Packet Tracer simulator. Packet Tracer can create two file formats: .pkt files (network simulation model files) and .pka files (activity files for practice). When you create your own networks in Packet Tracer, or modify existing files from your instructor or your peers, you will often use the .pkt file format. When you launched this activity from the curriculum, these instructions appeared. They are the result of the .pka Packet Tracer activity file format. At the bottom of these instructions are two buttons:

- **Check Results** gives you feedback on how much of the activity you have completed.

- **Reset Activity** restarts the activity if you want to clear your work or get more practice.

Task 1: Explore the PT Interface

Step 1: Examine the Logical Workplace.

Open the file LSG01-PTSkills1.pka on the CD-ROM that accompanies this book to perform this exercise using Packet Tracer. When Packet Tracer starts, it presents a logical view of the network in real-time mode. The main part of the PT interface is the Logical Workplace. This is the large area where devices are placed and connected.

Step 2:   Explore symbols navigation.

The lower-left portion of the PT interface, below the yellow bar, is the portion of the interface that you use to select and place devices into the Logical Workplace. The first box in the lower left contains symbols that represent groups of devices. As you move the mouse pointer over these symbols, the name of the group appears in the text box in the center. When you click one of these symbols, the specific devices in the group appear in the box to the right. As you point to the specific devices, a description of the device appears in the text box below the specific devices. Click each group, and study the various devices that are available and their symbols.

Task 2: Explore PT Operations

Step 1:   Connect the devices using auto connect.

Click the connections group symbol. The specific connection symbols provide different cable types that can be used to connect devices. The first specific type, the gold lightning bolt, automatically selects the connection type based on the interfaces available on the devices. When you click this symbol, the pointer resembles a cable connector.

To connect two devices, click the auto connection symbol, click the first device, and then click the second device. Using the auto connection symbol, make the following connection:

- Connect Eagle Server to the R1-ISP router.

- Connect PC-PT 1A to the S1-Central switch.

Step 2:   Examine device configuration with a mouseover.

Move the mouse over the devices found in the Logical Workplace. As you move the mouse pointer over these symbols, the device configurations appear in a text box:

- Router displays port configuration information, including IP address, port status, and MAC address.

- Server displays IP address, MAC address, and gateway information.

- Switch displays port configuration information, including IP address, MAC address, port status, and VLAN membership.

- PC displays IP address, MAC address, and gateway information.

Step 3:   Examine device configuration.

Click each device type found in the Logical Workplace to view the device configuration:

- **Router and Switch devices** contain three tabs—Physical, Config, and CLI (command-line interface).

    The Physical tab displays physical components of the device, such as modules. New modules can also be added using this tab.

    The Config tab displays the general configuration information, such as device name.

    The CLI tab allows the user to configure the device using the command-line interface.

- **Server and Hub devices** contain two tabs—Physical and Config.

    The Physical tab displays components of the device, such as ports. New modules can also be added using this tab.

    The Config tab displays the general information, such as device name.

- **PC devices** contain three tabs—Physical, Config, and Desktop.

    The Physical tab displays components of the device. New modules can also be added using this tab.

    The Config tab displays the device name, IP address, subnet mask, DNS, and gateway information.

    The Desktop tab allows the user to configure IP address, subnet mask, default gateway, DNS server, dialup, and wireless. A terminal emulator, the command prompt, and a simulated web browser can also be accessed using the Desktop tab.

Task 3: Review the Standard Lab Setup

The standard lab setup consists of two routers, one switch, one server, and two PCs. Each of these devices is preconfigured with such information as device names, IP addresses, gateways, and connections.

Task 4: Reflection

You have completed your first Packet Tracer lab. You are encouraged to obtain Packet Tracer from your instructor or Academy Connections, if you have not done so already.

Communicating over the Network

The Study Guide portion of this chapter uses a combination of multiple-choice, matching, fill-in-the-blank, and open-ended questions to test your knowledge of how devices communicate over the network.

The Labs and Activities portion of this chapter includes all the online curriculum activities and labs to further reinforce that you have mastered the practical, hands-on skills needed to use some critical tools to help evaluate network communications.

As you work through this chapter, use Chapter 2 in the Network Fundamentals CCNA Exploration online curriculum or use the corresponding Chapter 2 in the *Networking Fundamentals, CCNA Exploration Companion Guide*, for assistance.

Study Guide

The Platform for Communications

Communication begins with a message, or information, that must be sent from one individual or device to another. People exchange ideas using many different communication methods. All of these methods have three elements in common.

Concept Questions

1to4

1. What are the three elements of communication?

   _____

   _____

   _____

2. What is the process of breaking large messages, or flow of data, into smaller, easier-to-manage pieces called?

   Segmentation

3. What is the process used to allow many different conversations to be interleaved on a network called?

   Multiplexing

4. Modern networks primarily use three types of media to interconnect devices. What are these three types?

   1) Copper *—Host (end device) (Host + client)*

   2) Fiber-optic Client

   cable Intermediary devices

   3) Wireless network media

Vocabulary Exercise: Matching

In Table 2-1, match the definition on the right with a term on the left.

Table 2-1   Components of the Network

Term	Definition
a. Devices	__ Cat5 cable, wireless connection, fiber-optic cable
b. Media	__ Computer, switch, router
c. Services	__ E-mail, web browser

In Table 2-2, identify the definition on the left with either end devices or intermediary devices on the right.

Table 2-2   End or Intermediary Device

Definition	Device Type
Computers (work stations, laptops, file servers, web servers)	
Mobile handheld devices (such as wireless barcode scanners, PDAs)	
Network access devices (hubs, switches, and wireless access points)	
Network printers	
Internetworking devices (routers)	
VoIP phones	
Communication servers and modems	
Security cameras	
Security devices (firewalls)	

LANs, WANs, and Internetworks

Network infrastructures can vary greatly in terms of the following:

- The size of the area covered
- The number of users connected
- The number and types of services available

This section tests your knowledge of the differences between LANs, WANs, and internetworks.

Vocabulary Exercise: Completion

Fill in the blanks for the following statements.

1. The term _____ is often used to refer to a private connection of LANs and WANs that belongs to an organization, and is designed to be accessible only by the organization's members, employees, or others with authorization.

2. A _____ is usually administered by a single organization.

3. _____ use specifically designed network devices to make the interconnections between _____.

4. The media connecting the PC to the networking device plugs directly into the _____.

Vocabulary Exercise: Matching

In Table 2-3, match the definition on the right with a term on the left.

Table 2-3   LANs, WANs, and Internetworks

Term	Definition
a. LANs	__ When a company or organization has locations that are separated by large geographic distances, it might be necessary to use a telecommunications service provider (TSP) to interconnect the LANs at the different locations.
b. WANs	__ An individual network usually spans a single geographic area, providing services and applications to people within a common organizational structure, such as a single business, campus, or region.
c. Internetworks	__ A global mesh of interconnected networks.

In Table 2-4, match the term on the left with the correct symbol number from Figure 2-1.

Table 2-4   LANs, WANs, and Internetworks

Device	Number
Router	
Firewall	
Wireless access point	
LAN hub	
LAN switch	
IP phone	
Wireless router	
Wireless media	
Server	
Laptop	
LAN media	
Desktop computer	
WAN media	

Figure 2-1   Common Data Network Symbols

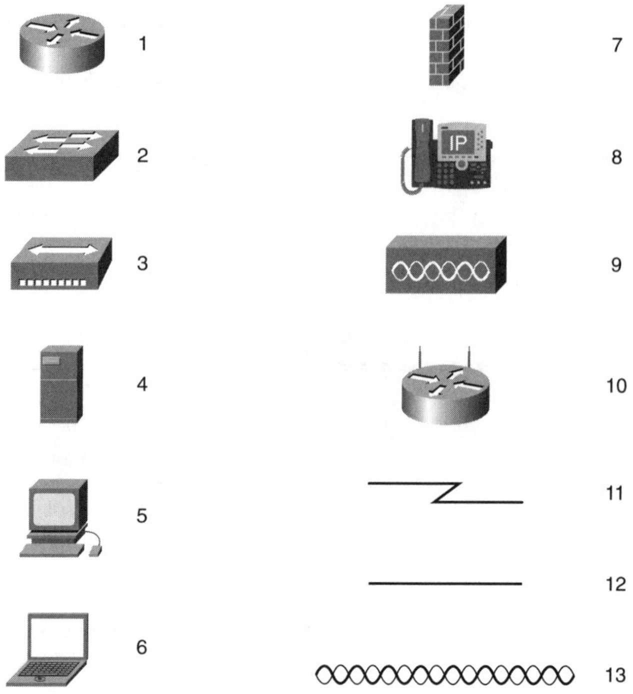

Protocols

All communication, whether face to face or over a network, is governed by predetermined rules called protocols. These protocols are specific to the characteristics of the conversation.

Vocabulary Exercise: Completion

Fill in the blanks for the following statements.

1. Successful communication between hosts on a network requires the interaction of many different protocols. A group of interrelated protocols that are necessary to perform a communication function is called a _____.

2. All communication, whether face to face or over a network, is governed by predetermined rules called _____.

3. A _____ is a process or protocol that has been endorsed by the networking industry and ratified by a standards organization.

4. The most common internetwork protocol is _____.

Concept Questions

1. What processes do networking protocol suites describe?

_____

_____

_____

2. What are some benefits to using a layered model to describe network protocols and operations?

_____

_____

_____

_____

_____

Using Layered Models

To visualize the interaction between various protocols, it is common to use a layered model. A layered model depicts the operation of the protocols occurring within each layer, and the interaction with the layers above and below it.

Vocabulary Exercise: Matching

In Table 2-5, match the definition on the right with a term on the left.

Table 2-5   TCP/IP Model

Term	Definition
a. Application layer	__ Uses packet sequencing and application mapping through port numbers
b. Transport layer	__ Represents data to the user plus encoding and dialog control
c. Internet layer	__ Controls the hardware devices and media that make up the network
d. Network access layer	__ Determines the best path through the network

In Table 2-6, match the definition on the right with a term on the left.

Table 2-6   OSI Model

Term	Definition
a. Application layer	__ Protocols describe methods for exchanging data frames between devices over a common media.
b. Presentation layer	__ Provides the means for end-to-end connectivity between individuals in the human network using data networks.
c. Session layer	__ Describes the mechanical, electrical, functional, and procedural means to activate, maintain, and deactivate physical connections for bit transmission to and from a network device.
d. Transport layer	__ Provides services to the presentation layer to organize its dialogue and to manage data exchange. Ensures that loss of connection can be recovered and reset if data flow is interrupted before all data is received.
e. Network layer	__ Provides for common representation of the data transferred between application layer services.

continues

Table 2-6   OSI Model *continued*

Term	Definition
f. Data link layer	___ Provides connectivity services that route packets from source network to destination network.
g. Physical layer	___ Defines services to segment, transfer, and reassemble the data for individual communications between the end devices.

Network Addressing

Various types of addresses must be included in a packet to successfully deliver the data from a source application running on one host to the correct destination application running on another. Using the OSI model as a guide, you can see the different addresses and identifiers that are necessary at each layer.

Vocabulary Exercise: Completion

Fill in the blanks for the following statements.

1. The first identifier, the host physical address, is contained in the header of the Layer 2 protocol data unit (PDU), called a _____. Layer 2 is concerned with the delivery of messages on a single local network. The Layer 2 address is unique on the local network and represents the address of the end device on the physical media. In a LAN using Ethernet, this address is called the _____ address.

2. A unique dialogue between devices is identified with a pair of Layer 4 source and destination _____ that are representative of the two communicating applications.

Multiple-Choice Questions

Choose the best answer for each of the questions that follow.

1. What kind of protocols are primarily designed to move data from one local network to another local network within an internetwork?

   a. Layer 1

   b. Layer 2

   c. Layer 3

   d. Layer 4

2. Which devices make Layer 3 decisions?

   a. Routers

   b. Switches

   c. Hubs

   d. Servers

Labs and Activities

Activity 2-1: Using NeoTrace to View Internetworks (2.2.5.1)

Upon completion of this activity, you will be able to do the following:

- Explain the use of route tracing programs, such as **tracert** and NeoTrace.

- Use **tracert** and NeoTrace to trace a route from its PC to a distant server.

- Describe the interconnected and global nature of the Internet with respect to data flow.

Background

Route-tracing software is a utility that lists the networks data has to traverse from the user's originating device to a distant destination network device.

This network tool is typically executed in UNIX and similar systems at the command line as follows:

traceroute *<destination network name or end device address>*

This network tool is typically executed in Microsoft Windows systems at the command line as follows:

tracert *<destination network name or end device address>*

This tool determines the route taken by packets across an IP network.

The **traceroute** (or **tracert**) tool is often used for network troubleshooting. By showing a list of routers traversed, it enables the user to identify the path taken to reach a particular destination on the network or across internetworks. Each router represents a point where one network connects to another network and the packet was forwarded through. The number of routers is known as the number of "hops" the data traveled from source to destination.

The displayed list can help identify data-flow problems when trying to access a service such as a website. It can also be useful when performing tasks such as downloading data. If multiple websites (mirrors) are available for the same file of data, one can trace each mirror to get a good idea of which mirror would be the fastest to use.

Note, however, that because of the "meshed" nature of the interconnected networks that make up the Internet and IP's capability to select different pathways over which to send packets, two trace routes between the same source and destination conducted some time apart might produce different results.

Tools such as **traceroute/tracert** are usually embedded within the operating system of the end device.

Others such as NeoTrace are proprietary programs that provide extra information. NeoTrace uses available online information to graphically display the route traced on a global map, for example.

Scenario

Using an Internet connection, you use two route-tracing programs to examine the Internet pathway to destination networks.

You should perform this activity on a computer that has Internet access and access to a command line. First, you use the Windows embedded **tracert** utility, and then the more enhanced NeoTrace program. This lab assumes the installation of NeoTrace. Remember, some computers running Windows XP might have firewall programs enabled that might prevent **tracert** and NeoTrace from operating; you might have to turn your firewalls off for this lab.

Task 1: Trace Route to Remote Server

Step 1.   Trace the route to a distant network.

To trace the route to a distant network, the PC being used must have a working connection to the class/lab network.

Step 2.   At the command-line prompt, enter **tracert www.cisco.com.**

The first output line should show the fully qualified domain name (FQDN) followed by the IP address. The lab Domain Name Service (DNS) server was able to resolve the name to an IP address. Without this name resolution, the **tracert** would have failed, because this tool operates at the TCP/IP layers, which understand valid IP addresses only.

If DNS is not available, the IP address of the destination device rather than the server name has to be entered after the **tracert** command.

Step 3.   Examine the output displayed.

How many hops between the source and destination? _____

Example 2-1 shows the successful result when running **tracert www.cisco.com** from a location in Bavaria, Germany.

Example 2-1   tracert Output

```
C:\> tracert www.cisco.com
Tracing route to www.cisco.com [198.133.219.25]
Over a maximum of 30 hops:
  1   <10 ms    10 ms   <10 ms   10-37-00-1.internal.alp.dillingen.de [10.317.0.11]
  2   <10 ms   <10 ms   <10 ms   194.95.207.11
  3    20 ms   <10 ms    10 ms   ar-augsburg2.g-win.dfn.de [188.1.37.145]
  4   <10 ms   <10 ms    10 ms   ar-augsburg1.g-win.dfn.de [188.1.74.193]
  5   <10 ms   <10 ms    10 ms   cr-muenchen1.g-win.dfn.de [188.1.74.33]
  6    10 ms    10 ms    10 ms   cr-frankfurt1.g-win.dfn.de [188.1.18.81]
  7    10 ms    10 ms    10 ms   so-6-0-0.ar2.FRA2.gblx.net [208.48.23.141]
  8    10 ms    10 ms    10 ms   pos3-0-622M.cr1.FRA2.gblx.net [62.16.32.73]
  9    30 ms    30 ms    20 ms   so0-0-0-2488M.cr2.LON3.gblx.net [195.8.96.174]
 10    30 ms    30 ms    20 ms   pos1-0-622M.br1.LON3.gblx.net [195.8.96.189]
 11    30 ms    30 ms    31 ms   sl-bb21-lon-5-0.sprintlink.net [213.206.131.25]
 12   100 ms   100 ms    90 ms   sl-bb20-msq-10-0.sprintlink.net [144.232.19.69]
 13   110 ms   110 ms   110 ms   sl-bb20-rly-15-1.sprintlink.net [144.232.19.694]
 14   171 ms   160 ms   170 ms   sl-bb22-sj-5-1.sprintlink.net [144.232.9.125]
 15   161 ms   160 ms   170 ms   sl-bb25-sj-12-0.sprintlink.net [144.232.3.210]
 16   160 ms   181 ms   160 ms   sl-gw11-sj-10-0.sprintlink.net [144.232.3.134]
 17   170 ms   151 ms   160 ms   sl-ciscopsn2-11-0-0.sprintllink.net [144.228.44.14]
 18   170 ms   151 ms   160 ms   sjck-dirty-gw1.cisco.com [128.107.239.5]
 19   160 ms   160 ms   161 ms   sjck-sdf-ciod-gw1.cisco.com [128.107.239.106]
 20   160 ms   150 ms   161 ms   www.cisco.com [198.133.219.25]

Trace complete.
```

The first output line shows the FQDN, followed by the IP address. Therefore, a DNS server was able to resolve the name to an IP address. Then, there are listings of all routers through which the **tracert** requests had to pass to get to the destination.

Step 4.   Try the same trace route on a PC connected to the Internet and examine your output:

Number of hops to www.cisco.com: _____

Step 5.   Try another trace route on the same PC, and examine your output.

Destination URL: _____

Destination IP address: _____

Task 2: Trace Route Using NeoTrace

Step 1.   Launch the NeoTrace program.

Step 2.   On the View menu, choose **Options**. Click the **Map** tab, and in the Home Location section click the **Set Home Location** button.

Step 3.   Follow the instructions to select your country and location within your country.

Alternatively, you can click the **Advanced** button, which enables you to enter the precise latitude and longitude of your location.

Step 4.   Enter **www.cisco.com** in the Target field and click **Go**.

Step 5.   From the View menu, List View displays the list of routers similar to **tracert**.

Node View from the View menu displays the connections graphically with symbols.

Map View from the View menu displays the links and routers in their geographic location on a global map.

Step 6.   Select each view in turn and note the differences and similarities.

Step 7.   Try a number of different URLs and view the routes to those destinations.

Task 3: Reflection

Review the purpose and usefulness of route-tracing programs.

Relate the displays of the output of NeoTrace to the concept of interconnected networks and the global nature of the Internet.

Task 4: Challenge

Consider and discuss possible network security issues that could arise from the use of programs such as **traceroute** and NeoTrace. Consider which technical details are revealed and how this information could perhaps be misused.

Task 5: Clean Up

Exit the NeoTrace program. Unless instructed otherwise by your instructor, properly shut down the computer.

Lab 2-1: Topology Orientation and Building a Small Network (2.6.1.1)

Upon completion of this lab, you will be able to do the following:

- Correctly identify cables for use in the network.

- Physically cable a peer-to-peer and switched network.

- Verify basic connectivity on each network.

Background

Many network problems can be fixed at the physical layer of a network. Therefore, you need to understand clearly which cables to use for your network connections.

At the physical layer (Layer 1) of the OSI model, end devices must be connected by media (cables). The type of media required depends on the type of device being connected. In the basic portion of this lab, you use straight-through or patch cables to connect workstations and switches.

In addition, two or more devices communicate through an address. The network layer (Layer 3) requires a unique address (also known as a logical address or IP address), which allows the data to reach the appropriate destination device.

Addressing for this lab is applied to the workstations and is used to enable communication between the devices.

Scenario

This lab starts with the simplest form of networking (peer to peer) and ends with the lab connecting through a switch, as shown in Figure 2-2.

Figure 2-2   Topology for Lab 2-1

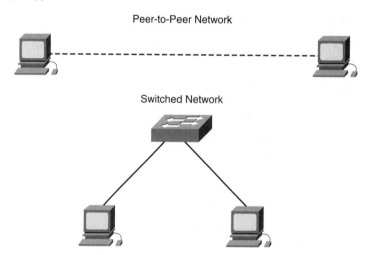

Task 1: Create a Peer-to-Peer Network

Step 1.   Select a lab partner.

Step 2.   Obtain the following equipment and resources for the lab:

- Two workstations

- Two straight-through (patch) cables

- One crossover cable

- One switch (or hub)

Task 2: Identify the Cables Used in a Network

Before the devices can be cabled, you must identify the types of media you intend to use. The cables used in this lab are crossover and straight-through.

Use a *crossover cable* to connect two workstations to each other through their network interface card (NIC) Ethernet port. This is an Ethernet cable. Notice when you look at the plug that the orange and green wires are in opposite positions on each end of the cable.

Use a *straight-through cable* to connect the router's Ethernet port to a switch port or a workstation to a switch port. This is also an Ethernet cable. Notice when you look at the plug that both ends of the cable are exactly the same in each pin position.

Task 3: Cable the Peer-to-Peer Network

Step 1.   Connect two workstations.

Using the correct Ethernet cable, connect two workstations together, as shown in Figure 2-3. Connect one end of the cable to the NIC port on PC1 and the other end of the cable to PC2.

Figure 2-3   Peer-to-Peer Cabling

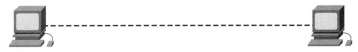

Which cable did you use? _____

Step 2.   Apply a Layer 3 address to the workstations.

To complete this task, use the following step-by-step instructions.

Note: These steps must be completed on *each* workstation. The instructions are for Windows XP. Steps may differ slightly if you are using a different operating system.

---

    a.   On your computer, click **Start**, right-click **My Network Places**, and then click **Properties.** The Network Connections window should appear, with icons showing the different network connections. See Figure 2-4.

Figure 2-4   Network Connections

b.   Right-click the **Local Area Connection** and click **Properties**.

c.   Select the **Internet Protocol (TCP/IP)** item as shown in Figure 2-5, and then click the **Properties** button.

Figure 2-5   Local Area Connection Properties

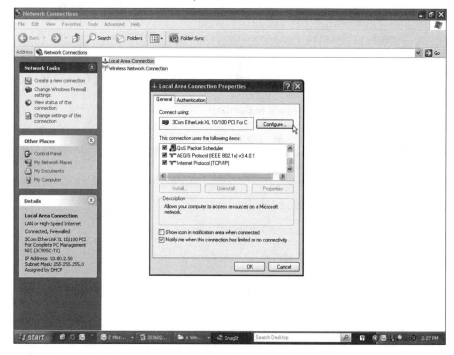

d.   On the General tab of the Internet Protocol (TCP/IP) Properties window, select the **Use the following IP address** option.

e.   In the IP address box, enter the IP address **192.168.1.2** for PC1. Enter the IP address **192.168.1.3** for PC2.

f. Press the Tab key; the subnet mask lists automatically. The subnet address should be 255.255.255.0, as shown in Figure 2-6. If this address is not automatically listed, enter the address manually.

Figure 2-6   Internet Protocol (TCP/IP) Properties

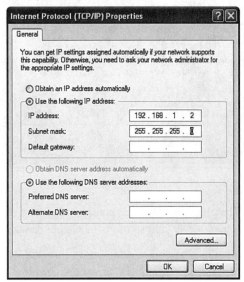

g. Click **OK**.

h. Close the Local Area Connection Properties window.

Step 3. Verify connectivity.

On your computer, click **Start**, and then click **Run**. The dialog box shown in Figure 2-7 appears.

Figure 2-7   Run Command

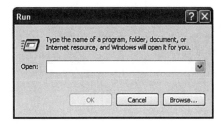

Enter **cmd** in the Open box, and then click **OK**.

The DOS command (cmd.exe) window will appear as shown in Figure 2-8. You can enter DOS commands using this window. For the purposes of this lab, you enter basic network commands to test your computer connections.

Figure 2-8   cmd Command

The **ping** command is a computer network tool used to test whether a host (workstation, router, server, and so on) is reachable across an IP network.

Step 4.   Use the **ping** command to verify that PC1 can reach PC2 and PC2 can reach PC1. From the PC1 DOS command prompt, enter **ping 192.168.1.3**. From the PC2 DOS command prompt, enter **ping 192.168.1.2**.

What is the output of the **ping** command?

_____

_____

_____

_____

_____

_____

_____

_____

_____

_____

If the **ping** command displays an error message or doesn't receive a reply from the other workstation, troubleshoot as necessary. Possible areas to troubleshoot include the following:

■ Verifying the correct IP addresses on both workstations

■ Ensuring that the correct type of cable is used between the workstations

What is the output of the **ping** command if you unplug the network cable and ping the other workstation?

_____

_____

_____

_____

_____

Task 4: Connect Your Workstations to the Classroom Lab Switch

Step 1.   Connect the workstation to a switch.

Using the correct cable, connect one end of the cable to the NIC port on the workstation and the other end to a port on the switch, as shown in Figure 2-9.

Figure 2-9   Switched Network

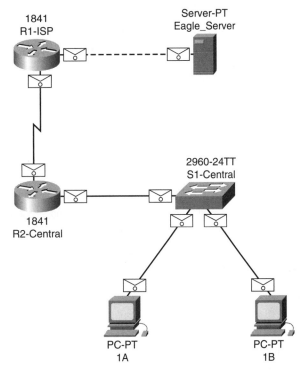

Step 2.   Repeat this process for each workstation on your network.

Which cable did you use? _____

Step 3.   Verify connectivity.

Verify network connectivity by using the **ping** command to reach the other workstations attached to the switch.

What is the output of the **ping** command?

_____

_____

_____

_____

_____

What is the output of the **ping** command if you ping an address that is not connected to this network?

_____

_____

_____

_____

_____

Step 4.   Share a document between PCs.

On your desktop, create a new folder and name it **test**.

Right-click the folder and click Sharing and Security. A hand symbol will appear under the icon.

Place a file in the folder.

On the desktop, double-click **My Network Places** and then **Computers Near Me**.

Double-click the workstation icon. The test folder should appear. You can access this folder across the network. When you can see it and work with the file, you have access through all seven layers of the OSI model.

Task 5: Reflection

What could prevent a ping from being sent between the workstations when they are directly connected?

_____

What could prevent the ping from being sent to the workstations when they are connected through the switch?

_____

Packet Tracer Companion: Topology Orientation and Building a Small Network (2.6.1.2)

You can now open the file LSG01-Lab2612.pka on the CD-ROM that accompanies this book to repeat this hands-on lab using Packet Tracer. Remember, however, that Packet Tracer is not a substitute for a hands-on lab experience with real equipment. A summary of the instructions is provided within the activity.

Lab 2-2: Using Wireshark to View Protocol Data Units (2.6.2.1)

Upon completion of this lab, you will be able to do the following:

- Explain the purpose of a protocol analyzer (Wireshark).

- Perform basic PDU capture using Wireshark.

- Perform basic PDU analysis on straightforward network data traffic.

- Experiment with Wireshark features and options such as PDU capture and display filtering.

Background

Wireshark is a software protocol analyzer, or "packet sniffer" application, used for network troubleshooting, analysis, software and protocol development, and education. Before June 2006, Wireshark was known as Ethereal.

A packet sniffer (also known as a *network analyzer* or *protocol analyzer*) is computer software that can intercept and log data traffic passing over a data network. As data streams travel back and forth over the network, the sniffer "captures" each protocol data unit (PDU) and can decode and analyze its content according to the appropriate RFC or other specifications.

Wireshark is programmed to recognize the structure of different network protocols. This enables it to display the encapsulation and individual fields of a PDU and interpret their meaning.

It is a useful tool for anyone working with networks and can be used with most labs in the CCNA courses for data analysis and troubleshooting. For information and to download the program, go to http://www.Wireshark.org.

Scenario

To capture PDUs, the computer on which Wireshark is installed must have a working connection to the network, and Wireshark must be running before any data can be captured.

When Wireshark is launched, the screen shown in Figure 2-10 displays.

Figure 2-10   Wireshark Opening Screen

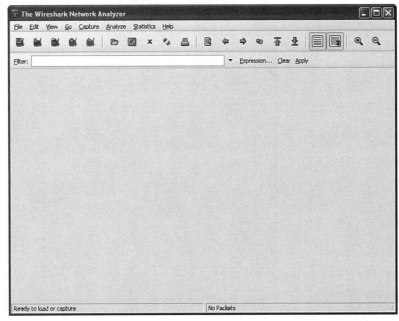

To start data capture, select **Options** from the Capture menu.

The Capture Options dialog box, shown in Figure 2-11, provides a range of settings and filters to determine which and how much data traffic is captured.

Figure 2-11   Wireshark: Capture Options Dialog Box

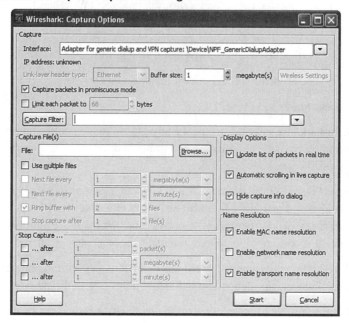

First, you must ensure that Wireshark is set to monitor the correct interface. From the Interface drop-down list, select the network adapter in use. Typically, for a computer this is the connected Ethernet adapter.

Then, you can set the other options. Among those available in the Capture Options dialog box, the two highlighted in Figure 2-12 deserve examination.

Figure 2-12   Wireshark Capture Options

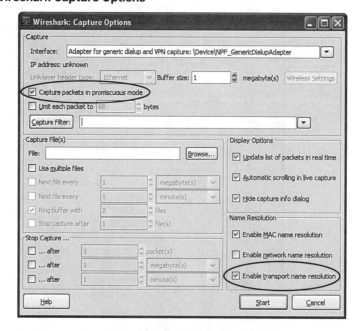

If the Capture packets in promiscuous mode feature is *not* checked, only PDUs destined for this computer will be captured. If this feature is checked, all PDUs destined for this computer *and* all those detected by the computer NIC on the same network segment (that is, those that "pass by" the NIC but are not destined for the computer) are captured.

Note: The capturing of these other PDUs depends on the intermediary device connecting the end-device computers on this network. As you use different intermediary devices (hubs, switches, routers) throughout these courses, you will experience the different Wireshark results.

The Enable transport name resolution option allows you to control whether Wireshark translates network addresses found in PDUs into names. Although this is a useful feature, the name-resolution process might add extra PDUs to your captured data, perhaps distorting the analysis.

Wireshark also provides a number of other capture-filtering and capture-process settings.

Clicking the **Start** button starts the data-capture process, and a message box displays the progress of this process (as shown in Figure 2-13).

Figure 2-13   Wireshark Capture Start

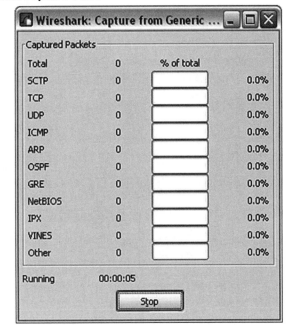

As data PDUs are captured, the types and number are indicated in the message box.

The examples in Figure 2-14 show the capture of a ping process (box on left) and then accessing a web page (box on right).

Figure 2-14   Wireshark Capture Output

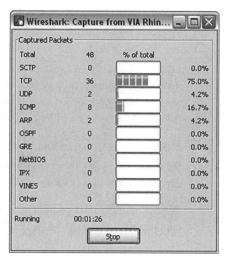

When the **Stop** button is clicked, the capture process is terminated and the main screen displays. This main display window of Wireshark has three panes, as shown in Figure 2-15.

Figure 2-15   Wireshark Capture Main Panes

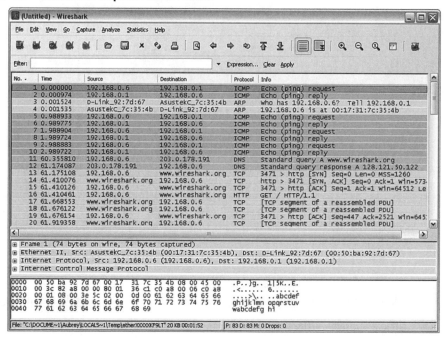

The PDU (or packet) list pane at the top of Figure 2-15 displays a summary of each packet captured. By clicking packets in this pane, you control what displays in the other two panes. Each line in the packet list corresponds to one PDU or packet of the captured data. If you select a line in this pane, more details will display in the packet details pane and in the packet bytes pane. The example in Figure 2-15 shows the PDUs captured when the ping utility was used and http://www.Wireshark.org was accessed. Packet number one is selected in this pane.

The PDU (or packet) details pane in the middle of Figure 2-15 displays the packet selected in the packet list pane in more detail. The packet details pane shows the current packet (selected in the packet list pane) in a more detailed form. This pane shows the protocols and protocol fields of the selected packet. The protocols and fields of the packet display in a tree form, which you can expand and collapse.

The PDU (or packet) bytes pane at the bottom of Figure 2-15 displays the actual data (in hexadecimal form representing the actual binary) from the packet selected in the packet list pane, and highlights the field selected in the packet details pane. The packet bytes pane shows the data of the current packet (selected in the packet list pane) in what is known as *hexdump* style. In this lab, this pane is not examined in detail. However, when a more in-depth analysis is required, you will find this displayed information useful for examining the binary values and content of PDUs.

You can save the information captured for the data PDUs in a file, and then open this file in Wireshark for later analysis without having to recapture the same data traffic. The information displayed when a capture file is opened is the same as the original capture.

When closing a data-capture screen or exiting Wireshark, a prompt asks whether you want to save the captured PDUs, as shown in Figure 2-16.

Figure 2-16   Wireshark Save Option

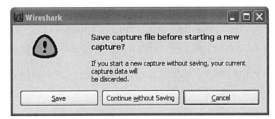

Clicking **Continue without Saving** closes the file and exits Wireshark without saving the captured data.

Task 1: Ping PDU Capture

Step 1.   After ensuring that the standard lab topology and configuration is correct, launch Wireshark on a computer in a lab pod.

Set the capture options as described in the preceding section, and then start the capture process.

From the command line, ping the IP address of another network-connected and powered-on end device in the lab topology. In this case, ping the Eagle Server using the command **ping 192.168.254.254**.

After receiving the successful replies to the ping in the command-line window, stop the packet capture.

Step 2.   Examine the packet list pane.

The packet list pane on Wireshark should now look something like Figure 2-17.

Figure 2-17   Wireshark Packet List Pane

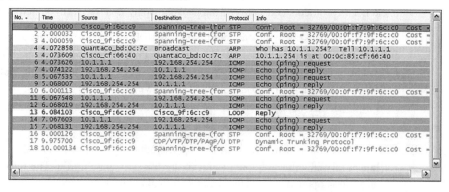

Look at the packets listed in Figure 2-17, particularly packet numbers 6, 7, 8, 9, 11, 12, 14, and 15.

Locate the equivalent packets on the packet list on your computer.

If you performed Step 1, match the messages displayed in the command-line window when the ping was issued with the six packets captured by Wireshark.

From the Wireshark packet list, answer the following:

What protocol is used by ping? _____

What is the full protocol name? _____

What are the names of the two ping messages?

_____

_____

Are the listed source and destination IP addresses what you expected? Why?

_____

_____

Step 3.   Select (highlight) the first echo request packet on the list.

The packet details pane will now display something similar to Figure 2-18.

Figure 2-18   Wireshark Packet Details Pane

```
⊞ Frame 6 (74 bytes on wire, 74 bytes captured)
⊞ Ethernet II, Src: QuantaCo_bd:0c:7c (00:c0:9f:bd:0c:7c), Dst: Cisco_cf:66:40 (00:0c:85:cf:66:40)
⊞ Internet Protocol, Src: 10.1.1.1 (10.1.1.1), Dst: 192.168.254.254 (192.168.254.254)
⊞ Internet Control Message Protocol
```

Click each of the four plus sign (+) buttons to expand the information.

The packet details pane will now display something similar to Figure 2-19.

Figure 2-19   Wireshark Packet Details Pane, Expanded

```
⊟ Frame 6 (74 bytes on wire, 74 bytes captured)
    Arrival Time: Jan 10, 2007 01:54:07.860436000
    [Time delta from previous packet: 0.000017000 seconds]
    [Time since reference or first frame: 4.073626000 seconds]
    Frame Number: 6
    Packet Length: 74 bytes
    Capture Length: 74 bytes
    [Frame is marked: False]
    [Protocols in frame: eth:ip:icmp:data]
    [Coloring Rule Name: ICMP]
    [Coloring Rule String: icmp]
⊟ Ethernet II, Src: QuantaCo_bd:0c:7c (00:c0:9f:bd:0c:7c), Dst: Cisco_cf:66:40 (00:0c:85:cf:66:40)
  ⊞ Destination: Cisco_cf:66:40 (00:0c:85:cf:66:40)
  ⊞ Source: QuantaCo_bd:0c:7c (00:c0:9f:bd:0c:7c)
    Type: IP (0x0800)
⊟ Internet Protocol, Src: 10.1.1.1 (10.1.1.1), Dst: 192.168.254.254 (192.168.254.254)
    Version: 4
    Header length: 20 bytes
  ⊞ Differentiated Services Field: 0x00 (DSCP 0x00: Default; ECN: 0x00)
    Total Length: 60
    Identification: 0x0bf7 (3063)
  ⊞ Flags: 0x00
    Fragment offset: 0
    Time to live: 128
    Protocol: ICMP (0x01)
  ⊞ Header checksum: 0x6421 [correct]
    Source: 10.1.1.1 (10.1.1.1)
    Destination: 192.168.254.254 (192.168.254.254)
⊟ Internet Control Message Protocol
    Type: 8 (Echo (ping) request)
    Code: 0
    Checksum: 0x2a5c [correct]
    Identifier: 0x0300
    Sequence number: 0x2000
```

As you can see, you can further expand the details for each section and protocol. Spend some time scrolling through this information. Although at this stage of the course you might not fully understand the displayed information, make a note of the information you do recognize.

Locate the two different types of "source" and "destination." Why are there two types?

_____

What protocols are in the Ethernet frame?

_____

As you select a line in the packet details pane, all or part of the information in the packet bytes pane also becomes highlighted. For example, if you select (highlight) the second line (+ Ethernet II) in the details pane, the bytes pane highlights the corresponding values, as shown in Figure 2-20.

Figure 2-20   Wireshark Packet Expanded, Highlighted Pane

```
0000  00 0c 85 cf 66 40 00 c0  9f bd 0c 7c 08 00 45 00   ....f@.....|..E.
0010  00 3c 0b f7 00 00 80 01  64 21 0a 01 01 01 c0 a8   .<......d!......
0020  fe fe 08 00 2a 5c 03 00  20 00 61 62 63 64 65 66   ....*\.. .abcdef
0030  67 68 69 6a 6b 6c 6d 6e  6f 70 71 72 73 74 75 76   ghijklmn opqrstuv
0040  77 61 62 63 64 65 66 67  68 69                     wabcdefg hi
```

This line shows the particular binary values that represent that information in the PDU. At this stage of the course, it is not necessary to understand this information in detail.

Step 4.   Go to the File menu and select **Close**.

Click **Continue without Saving** when the message box shown in Figure 2-16 appears.

Task 2: FTP PDU Capture

Step 1.   Start packet capture.

Assuming Wireshark is still running from the previous steps, start packet capture by clicking the **Start** option on the Capture menu of Wireshark.

At the command line on your computer running Wireshark, enter **ftp 192.168.254.254.**

When the connection is established, enter **anonymous** as the user without a password, as follows:

Userid: **anonymous**

Password: <ENTER>

You may alternatively log in with userid cisco and password cisco.

When successfully logged in, enter get /pub/eagle_labs/eagle1/chapter1/gaim-1.5.0.exe and press the Enter key <ENTER> to start downloading the file from the FTP server. The output will look similar to Example 2-2.

Example 2-2   Eagle Server Output

```
C:\Documents and Settings\ccna1>ftp eagle-server.example.com
Connected to eagle-server.example.com.
220 Welcome to the eagle-server FTP service.
User (eagle-server.example.com:(none)): anonymous
331 Please specify the password.
Password:<ENTER>
230 Login successful.
ftp> get /pub/eagle_labs/eagle1/chapter1/gaim-1.5.0.exe
200 PORT command successful. Consider using PASV.
150 Opening BINARY mode data connection for pub/eagle_labs/eagle1/chapter1/gaim-
1.5.0.exe (6967072 bytes).
226 File send OK.
ftp: 6967072 bytes received in 0.59Seconds 11729.08Kbytes/sec.
When the file download is complete, enter quit, as follows:
ftp> quit
221 Goodbye.
C:\Documents and Settings\ccna1>
```

When the file has successfully downloaded, stop the PDU capture in Wireshark.

Step 2.   Increase the size of the Wireshark packet list pane and scroll through the PDUs listed.

Locate and note those PDUs associated with the file download.

These will be the PDUs from the Layer 4 protocol, TCP, and the Layer 7 protocol, FTP.

Identify the three groups of PDUs associated with the file transfer.

If you performed Step 2, match the packets with the messages and prompts in the FTP command-line window.

The first group is associated with the "connection" phase and logging in to the server.

List examples of messages exchanged in this phase.

_____

_____

_____

Locate and list examples of messages exchanged in the second phase (that is, the actual download request and the data transfer).

_____

The third group of PDUs relate to logging out and "breaking the connection."

List examples of messages exchanged during this process.

_____

_____

Locate recurring TCP exchanges throughout the FTP process. What feature of TCP does this indicate?

_____

Step 3.   Examine packet details.

Select (highlight) a packet on the list associated with the first phase of the FTP process.

View the packet details in the details pane.

What protocols are encapsulated in the frame?

_____

Highlight the packets containing the username and password.

Examine the highlighted portion in the packet bytes pane.

What does this indicate about the security of this FTP login process?

_____

Highlight a packet associated with the second phase.

From any pane, locate the packet containing the filename.

_____

Highlight a packet containing the actual file content; note the plain text visible in the bytes pane.

In the details and bytes panes, highlight and examine some packets exchanged in the third phase of the file download.

Which features distinguish the content of these packets?

_____

When finished, close the Wireshark file and continue without saving.

Task 3: HTTP PDU Capture

Step 1.   Start packet capture.

Assuming Wireshark is still running from the previous steps, start packet capture by clicking the Start option on the Capture menu of Wireshark.

_____

Note: Capture options do not have to be set if you are continuing from previous steps of this lab.

Launch a web browser on the computer that is running Wireshark.

Enter the URL of the Eagle Server as **example.com** or enter the IP address **192.168.254.254**. After the web page has fully downloaded, stop the Wireshark packet capture.

Step 2.   Increase the size of the Wireshark packet list pane and scroll through the PDUs listed.

Locate and identify the TCP and HTTP packets associated with the downloaded web page.

Note the similarity between this message exchange and the FTP exchange.

Step 3.   In the packet list pane, highlight an HTTP packet that has the notation "(text/html)" in the Info column.

In the packet details pane, click the + box next to Line-based text data: html.

When this information expands, what is displayed?

_____

Examine the highlighted portion of the bytes pane. This shows the HTML data carried by the packet.

When you have finished, close the Wireshark file and continue without saving.

Task 4: Reflection

Consider the encapsulation information pertaining to captured network data Wireshark can provide. Relate this to the OSI and TCP/IP layer models. It is important that you can recognize and link both the protocols represented and the protocol layer and encapsulation types of the models with the information provided by Wireshark.

Task 5: Challenge

Discuss how you could use a protocol analyzer such as Wireshark to troubleshoot the failure of a web page to download successfully to a browser on a computer.

Also, identify data traffic on a network that is requested by users.

_____

Task 6: Cleanup

Unless instructed otherwise by your instructor, exit Wireshark and properly shut down the computer.

Packet Tracer Companion: Using Packet Tracer to View Protocol Data Units (2.6.2.2)

You can now open the file LSG01-Lab2622.pka on the CD-ROM that accompanies this book to repeat this hands-on lab using Packet Tracer. Remember, however, that Packet Tracer is not a substitute for a hands-on lab experience with real equipment. A summary of the instructions is provided within the activity.

Skills Integration Challenge: Examining Packets (2.7.1.3)

In this activity, you start building, testing, and analyzing a model of the Exploration lab network. You can now open the file LSG01-PTSkills2.pka on the CD-ROM that accompanies this book to do the challenge lab using Packet Tracer. Remember, however, that Packet Tracer is not a substitute for a hands-on lab experience with real equipment. A summary of the instructions is provided within the activity.

Figure 2-21 shows the topology for this challenge, and Table 2-7 reflects the addressing information.

Figure 2-21   Topology for Challenge

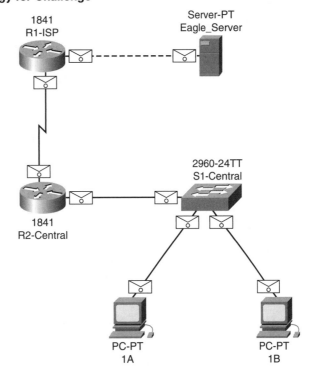

Table 2-7   Addressing Table

Device	Interface	IP Address	Subnet Mask	Default Gateway
R1-ISP	Fa0/0	192.168.254.253	255.255.255.0	N/A
	S0/0/0	10.10.10.6	255.255.255.252	N/A
R2-Central	Fa0/0	172.16.255.254	255.255.0.0	10.10.10.6
	S0/0/0	10.10.10.5	255.255.255.252	10.10.10.6
S1-Central	VLAN 1	172.16.254.1	255.255.0.0	172.16.255.254
PC 1A	NIC	172.16.1.1	255.255.0.0	172.16.255.254
PC 1B	NIC	172.16.1.2	255.255.0.0	172.16.255.254
Eagle Server	NIC	192.168.254.254	255.255.255.0	192.168.254.253

Upon completion of this activity, you will be able to do the following:

- Complete the topology.

- Add simple PDUs in real-time mode.

- Analyze PDUs in simulation mode.

- Experiment with the model of the standard lab setup.

Background

Throughout the course, you will be using a standard lab setup created from actual PCs, servers, routers, and switches to learn networking concepts. In this activity, you continue learning how to build and analyze this standard lab topology. If you have not done so already, you are encouraged to examine the Help files available from the Help pull-down menu at the top of the Packet Tracer GUI. Resources include a "My First PT Lab" to help you learn the basic operation of Packet Tracer, tutorials to guide you through various tasks, and information about the strengths and weaknesses of using Packet Tracer to model networks.

This activity provides an opportunity to explore the standard lab setup using the Packet Tracer simulator. Packet Tracer can create two file formats: PKT files (network simulation model files) and PKA files (activity files for practice). When you create your own networks in Packet Tracer, or modify existing files from your instructor or your peers, you will often use the PKT file format. When you launched this activity from the curriculum, these instructions appeared. They are the result of the PKA Packet Tracer activity file format. Two buttons appear at the bottom of these instructions: Check Results (which gives you feedback on how much of the activity you have completed) and Reset Activity (which starts the activity over, in case you want to clear your work or gain more practice).

Task 1: Complete the Topology

Add a PC to the workspace. Configure it using the following parameters: IP address 172.16.1.2, subnet mask 255.255.0.0, default gateway 172.16.255.254, DNS server 192.168.254.254, display name 1B. Connect PC 1B to the Fa0/2 port of the S1-Central Switch and check your work with the **Check Results** button to see that the topology is complete.

Task 2: Add Simple PDUs in Real-Time Mode

Using the Add Simple PDU, send a test message: one between PC 1B and Eagle Server. Note that this packet will appear in the event list as something that was "detected" or "sniffed" on the network, and in the lower right as a user-created PDU that can be manipulated for testing purposes.

Task 3: Analyze PDUs in Simulation Mode (Packet Tracing)

Switch to simulation mode. Double-click the red "Fire" button in the User-Created PDU window. Use the **Capture / Forward** button to move the packet through the network. Click the packet envelope, or click the colored square in the Info column of the event list, to examine the packet at each step in its journey.

Task 4: Experiment with the Model of the Standard Lab Setup

The standard lab setup will consist of two routers, one switch, one server, and two PCs. Each of these devices is preconfigured. Try creating different combinations of test packets and analyzing their journey through the network.

Task 5: Reflection

If you have not already done so, you are encouraged to obtain Packet Tracer from your instructor and complete My First PT Lab (available by accessing the Help pull-down menu and choosing Contents).

Application Layer Functionality and Protocols

The Study Guide portion of this chapter uses a combination of multiple-choice, matching, fill-in-the-blank, and open-ended questions to test your knowledge of the TCP/IP model application layer and the OSI model application, presentation, and session layers.

The Labs and Activities portion of this chapter includes all the online curriculum labs to further reinforce that you have mastered the practical, hands-on skills needed to work with the application layer of the OSI model.

As you work through this chapter, use Chapter 3 in the Network Fundamentals CCNA Exploration online curriculum, or use the corresponding Chapter 3 in the *Network Fundamentals CCNA Exploration Companion Guide*, for assistance.

Study Guide

Applications: The Interface Between the Networks

Visualizing the mechanisms that enable communication across the network is easier if you use the layered framework of the Open Systems Interconnection (OSI) model. In this section you explore the upper layers of both the OSI and TCP/IP models. How the human network generates data and how that data then enters the computer network is discussed. Application layer software and application layer services and protocols are examined in the labs.

When placed side by side, as shown in Figure 3-1, the OSI and TCP/IP models provide a means by which you can visualize and discuss the flow of networking.

Figure 3-1   OSI and TCP/IP Models

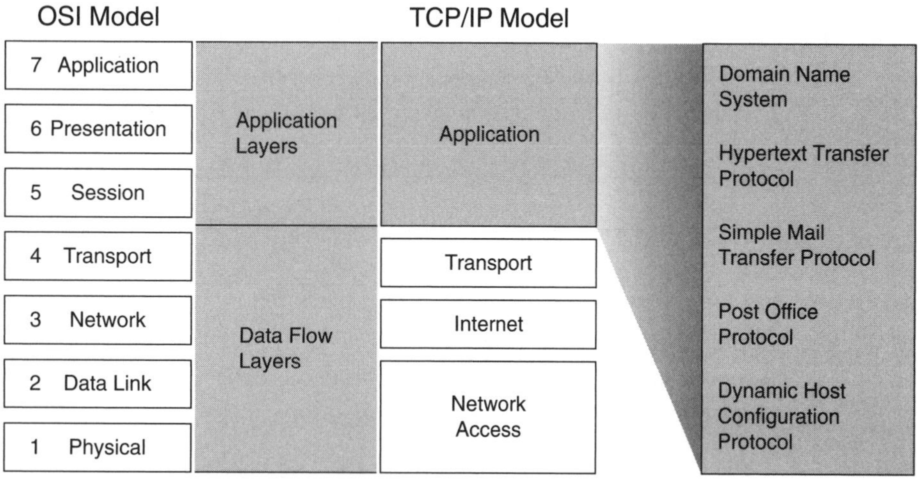

Vocabulary Exercise: Matching

In Table 3-1, match the term on the left with its definition on the right.

Table 3-1   OSI and TCP/IP Model Comparison

Term	Definition
a. Application layer	__ Generally defines the protocols in the TCP/IP suite
b. Layer 7	__ Top layer of both the OSI and TCP/IP models
c. Presentation layer	__ Functions at this layer create and maintain dialogs between source and destination applications
d. Session layer	__ The most widely known TCP/IP application layer protocols that provide for the exchange of user information
e. GIF, JPEG, TIFF	__ Top layer of the OSI model
f. DNS, HTTP, SMTP, FTP	__ Protocol used to provide remote access to servers and network work devices
g. Telnet	__ This layer provides coding, compression, and encryption
h. Request For Comments (RFC)	__ Graphic image formats

Concept Questions

1. What does the term network-aware application mean? List a few examples.

_____

_____

_____

_____

2. What is meant by the term application layer services? Why are protocols important when used in conjunction with application layer services?

_____

_____

_____

_____

3. It is difficult to generalize about protocols because they vary so greatly in purpose, but what properties do application protocols display?

_____

_____

_____

_____

Making Provisions for Applications and Services

When people attempt to access information on their device, whether it is a PC, laptop, PDA, cell phone, or some other device connected to a network, the data may not be physically stored on their device. If that is the case, a request to access that information must be made to the device where the data resides.

Vocabulary Exercise: Matching

In Table 3-2, match the term on the left with its definition on the right.

Table 3-2   Application Layer Terms

Term	Definition
a. Client	__ Device responding to the request
b. Server	__ Hosted on a client
c. Web services	__ Can be on a client and/or a server
d. Web browser	__ Device requesting information
e. Telnet services	__ Hosted on a web server
f. Peer-to-peer networks	__ Two or more computers are connected via a network and can share resources (such as printers and files) without having a dedicated server.

Multiple-Choice Questions

Choose the best answer(s) for each of the following questions.

1. Peer-to-peer applications can be used on which of the following? (Choose all that apply.)

   a. Peer-to-peer networks

   b. Client/server networks

   c. Across the Internet

   d. Across the intranet only

   e. Across the peer-to-server network

2. A Telnet server may have _____.

   a. a single client requesting a service

   b. multiple clients requesting services, but not at the same time

   c. multiple clients requesting services, simultaneously but as separate transactions

   d. multiple clients requesting services, simultaneously and as a single transaction

Application Layer Protocols and Services Examples

As you will see later in this course, the transport layer uses an addressing scheme called a port number. Port numbers identify applications and application layer services that are the source and destination of data. Server programs generally use predefined port numbers that are commonly known by clients.

Vocabulary Exercise: Matching

In Table 3-3, match the port number on the left with its protocol on the right.

Table 3-3   Port Numbers and Protocols

Port Number	Protocol
a. TCP/UDP port 53	__ Hypertext Transfer Protocol (HTTP)
b. TCP port 80	__ Post Office Protocol (POP)
c. TCP port 25	__ Telnet
d. UDP port 110	__ Domain Name System (DNS)
e. TCP port 23	__ Dynamic Host Configuration Protocol (DHCP)
f. UDP port 67	__ File Transfer Protocol (FTP)
g. TCP ports 20 and 21	__ Simple Mail Transfer Protocol (SMTP)

Vocabulary Exercise: Completion

Fill in the blanks in the following statements.

1. A DNS server provides name _____ using the name daemon.

2. DNS uses a _____ system to create a name database to provide name resolution.

3. When a web address (or URL) is entered into a web browser, the web browser establishes a connection to the web service running on the server using the _____ protocol.

4. When a client, typically a web browser, sends a _____ message to a server, HTTP defines the message types that the client uses to request the web page and also the message types the server uses to _____.

5. _____, the most popular network service, has revolutionized how people communicate through its simplicity and speed.

6. The e-mail server operates two separate processes: _____ and _____.

7. The _____ client is an application that runs on a computer that is used to push files to and pull files from a server.

8. _____ allows a host to obtain an IP address dynamically when it connects to the network.

9. The Server Message Block (SMB) is a _____ file-sharing protocol.

10. Sharing files over the Internet has become extremely popular. With _____applications based on the Gnutella protocol, people can make files on their hard disks available to others for downloading.

11. _____ provides a standard method of emulating text-based terminal devices over the data network.

Multiple-Choice Questions

Choose the best answer(s) for each of the following questions.

1. The Open Systems Interconnection reference model is a layered, abstract representation created as a guideline for network protocol design. The OSI model divides the networking process into which seven layers?

   a. Application, presentation, session, transport, network, data link, and physical

   b. Application, presentation, session, transport, Internet, data link, and physical

   c. Application, presentation, session, transport, network, Internet, and physical

   d. Application, presentation, Internet, transport, network, data link, and physical

2. What is the most popular application service?

   a. World Wide Web

   b. E-mail

   c. P2P

   d. eBay

3. The e-mail server operates which two separate processes?

   a. Mail Transfer Agent (MTA)

   b. Mail Transfer Bridge (MTB)

   c. Mail User Agent (MUA)

   d. Mail Delivery Agent (MDA)

4. Data transfer from a client to a server is referred to as which of the following?

   a. Query

   b. Download

   c. Upload

   d. Pull

5. Which of the following best describes a peer-to-peer network?

   a. It decentralizes the resources on a network.

   b. It centralizes the resources on a network.

   c. It uses file servers.

   d. It uses the client/server model.

6. The Domain Name System (DNS) was created to do what?

   a. Resolve domain names to e-mail addresses.

   b. Resolve domain names to MAC addresses.

   c. Resolve domain names to computer names.

   d. Resolve domain names to IP addresses.

7. The different top-level domains represent which of the following? (Choose all correct answers.)

   a. Type of organization

   b. Country of origin

   c. Company or brand name

   d. File server name

8. For secure communication across the Internet, which protocol is used to access or post web server information?

   a. HTTPS

   b. SHTTP

   c. Telnet

   d. STelnet

9. To receive e-mail messages from an e-mail server, the e-mail client can use which of the following protocols?

   a. SMTP

   b. SSH

   c. STP

   d. POP

10. Which service automates the assignment of IP addresses, subnet masks, gateway, and other IP networking parameters?

   a. SMTP

   b. TFTP

   c. HTTP

   d. DHCP

Labs and Activities

Activity 3-1: Data Stream Capture (3.4.1.1)

Upon completion of this activity, you will be able to

- Capture or download an audio stream.

- Record the file's characteristics.

- Examine data transfer rates associated with the file.

Background

When an application creates a file, the data that comprises that file must be stored somewhere. The data can be stored on the end device where it was created, or it can be transferred for storage on another device.

In this activity, you will use a microphone and Microsoft Sound Recorder to capture an audio stream. Microsoft Sound Recorder is a Windows accessory. You can find it in Windows XP by choosing **Start > Programs > Accessories > Entertainment > Sound Recorder**. If a microphone and Microsoft Sound Recorder are not available, you can download an audio file to use in this activity from http://newsroom.cisco.com/dlls/podcasts/audio_feeds.html.

Scenario

Perform this activity on a computer that has a microphone and Microsoft Sound Recorder or Internet access so that you can download an audio file.

Estimated completion time, depending on network speed, is 30 minutes.

Task 1: Create a Sound File

Step 1.   Open the Windows Sound Recorder application.

You can find the application in Windows XP by choosing **Start > Programs > Accessories > Entertainment > Sound Recorder**. The Sound Recorder interface is shown in Figure 3-2.

Figure 3-2   Sound Recorder Interface

Step 2.   Record an audio file.

To begin recording, click the Record button on the Sound Recorder interface.

Speak into the microphone, or create sounds that the microphone can pick up. As the audio is recorded, the sound's waveform should appear on the Sound Recorder interface, as shown in Figure 3-3.

Figure 3-3   Recording in Progress

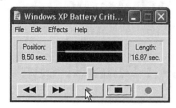

Click the Stop button when you are finished.

Step 3.   Check the audio file that was recorded.

Click the Play button to listen to the recording. The recording should be played back, as shown in Figure 3-4.

Figure 3-4   Playback

If you are unable to hear the recording, check the microphone's configuration, the speakers, and the volume settings, and attempt to create the recording again.

If you are unable to create a recording, download an audio file from News@Cisco at http://newsroom.cisco.com/dlls/podcasts/audio_feeds.html.

Save the audio file to the desktop, and proceed to Task 2.

Step 4.   Save the audio file.

Save to the desktop the audio file you created. Name the file myaudio.wav.

After saving the file, close the Sound Recorder application.

Task 2: Observe the Properties of the Audio File

Step 1.   View audio file properties.

Right-click the audio file you saved to the desktop, and choose **Properties** from the popup menu.

What is the file size in kilobytes? _____

What is the file size in bytes? _____

What is the file size in bits? _____

Step 2.   Open the audio file in Windows Media Player.

Right-click the audio file and choose **Open With > Windows Media Player**.

When the file is open, right-click at the top of the Media Player interface, and choose **File > Properties** from the popup menu.

What is the length of the audio file in seconds?

Calculate the amount of data per second in the audio file, and record the result.

Task 3: Reflection

Data files do not have to remain on the end devices where they are created. For example, you may want to copy the audio file that you created to another computer or a portable audio device.

If the audio file that you saved to the desktop were to be transferred at a rate of 100 megabits per second (Mbps), how long would it take for the file transfer to be completed?

Even with an Ethernet connection operating at 100 Mbps, the data that makes up a file is not transferred at this speed. All Ethernet frames contain other information, such as source and destination addresses, that is necessary for the frame's delivery.

If the Ethernet overhead uses 5 percent of the available 100 Mbps bandwidth, and 95 percent of the bandwidth is left for the data payload, how long would it take the file transfer to be completed?

Task 4: Clean Up

You may be required to remove from the computer the audio file you saved. If so, delete the file from the desktop.

Unless instructed otherwise, turn off the computer.

Lab 3-1: Managing a Web Server (3.4.2.1)

Upon completion of this lab, you will be able to

- Download, install, and verify a web server application.
- Verify the default web server configuration file.
- Capture and analyze HTTP traffic with Wireshark.

Background

Web servers are an important part of the business plan for any organization with a presence on the Internet. Consumers use web browsers to access business websites. However, web browsers make up only half the communication channel. The other half is web server support. Web server support is a valuable skill for network administrators. Based on a survey by Netcraft in January 2007, Table 3-4 shows the top three web server applications by percentage of use.

Table 3-4   Web Server Choices

Web Server	Percent of Use
Apache	60 percent
Microsoft	31 percent
Sun	1.6 percent

Scenario

In this lab you will download, install, and configure the popular Apache web server. You will use a web browser to connect to the server, using Wireshark to capture the communication. Analyzing the capture will help you understand how the HTTP protocol operates.

The lab should be configured as shown in Figure 3-5 and Table 3-5. If it is not, ask the instructor for assistance before proceeding.

Figure 3-5   Topology for Lab 3-1

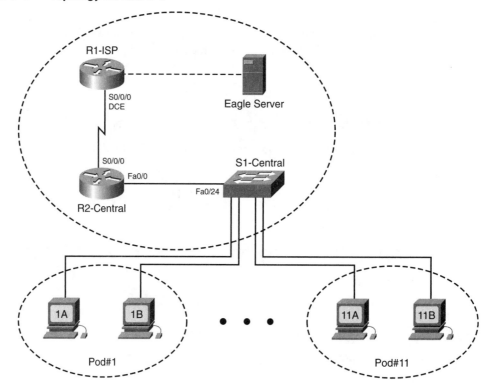

Table 3-5   Addressing Table

Device	Interface	IP Address	Subnet Mask	Default Gateway
R1-ISP	S0/0/0	10.10.10.6	255.255.255.252	—
	Fa0/0	192.168.254.253	255.255.255.0	—
R2-Central	S0/0/0	10.10.10.5	255.255.255.252	10.10.10.4
	Fa0/0	172.16.255.254	255.255.0.0	—
Eagle Server	—	192.168.254.254	255.255.255.0	192.168.254.253
	—	172.31.24.254	255.255.255.0	—
Host *Pod#*A	—	172.16.*Pod#*.1	255.255.0.0	172.16.255.254
Host *Pod#*B	—	172.16.*Pod#*.2	255.255.0.0	172.16.255.254
S1-Central	—	172.16.254.1	255.255.0.0	172.16.255.254

Task 1: Download, Install, and Verify the Apache Web Server

Step 1.   Download the software from Eagle Server.

The Apache web server application is available for download from Eagle Server.

Using a web browser, go to ftp://eagle-server.example.com/pub/eagle_labs/eagle1/chapter3 to access and download the software.

Right-click the file, and save the software on the pod host computer.

Step 2.   Install the Apache web server on the pod host computer.

Open the folder where the software was saved, and double-click the Apache file to begin installation. Choose default values and consent to the licensing agreement. The next installation step requires customized configuration of the web server, as shown in Figure 3-6.

Figure 3-6   Customized Configuration Screen

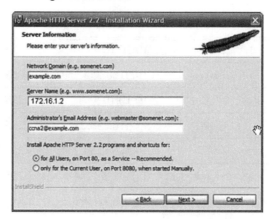

Use the values shown in Table 3-6.

Table 3-6   Apache Server Values

Information	Value
Network Domain	example.com
Server Name	The computer's IP address
Administrator's E-mail Address	ccna*xx*@example.com. For example, for users 1 through 22, if the computer is on Pod 5, Host B, the administrator's e-mail address is ccna10@example.com.

Accept the recommended port and service status. Click **Next**.

Accept the default typical installation, and click **Next**.

What is the default installation folder?

_____

Accept the default installation folder, click **Next**, and click **Install**. When the installation has finished, close the screen.

Note: If a Windows Security Alert is displayed, as shown in Figure 3-7, click Unblock. This permits connections to the web server.

Figure 3-7   Windows Security Alert

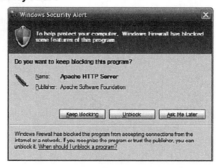

Step 3.   Verify the web server.

The **netstat** command displays protocol statistics and connection information for this lab computer.

Choose **Start > Run** and open a command-line window. Enter **cmd**, and then click **OK**. Use the **netstat -a** command to discover open and connected ports on your computer, as shown in Example 3-1.

Example 3-1   netstat -a Output

```
C:\> netstat -a
Active Connections


Proto    Local Address            Foreign Address          State
TCP      GW-desktop-hom:http      GW-desktop-hom:0         LISTENING
TCP      GW-desktop-hom:epmap     GW-desktop-hom:0         LISTENING
TCP      GW-desktop-hom:microsoft-ds  GW-desktop-hom:0 LISTENING
TCP      GW-desktop-hom:3389      GW-desktop-hom:0         LISTENING
<output omitted>
C:\>
```

Using the command **netstat -a**, verify that the web server is operating properly on the pod host computer.

The Apache web server monitor icon should be visible on the lower-right side of the screen, near the time.

Open a web browser, and connect to your computer's URL. A web page similar to Figure 3-8 appears if the web server is working properly.

Figure 3-8   Web Server Default Page

The 127.0.0.0 /8 network address is reserved and is used for local IP addresses. The same page should be displayed if the URL is changed to the IP address on the Ethernet interface or to any host IP address in the 127.0.0.0 /8 network range.

Test the web server on several different IP addresses from the 127.0.0.0 /8 network range. Fill in Table 3-7 with the results.

Table 3-7   Web Server Test

IP Address	Status	Description
127.0.0.1		
127.255.255.254		
127.255.255.255		
127.0.0.0		

Task 2: Verify the Default Web Server Configuration File

Step 1.   Access the httpd.conf file.

A system administrator may need to verify or modify the default configuration file.

Open the Apache web server configuration file, C:\Program Files\Apache Software Foundation\Apache2.2\conf\httpd.conf, as shown in Figure 3-9.

Figure 3-9   Apache Web Server Configuration File

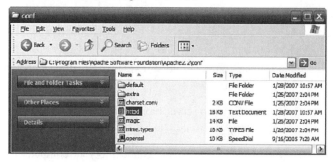

Step 2.   Review the httpd.conf file.

Numerous configuration parameters allow the Apache web server to be fully customizable. The # character indicates a comment for system administrators; the web server ignores the comment. Scroll down the configuration file, and verify the settings listed in Table 3-8.

Table 3-8   Apache Web Server Settings

Value	Description
#Listen 12.34.56.78:80	
Listen 80	Listen on TCP port 80 for all incoming connections. To accept connections from only this host, change the line to Listen 127.0.0.1 80.
ServerAdmin ccna2@example.com	If there are problems, e-mail the web server at this e-mail address.
ServerName 172.16.1.2:80	For servers without DNS names, use the IP *address:port number*.
DocumentRoot "C:/Program Files/Apache Software Foundation/ Apache2.2/htdocs"	This is the root directory for the web server.

Table 3-8   Apache Web Server Settings   *continued*

Value	Description
\<IfModule dir_module\>	
DirectoryIndex index.html	
\</IfModule\>	DirectoryIndex sets the file that Apache serves if a directory is requested. If no page is requested from that directory, display index.html if it is present.

Step 3.   Modify the web server default page.

Figure 3-8 shows the default web page from file index.html. Although this page is sufficient for testing, something more personal should be displayed.

Open folder C:\Program Files\Apache Software Foundation\Apache2.2\htdocs. The file index.html should be present. Right-click the file, and choose **Open With**. From the pull-down list, choose **notepad**. Change the file content to something similar to Example 3-2.

Example 3-2   htdocs Edit

```
<html><body><h1>Welcome to the Pod1HostB Web Server!!!</h1>
<center><bold>
Operated by me!
</center></bold>
Contact web administrator: ccna2@example.com
</body></html>
```

Save the file, and refresh the web browser. Or, go to http://127.0.0.1. The new default page should be displayed. As you make and save changes to index.html, refresh the web browser to view the new content.

Task 3: Capture and Analyze HTTP Traffic with Wireshark

Wireshark will not capture packets sent from or to the 127.0.0.0 network on a Windows computer. The interface will not appear. To complete this task, access the web server by running Apache from a separate client machine.

Step 1.   Analyze HTTP traffic.

Start Wireshark, and set the capture interface to the interface destined for the 172.16 network. Open a web browser, and connect to another computer with an active web server.

Why does index.html *not* have to be entered in the URL for the file contents to be displayed?

_____

_____

Deliberately enter a web page that is not on the web server. Note that an error message is displayed in the web browser, as shown in Figure 3-10.

Figure 3-10   404 Not Found Error

Figure 3-11 shows a captured HTTP session. File index.htm was requested from the web server, but the server did not have it. Therefore, the server sent a 404 error. The web browser simply displayed the server response "The page cannot be found."

Figure 3-11   Wireshark Capture of HTTP Traffic

No. -	Time	Source	Destination	Protocol	Info
20	14.384747	172.16.1.2	172.16.1.1	TCP	1149 > http [SYN] seq=0 Len=0 MSS=1360
21	14.384993	172.16.1.1	172.16.1.2	TCP	http > 1149 [SYN, ACK] Seq=0 Ack=1 Win=65535 Len=0 MSS=1460
22	14.385030	172.16.1.2	172.16.1.1	TCP	1149 > http [ACK] seq=1 Ack=1 win=64240 Len=0
23	14.388292	172.16.1.2	172.16.1.1	HTTP	GET /index.htm HTTP/1.1
24	14.389299	172.16.1.1	172.16.1.2	HTTP	HTTP/1.1 404 Not Found (text/html)
25	14.541723	172.16.1.2	172.16.1.1	TCP	1149 > http [ACK] seq=256 Ack=423 Win=63818 Len=0

What are the contents of the HTTP session?

_____

_____

_____

_____

_____

_____

_____

_____

Task 4: Challenge

Modify the default web server configuration file httpd.conf by changing the **Listen 80** line to **Listen 8080**. Open a web browser and go to http://127.0.0.1:8080. Verify with the **netstat** command that the new web server TCP port is 8080.

Task 5: Reflection

Web servers are an important component of e-commerce. Depending on the organization, the network or web administrator has the responsibility of maintaining the corporate web server. This lab has demonstrated how to install and configure the Apache web server, test for proper operation, and identify several key configuration parameters.

You modified the default web page index.html and observed the effect on the web browser output.

Finally, you used Wireshark to capture an HTTP session of a file that could not be found. The web server responded with an HTTP 1.1 error 404 and returned a file not found message to the web browser.

Task 6: Clean Up

During this lab the Apache web server was installed on the pod host computer. It should be uninstalled. To uninstall the web server, choose **Start > Control Panel > Add or Remove Programs**. Click **Apache Web Server**, and then click **Remove**.

Unless directed otherwise by the instructor, turn off power to the host computers. Remove anything that was brought into the lab, and leave the room ready for the next class.

Lab 3-2: E-mail Services and Protocols (3.4.3.1)

Upon completion of this lab, you will be able to

- Configure the pod host computer for e-mail service.

- Capture and analyze e-mail communication between the pod host computer and a mail server.

Background

E-mail is one of the most popular network services that uses a client/server model. The e-mail client is configured on a user's computer and is configured to connect to an e-mail server. Most Internet service providers (ISP) provide step-by-step instructions for using e-mail services. Consequently, the typical user may be unaware of the complexities of e-mail or the protocols used.

In network environments where the Mail User Agent (MUA) client must connect to an e-mail server on another network to send and receive e-mail, the following protocols are used:

- Simple Mail Transfer Protocol (SMTP) was originally defined in RFC 821 in August 1982. It has undergone many modifications and enhancements. RFC 2821, from April 2001, consolidates and updates previous e-mail-related RFCs. The SMTP server listens on well-known TCP port 25. SMTP is used to send e-mail messages from the external e-mail client to the e-mail server, deliver e-mail to local accounts, and relay e-mail between SMTP servers.

- Post Office Protocol version 3 (POPv3) is used when an external e-mail client wants to receive e-mail messages from the e-mail server. The POPv3 server listens on well-known TCP port 110.

- Internet Message Access Protocol (IMAP) is an Internet protocol that allows a central server to provide remote access to e-mail messages. IMAP servers listen on well-known TCP port 143.

  In this lab, you will use IMAP instead of POPv3 for e-mail delivery to the client.

  Earlier versions of both protocols should not be used. Also, secure versions of both protocols employ Secure Socket Layer/Transport Layer Security (SSL/TLS) for communication.

E-mail is subject to multiple computer security vulnerabilities. Spam attacks flood networks with useless, unsolicited e-mail, consuming bandwidth and network resources. E-mail servers have had numerous vulnerabilities, which have left computers open to compromise.

Scenario

In this lab, you will configure and use an e-mail client application to connect to eagle-server network services. You will monitor the communication with Wireshark and analyze the captured packets.

You will use an e-mail client such as Outlook Express or Mozilla Thunderbird to connect to the eagle-server network service. Eagle-server has SMTP mail services preconfigured, with user accounts that can send and receive external e-mail messages.

The lab should be configured as shown in Figure 3-12 and Table 3-9. If it is not, ask the instructor for assistance before proceeding.

Figure 3-12   Topology for Lab 3-2

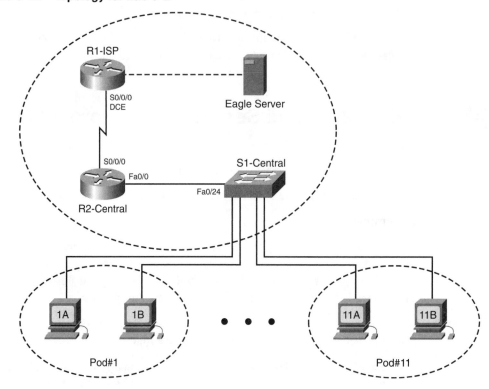

Table 3-9   Addressing Table

Device	Interface	IP Address	Subnet Mask	Default Gateway
R1-ISP	S0/0/0	10.10.10.6	255.255.255.252	—
	Fa0/0	192.168.254.253	255.255.255.0	—
R2-Central	S0/0/0	10.10.10.5	255.255.255.252	10.10.10.4
	Fa0/0	172.16.255.254	255.255.0.0	—
Eagle Server	—	192.168.254.254	255.255.255.0	192.168.254.253
	—	172.31.24.254	255.255.255.0	—
Host *Pod#*A	—	172.16.*Pod#*.1	255.255.0.0	172.16.255.254
Host *Pod#*B	—	172.16.*Pod#*.2	255.255.0.0	172.16.255.254
S1-Central	—	172.16.254.1	255.255.0.0	172.16.255.254

Task 1: Configure the Pod Host Computer for E-mail Service

Step 1.   Download and install Mozilla Thunderbird.

If Thunderbird is not installed on the pod host computer, you can download it from eagle-server.example.com, as shown in Figure 3-13. The download URL is **ftp://eagle-server.example.com/pub/eagle_labs/eagle1/chapter3.**

Figure 3-13   FTP Download for Wireshark

Double-click the Thunderbird filename, and then select Save the file to the host pod computer.

Note: Depending on the connection speed of the link between the two routers and the number of students downloading the file, this download may be slow.

When the file has downloaded, double-click the filename and install Thunderbird with the default settings.

When finished, start Thunderbird.

Step 2.   Configure Thunderbird to receive and send e-mail messages.

If prompted for Import Options, select **Don't import anything**, and click **Next**.

When Thunderbird starts, you must configure an e-mail account. In the New Account Setup, select **Email account**, and then click **Next**.

Fill in the account information, as prompted, with the information shown in Table 3-10.

Table 3-10   Account Information

Field	Value
Account Name	The account name is based on the pod and host computer. A total of 22 accounts are configured on Eagle Server, labeled ccna[1...22]. If this pod host is on Pod1, Host A, the account name is **ccna1**. If the pod host is on Pod 3, Host B, the account name is **ccna6**, and so on.
Your Name	Use the same name as the Account Name.
E-mail address	*your_name*@**eagle-server.example.com**
Type of incoming server you are using	**IMAP**
Incoming Server (SMTP)	**eagle-server.example.com**
Outgoing Server (SMTP)	**eagle-server.example.com**
Incoming User Name	**Use the same name as above (see Account name discussion).**
Account Name	*your_name*@**eagle-server.example.com**

When Thunderbird starts, you may be prompted for a password for your e-mail account. Click **Cancel**.

The Thunderbird client needs to have SMTP server login disabled. To do this, choose **Tools > Account Settings > Outgoing Server (SMTP)**. From the outgoing server screen, shown in Figure 3-14, click **Edit**.

Figure 3-14   Thunderbird SMTP Server Settings

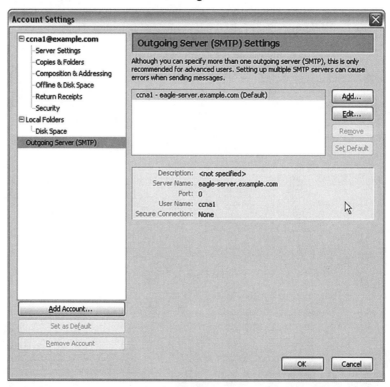

On the SMTP Server screen, shown in Figure 3-15, uncheck the **Use name and password** box. Click **OK**, and then click **OK** again.

Figure 3-15 SMTP Server Edit

You may also want to verify account settings, as shown in Figure 3-16, by choosing **Tools > Account Settings**.

Figure 3-16 Thunderbird Account Settings

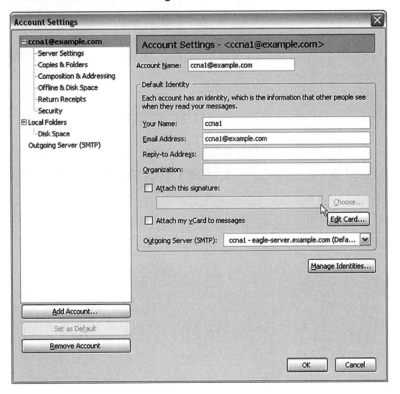

In the left pane of the Account Settings screen, click Server Settings. A screen similar to Figure 3-17 appears.

Figure 3-17   Thunderbird Server Settings

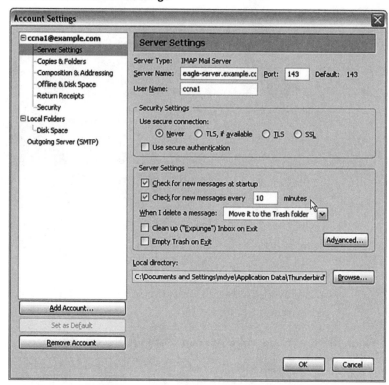

What is the purpose of the SMTP protocol, and what is the well-known TCP port number?

_____

_____

Task 2: Capture and Analyze E-mail Communication Between the Pod Host Computer and an E-mail Server

Step 1.   Send an uncaptured e-mail.

Ask another student in the class for his or her e-mail name.

To create and send an e-mail, click the **Write** icon. Using the name provided in the preceding task, each of you should compose and send an e-mail message to the other.

When the e-mails have been sent, check your e-mail. To do so, you must be logged in. If you have not previously logged in, enter **cisco** as the password. Please note that this is the default password that is embedded in the Eagle Server.

Step 2.   Start Wireshark captures.

When you are certain that the e-mail operation is working properly for both sending and receiving, start a Wireshark capture. Wireshark displays captures based on packet type.

Step 3.   Analyze a Wireshark capture session of SMTP.

Using the e-mail client, again send and receive e-mail from a classmate. This time, however, the e-mail transactions will be captured.

After sending and receiving one e-mail message, stop the Wireshark capture. A partial Wireshark capture of an outgoing e-mail message using SMTP is shown in Figure 3-18.

Figure 3-18   SMTP Capture

No.	Time	Source	Destination	Protocol	Info
1	0.000000	172.16.1.1	172.16.255.255	NBNS	Name query NB WORKGROUP<1b>
2	0.741371	172.16.1.1	172.16.255.255	NBNS	Name query NB WORKGROUP<1b>
3	1.492443	172.16.1.1	172.16.255.255	NBNS	Name query NB WORKGROUP<1b>
4	3.306445	172.16.1.1	192.168.254.254	TCP	1250 > smtp [SYN] Seq=0 Len=0 MSS=1460
5	3.306968	192.168.254.254	172.16.1.1	TCP	smtp > 1250 [SYN, ACK] Seq=0 Ack=1 Win=5840 Len=0 MSS=1
6	3.307012	172.16.1.1	192.168.254.254	TCP	1250 > smtp [ACK] Seq=1 Ack=1 Win=64240 Len=0
7	3.313519	192.168.254.254	172.16.1.1	SMTP	Response: 220 localhost.localdomain ESMTP Sendmail 8.13.1/8.13
8	3.353004	172.16.1.1	192.168.254.254	SMTP	Command: EHLO [172.16.1.1]
9	3.353436	192.168.254.254	172.16.1.1	TCP	smtp > 1250 [ACK] Seq=90 Ack=20 Win=5840 Len=0
10	3.353657	192.168.254.254	172.16.1.1	SMTP	Response: 250-localhost.localdomain Hello host-1.example.com [1?
11	3.356823	172.16.1.1	192.168.254.254	SMTP	Command: MAIL FROM:<ccna1@example.com> SIZE=398
12	3.359743	192.168.254.254	172.16.1.1	SMTP	Response: 250 2.1.0 <ccna1@example.com>... Sender ok
13	3.363127	172.16.1.1	192.168.254.254	SMTP	Command: RCPT TO:<ccna2@example.com>
14	3.365007	192.168.254.254	172.16.1.1	SMTP	Response: 250 2.1.5 <ccna2@example.com>... Recipient ok
15	3.367680	172.16.1.1	192.168.254.254	SMTP	Command: DATA
16	3.368230	192.168.254.254	172.16.1.1	SMTP	Response: 354 Enter mail, end with "." on a line by itself
17	3.376881	172.16.1.1	192.168.254.254	SMTP	Message Body
18	3.387830	192.168.254.254	172.16.1.1	SMTP	Response: 250 2.0.0 l0S8dIOY005299 Message accepted for deliver
19	3.395347	172.16.1.1	192.168.254.254	SMTP	Message Body
20	3.395855	192.168.254.254	172.16.1.1	SMTP	Response: 221 2.0.0 localhost.localdomain closing connection
21	3.395897	192.168.254.254	172.16.1.1	TCP	smtp > 1250 [FIN, ACK] Seq=564 Ack=502 Win=6432 Len=0
22	3.395929	172.16.1.1	192.168.254.254	TCP	1250 > smtp [ACK] Seq=502 Ack=565 Win=63677 Len=0
23	3.405772	172.16.1.1	192.168.254.254	TCP	1250 > smtp [FIN, ACK] Seq=502 Ack=565 Win=63677 Len=0
24	3.406204	192.168.254.254	172.16.1.1	TCP	smtp > 1250 [ACK] Seq=565 Ack=503 Win=6432 Len=0

Highlight the first SMTP capture in the top Wireshark window. In Figure 3-18, this is line 7.

In the second Wireshark window, expand the Simple Mail Transfer Protocol record.

Many different types of SMTP servers exist. Malicious attackers can gain valuable knowledge simply by learning the SMTP server type and version.

What are the SMTP server name and version?

_____

E-mail client applications send commands to e-mail servers, and e-mail servers send responses. In every first SMTP exchange, the e-mail client sends the command **EHLO**. The syntax may vary between clients, however, and the command may also be **HELO** or **HELLO**. The e-mail server must respond to the command.

What is the SMTP server response to the **EHLO** command?

_____

The next exchanges between the e-mail client and server contain e-mail information. Using your Wireshark capture, fill in the e-mail server responses to the e-mail client commands shown in Table 3-11.

Table 3-11   Response Table

E-mail Client	E-mail Server
MAIL FROM:<ccna1@example.com>	
RCPT TO:<ccna2@example.com>	
DATA	
(message body is sent)	

What are the contents of the last message body from the e-mail client?

_____

How does the e-mail server respond?

_____

Task 3: Challenge

Access a computer that has Internet access. Look up the SMTP server name and version for known weaknesses or compromises. Are any newer versions available?

Task 4: Reflection

E-mail is probably the most common network service used. Understanding the flow of traffic with the SMTP protocol will help you understand how the protocol manages the client/server data connection. E-mail can also experience configuration issues. Is the problem with the e-mail client or the e-mail server? One simple way to test SMTP server operation is to use the Windows command-line Telnet utility to telnet into the SMTP server.

To test SMTP operation, open the Windows command-line window, and begin a Telnet session with the SMTP server, as shown in Example 3-3. The highlighted lines are what you enter into the blank Telnet window.

Example 3-3   Telnet Session

```
C:\> telnet eagle-server.example.com 25
220 localhost.localdomain ESMTP Sendmail 8.13.1/8.13.1; Sun, 28 Jan 2007
20:41:0
3 +1000
HELO eagle-server.example.com
250 localhost.localdomain Hello [172.16.1.2], pleased to meet you
MAIL From: ccna2@example.com
250 2.1.0 ccna2@example.com... Sender ok
RCPT To: instructor@example.com
250 2.1.5 instructor@example.com... Recipient ok
DATA
354 Please start mail input.
e-mail SMTP server test...
.
250 Mail queued for delivery.
QUIT
221 Closing connection. Good bye.
Connection to host lost.
C:\ >
```

Task 5: Clean Up

If Thunderbird was installed on the pod host computer for this lab, the instructor may want the application removed. To remove Thunderbird, choose **Start > Control Panel > Add or Remove Programs**. Scroll to and click **Thunderbird**, and then click **Remove**.

Unless directed otherwise by the instructor, turn off power to the host computers. Remove anything that was brought into the lab, and leave the room ready for the next class.

Skills Integration Challenge: Configuring Hosts and Services (3.5.1.3)

Open the file LSG01-PTSkills3.pka on the CD-ROM that accompanies this book to perform this exercise using Packet Tracer.

Upon completion of this activity, you will be able to

- Configure hosts and services.

- Add, configure, and connect hosts and servers.

- Explore how DNS and HTTP work together.

- Use simulation mode to view the details of packets generated by DNS and HTTP.

Background

Throughout the course, you will use a standard lab setup created from actual PCs, servers, routers, and switches to learn networking concepts. At the end of each chapter, you will build increasingly larger parts of this topology in Packet Tracer.

Figure 3-19 shows the topology for this Skills Integration Challenge, and Table 3-12 shows the corresponding addressing table.

Figure 3-19   Topology for the Challenge

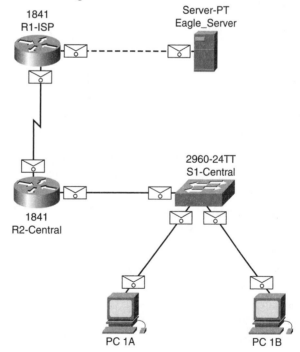

Table 3-12   Addressing Table

Device	Interface	IP Address	Subnet Mask	Default Gateway
R1-ISP	Fa0/0	192.168.254.253	255.255.255.0	—
	S0/0/0	10.10.10.6	255.255.255.252	—
R2-Central	Fa0/0	172.16.255.254	255.255.0.0	10.10.10.6
	S0/0/0	10.10.10.5	255.255.255.252	10.10.10.6
S1-Central	VLAN 1	172.16.254.1	255.255.0.0	172.16.255.254
PC 1A	NIC	172.16.1.1	255.255.0.0	172.16.255.254
PC 1B	NIC	172.16.1.2	255.255.0.0	172.168.255.254
Eagle Server	NIC	192.168.254.254	255.255.255.0	192.168.254.253

Task 1: "Repair" and Test the Topology

Add a PC with a display name of 1B to the topology. Configure it with the following settings:

- IP address: 172.16.1.2

- Subnet mask: 255.255.0.0

- Default gateway: 172.16.255.254

- DNS server: 192.168.254.254

Connect PC 1B to the Fa0/2 port of the S1-Central switch. Connect Eagle Server to the Fa0/0 port on the R1-ISP router. Turn on web services on the server by enabling HTTP. Enable DNS services, and add a DNS entry that associates eagle-server.example.com with the server's IP address. Verify your work using feedback from the **Check Results** button and the **Assessment Items** tab.

Test connectivity in real time by using ADD SIMPLE PDU to test connectivity between PC 1B and the Eagle Server. Note that when you add a simple PDU, it appears in the PDU List Window as part of "Scenario 0." The first time you issue this one-shot ping message, it shows Failed because of the ARP process. Double-click the **Fire** button in the PDU List Window to send this single test ping a second time. This time it succeeds.

In Packet Tracer, the term *scenario* means a specific configuration of one or more test packets. You can create different test packet scenarios by clicking the **New** button. For example, Scenario 0 might have one test packet from PC 1B to Eagle Server, and Scenario 1 might test packets between PC 1A and the routers. You can remove all test packets in a particular scenario by clicking the **Delete** button. For example, if you use the **Delete** button for Scenario 0, the test packet you just created between PC 1B and Eagle Server is removed. Do this before the next task.

Task 2: Explore How DNS and HTTP Work Together

Switch from Realtime mode to Simulation mode. Open a web browser from the desktop of PC 1B. Enter **eagle-server.example.com**, press **Enter**, and then use the **Capture / Forward** button in the Event List to capture the interaction of DNS and HTTP.

Play this animation. Examine the Packet contents (PDU Information Window, Inbound PDU Details, Outbound PDU Details) for each event in the event list, especially when the packets are at PC 1B or at Eagle Server. If you receive a "Buffer Full" message, click the **View Previous Events** button. Even though the processing of the packets by the switch and the routers may not make sense to you yet, you should be able to see how DNS and HTTP work together.

Task 3: Reflection

Can you now explain the process that occurs when you enter a URL into a browser and a web page returns? What types of client/server interactions are involved? If you have not already done so, you are encouraged to obtain Packet Tracer from your instructor and complete My First PT Lab (choose **Help > Contents**).

CHAPTER 4

OSI Transport Layer

The Study Guide portion of this chapter uses a combination of multiple-choice, matching, fill-in-the-blank, and open-ended questions to test your knowledge of the OSI transport layer.

The Labs and Activities portion of this chapter includes all the online curriculum labs to further reinforce that you have mastered the practical, hands-on skills needed.

As you work through this chapter, use Chapter 4 in the Network Fundamentals CCNA Exploration online curriculum or use the corresponding Chapter 4 in the *Network Fundamentals CCNA 1 Exploration Companion Guide* for assistance.

Study Guide

Roles of the Transport Layer

The transport layer provides vital control over the network: It enables multiple applications to work at the same time over the same network. That way, one computer can use instant messaging, surf the web, use a Voice over IP (VoIP) phone, stream video, and check e-mail.

The transport layer provides for data network needs by

- Dividing data received from an application into segments
- Adding a header to identify and manage each segment
- Using the header information to reassemble the segments back into application data
- Passing the assembled data to the correct application

Vocabulary Exercise: Matching

In Table 4-1, match the definitions on the right with the terms on the left.

Table 4-1   Transport Layer Matching Exercise

Term	Definition
a. Multiplexing	__ Ensures the application is ready to receive data.
b. Data segmentation	__ Manages data delivery if there is congestion on the host.
c. Error checking	__ Facilitates data preparation for delivery by the lowest four OSI layers.
d. Establishing a session	__ Multiple network-aware applications can use the network at the same time.
e. Same order delivery	__ Performed on the data in the segment to check if the segment was changed during transmission.
f. Reliable delivery	__ Means lost segments are present so the data is received complete.
g. Flow control	__ Ensures segment sequencing so that data can be presented by the session layer to the application layer with all data intact and ready for processing.

Concept Questions

1. How does the transport layer multiplex different applications' communication?

   using segmentation, where T.L breaks the large data sent for app. layer into smaller peices called segments.

2. How does the transport layer tell the difference between different data segments?

   Port number.

Vocabulary Exercise: Completion

Fill in the blanks for the following questions.

1. The pieces of communication in UDP are called _____.

2. Additional functions specified by TCP are _____, reliable delivery, and _____.

3. A TCP segment has ___ bytes of overhead in the header encapsulating the application layer data, whereas each UDP segment only has ___ bytes of overhead.

Port Type Ranges Exercise

Table 4-2 lists port types. Fill in the port number ranges in the Numbers column.

Table 4-2   Port Type Ranges

Port Type	Numbers
Well-known ports	
Registered ports	
Dynamic or private ports	

The TCP Protocol: Communicating with Reliability

The key distinction between TCP and UDP is reliability. This reliability is achieved by having fields in the TCP segment, each with a specific function. A complete TCP conversation requires the establishment of a session between the source and the destination in both directions. As the source receives an acknowledgment from the destination, it knows that the data has been successfully delivered and can quit tracking that data. If the source does not receive an acknowledgment within a predetermined amount of time, it retransmits that data to the destination.

Concept Questions

1. When the host is using TCP, why does the transport layer initiate a process to create a connection with the destination?

    _____

    _____

2. A key feature of TCP is its reliability. Define *reliability*.

    _____

    _____

Vocabulary Exercise: Matching

In Table 4-3, match the definition on the right with a flag on the left.

Table 4-3   Flag-Matching Exercise

Flags	Definition
a. ACK	__ Urgent pointer field significant
b. PSH	__ Acknowledgment field significant
c. SYN	__ Push function
d. URG	__ Reset the connection
e. FIN	__ Synchronize sequence numbers
f. RST	__ No more data from sender

Managing TCP Sessions

When services send data using TCP, segments may arrive at their destination out of order. For the original message to be understood by the recipient, the data in these segments is reassembled into the original order. Sequence numbers are assigned in the header of each packet to achieve this goal. Segment sequence numbers enable reliability by indicating how to reassemble and reorder received segments.

Internet Research Exercise

Using your favorite search engine, enter the keywords "TCP segment reassembly," and find a website that explains it. Using this site, be prepared to share your findings with the class.

Concept Questions

1. What is expectational acknowledgment?

   _____

   _____

2. In what case would it be possible for the destination to acknowledge bytes in discontiguous segments and request that the host retransmit only the missing data?

   _____

3. What is flow control, and what does it do?

   _____

   _____

The UDP Protocol: Communicating with Low Overhead

User Datagram Protocol (UDP) is a simple protocol that provides the basic transport layer functions. It has much lower overhead than TCP because it is not connection oriented and does not provide the sophisticated retransmission, sequencing, and flow-control mechanisms.

Some applications, such as online games and VoIP, can tolerate some loss of data. If these applications use TCP, they might experience large delays while TCP detects data loss and retransmits data. These delays would be more detrimental to the application than small data losses. The low overhead of UDP makes it very desirable for such applications. Some applications, such as DNS, simply retry the request if they do not receive a response, and therefore they do not need TCP to guarantee the message delivery.

Vocabulary Exercise: Completion

Fill in the blanks in the following sentences.

1. UDP is said to be _____ based.

2. After a client has chosen the source and destination ports, the same pair of ports is used in the _____ of all _____ used in the transaction.

3. For the data returning to the client from the server, the _____ and _____ port numbers in the datagram header are _____.

Labs and Activities

Lab 4-1: Observing TCP and UDP Using netstat (4.5.1.1)

Upon completion of this lab, you will be able to do the following:

- Explain common **netstat** command parameters and outputs.

- Use **netstat** to examine protocol information on a pod host computer.

Background

netstat is an abbreviation for the network statistics utility, available on both Windows and UNIX/Linux computers. Passing optional parameters with the command will change output information. **netstat** displays incoming and outgoing network connections (TCP and UDP), host computer routing table information, and interface statistics.

Scenario

In this lab, you examine the **netstat** command on a pod host computer, and adjust **netstat** output options to analyze and understand TCP/IP transport layer protocol status.

Figure 4-1 shows the topology for this lab. Table 4-4 shows the corresponding addressing table.

Figure 4-1   Topology for Lab 4-1

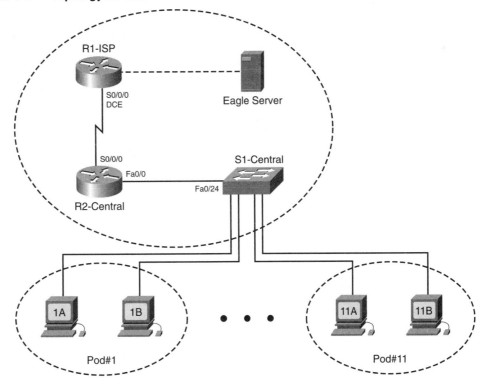

Table 4-4   Addressing Table

Device	Interface	IP Address	Subnet Mask	Default Gateway
R1-ISP	S0/0/0	10.10.10.6	255.255.255.252	N/A
	Fa0/0	192.168.254.253	255.255.255.0	N/A
R2-Central	S0/0/0	10.10.10.5	255.255.255.252	10.10.10.4
	Fa0/0	172.16.255.254	255.255.0.0	N/A
Eagle Server	N/A	192.168.254.254	255.255.255.0	192.168.254.253
	N/A	172.31.24.254	255.255.255.0	N/A
Host *Pod#*A	N/A	172.16.*Pod#*.1	255.255.0.0	172.16.255.254
Host *Pod#*B	N/A	172.16.*Pod#*.2	255.255.0.0	172.16.255.254
S1-Central	N/A	172.16.254.1	255.255.0.0	172.16.255.254

Task 1: Explain Common netstat Command Parameters and Outputs

Open a terminal window by clicking **Start** > **Run**. Enter **cmd**, and click **OK**.

To display help information about the **netstat** command, use the **/?** options, as shown here:

```
C:\> netstat /?
```

Use the output of the **netstat /?** command as reference to fill in the appropriate option that best matches the description in Table 4-5.

Table 4–5   netstat Table

Option	Description
	Displays all connections and listening ports.
	Displays addresses and port numbers in numeric form.
	Redisplays statistics every 5 seconds. Press Ctrl+C to stop redisplaying statistics.
	Shows connections for the protocol specified by proto; proto may be any of TCP, UDP, TCPv6, or UDPv6. If used with the –s option to display per-protocol statistics, proto may be any of IP, IPv6, ICMP, ICMPv6, TCP, TCPv6, UDP, or UDPv6.
	Redisplays all connections and listening ports every 30 seconds.
	Display only open connections. This is a tricky problem.

When netstat statistics are displayed for TCP connections, the TCP state is displayed. During the life of a TCP connection, the connection passes through a series of states. Table 4-6 is a summary of TCP states, compiled from RFC 793, Transmission Control Protocol, September 1981, as reported by netstat.

Table 4-6   Packet State Table

State	Connection Description
LISTEN	The local connection is waiting for a connection request from any remote device.
ESTABLISHED	The connection is open, and data may be exchanged through the connection. This is the normal state for the data-transfer phase of the connection.
TIME-WAIT	The local connection is waiting a default period of time after sending a connection termination request before closing the connection. This is a normal condition, and will normally last between 30 and 120 seconds.
CLOSE-WAIT	The connection is closed, but is waiting for a termination request from the local user.
SYN-SENT	The local connection is waiting for a response after sending a connection request. The connection should transition quickly through this state.
SYN_RECEIVED	The local connection is waiting for a confirming connection request acknowledgment. The connection should transition quickly through this state. Multiple connections in SYN_RECEIVED state may indicate a TCP SYN attack.

IP addresses displayed by **netstat** fall into several categories, as shown in Table 4-7.

Table 4-7   Packet State Table

IP Address	Description
127.0.0.1	This address refers to the local host, or this computer.
0.0.0.0	A global address, meaning any.
Remote Address	The address of the remote device that has a connection with this computer.

Task 2: Use netstat to Examine Protocol Information on a Pod Host Computer

Step 1.   Use **netstat** to view existing connections.

From the terminal window in Task 1, issue the command **netstat –a**:

```
C:\> netstat -a
```

A table will display that lists the protocol (TCP and UDP), local address, foreign address, and state information. Addresses and protocols that can be translated into names are displayed.

The **–n** option forces **netstat** to display output in raw format. From the terminal window, issue the command **netstat –an**:

```
C:\> netstat -an
```

Use the window vertical scrollbar to go back and forth between the outputs of the two commands. Compare outputs, noting how well-known port numbers are changed to names.

Write down three TCP and three UDP connections from the netstat –a output and the corresponding translated port numbers from the netstat –an output. If fewer than three connections translate, note that in Table 4-8.

Table 4-8   netstat Output Table

Connection Protocol	Local Address	Foreign Address	State
TCP			
TCP			
TCP			
UDP			
UDP			
UDP			

Refer to the following **netstat** output shown in Example 4-1.

Example 4-1   Netstat Output

```
C:\> netstat -n
Active Connections
Proto  Local Address        Foreign Address       State
TCP    127.0.0.1:1070       127.0.0.1:1071        ESTABLISHED
TCP    127.0.0.1:1071       127.0.0.1:1070        ESTABLISHED
C:\>
```

A new network engineer suspects that his host computer has been compromised by an outside attack against ports 1070 and 1071. How would you respond?

Step 2.   Establish multiple concurrent TCP connections and record **netstat** output.

In this task, several simultaneous connections will be made with Eagle Server. The venerable **telnet** command is used to access Eagle Server network services, thus providing several protocols to examine with **netstat**.

Open four additional terminal windows. Arrange the windows so that all are visible. The four terminal windows that will be used for Telnet connections to Eagle Server can be relatively small, approximately ½ screen width by ¼ screen height. The terminal windows that will be used to collect connection information should be ½ screen width by full screen height.

Several network services on Eagle Server will respond to a Telnet connection. You will use the following:

- **DNS**: Domain Name System server, port 53

- **FTP**: FTP server, port 21

- **SMTP**: SMTP mail server, port 25

- **Telnet**: Telnet server, port 23

Why should Telnet to UDP ports fail?

To close a Telnet connection, press the Ctrl+] keys together. That will bring up the t=Telnet prompt, Microsoft Telnet>. Type **quit** and press **Enter** to close the session.

In the first Telnet terminal window, telnet to Eagle Server on port 53. In the second terminal window, telnet on port 21. In the third terminal window, telnet on port 25. In the fourth terminal window, telnet on port 23. The command for a Telnet connection on port 21 follows:

```
C:\> telnet eagle-server.example.com 53
```

In the large terminal window, record established connections with Eagle Server. Output should look similar to the output in Example 4-1. If typing is slow, a connection might close before all connections have been made. Eventually, connections should terminate from inactivity.

Example 4-2   Eagle Server Output Table

```



```

Task 3: Reflection

The **netstat** utility displays incoming and outgoing network connections (TCP and UDP), host computer routing table information, and interface statistics. Ponder the utility of **netstat** in small and large networks and consider how **netstat** can help you diagnose problems.

Task 4: Challenge

Close established sessions abruptly (close the terminal window), and issue the **netstat –an** command. Try to view connections in stages different from ESTABLISHED.

Task 5: Cleanup

Unless directed otherwise by the instructor, turn off power to the host computers. Remove anything that was brought into the lab and leave the room ready for the next class.

Lab 4-2: TCP/IP Transport Layer Protocols, TCP and UDP (4.5.2.1)

Upon completion of this activity, you will be able to do the following:

- Identify TCP header fields and operation using a Wireshark FTP session capture.

- Identify UDP header fields and operation using a Wireshark TFTP session capture.

Background

The two protocols in the TCP/IP transport layer are the Transmission Control Protocol (TCP), defined in RFC 761, January 1980, and User Datagram Protocol (UDP), defined in RFC 768, August 1980. Both protocols support upper-layer protocol communication. For example, TCP is used to provide transport layer support for the HTTP and FTP protocols, among others. UDP provides transport layer support for Domain Name System (DNS) services and Trivial File Transfer Protocol (TFTP), among others.

The ability to understand the parts of the TCP and UDP headers and operation is a critical skill for network engineers.

Scenario

Using Wireshark capture, analyze TCP and UDP protocol header fields for file transfers between the host computer and Eagle Server. If Wireshark has not been loaded on the host pod computer, you can download it from ftp://eagle-server.example.com/pub/eagle_labs/eagle1/chapter4/, file wireshark-setup-0.99.4.exe.

Windows command-line utilities FTP and TFTP will be used to connect to Eagle Server and download files.

Figure 4-2 shows the topology for this lab, and Table 4-9 shows the corresponding addressing table.

Figure 4–2   Topology for Lab 4-2

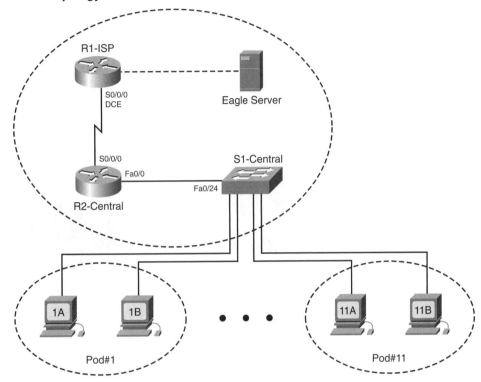

Table 4-9   Addressing Table

Device	Interface	IP Address	Subnet Mask	Default Gateway
R1-ISP	S0/0/0	10.10.10.6	255.255.255.252	N/A
	Fa0/0	192.168.254.253	255.255.255.0	N/A
R2-Central	S0/0/0	10.10.10.5	255.255.255.252	10.10.10.4
	Fa0/0	172.16.255.254	255.255.0.0	N/A
Eagle Server	N/A	192.168.254.254	255.255.255.0	192.168.254.253
	N/A	172.31.24.254	255.255.255.0	N/A
Host *Pod#*A	N/A	172.16.*Pod#*.1	255.255.0.0	172.16.255.254
Host *Pod#*B	N/A	172.16.*Pod#*.2	255.255.0.0	172.16.255.254
S1-Central	N/A	172.16.254.1	255.255.0.0	172.16.255.254

Task 1: Identify TCP Header Fields and Operation Using a Wireshark FTP Session Capture

Step 1.   Capture an FTP session.

TCP sessions are well controlled and managed by information exchanged in the TCP header fields. In this task, an FTP session is made to Eagle Server. When finished, the session capture will be analyzed. Windows computers use the FTP client, **ftp**, to connect to the FTP server. A command-line window will start the FTP session, and the text configuration file for S1-Central from Eagle Server will be downloaded, /pub/eagle_labs/eagle1/chapter4/s1-central, to the host computer.

Open a command-line window by clicking **Start > Run**, **type** cmd, and then click **OK**.

A window similar to Figure 4-3 should open.

Figure 4–3   Command-Line Window

Start a Wireshark capture on the interface that has IP address 172.16.Pod#.[1-2].

Start an FTP connection to Eagle Server. Enter the following command:

```
> ftp eagle-server.example.com
```

When prompted for a user ID, type **anonymous**. When prompted for a password, press **Enter**.

Change the FTP directory to /pub/eagle_labs/eagle1/chapter4/:

```
ftp> cd /pub/eagle_labs/eagle1/chapter4/
```

Download the file s1-central:

```
ftp> get s1-central
```

When finished, terminate the FTP sessions in each command-line window with the FTP **quit** command:

```
ftp> quit
```

Close the command-line window with the command **exit**:

```
> exit
```

Stop the Wireshark capture.

Step 2.   Analyze the TCP fields.

Switch to the Wireshark capture windows. The top window contains summary information for each captured record. Your capture should be similar to the capture shown in Figure 4-4. Before we delve into TCP packet details, an explanation of the summary information is needed. When the FTP client is connected to the FTP server, the transport layer protocol TCP created a reliable session. TCP is routinely used during a session to control datagram delivery, verify datagram arrival, and manage window size. For each exchange of data between the FTP client and FTP server, a new TCP session is started. At the conclusion of the data transfer, the TCP session is closed. Finally, when the FTP session is finished, TCP performs an orderly shutdown and termination.

Figure 4-4   FTP Capture

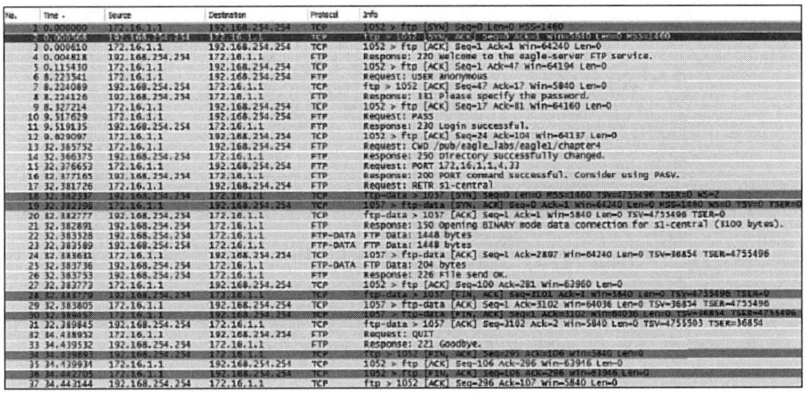

In Wireshark, detailed TCP information is available in the middle window. Highlight the first TCP datagram from the host computer, and move the cursor to the middle window. You might need to adjust the middle window and expand the TCP record by clicking the protocol expand box. The expanded TCP datagram should look similar to Example 4-3.

Example 4-3   Wireshark Capture of a TCP Datagram

```
>Transmission Control Protocol, Src Port: 1052 (1052), Dst port: ftp (21), Seq: 0,
 Len: 0
        Source Port: 1052 (1052)
        Destination Port: ftp (21)
        Sequence number: 0 (relative sequence number)
        Header length: 28 bytes
        >Flags: 0x02 (SYN)
            0... .... = Congestion Window Reduced (CWR): Not Set
            .0.. .... = ECN-Echo: Not set
            ..0. .... = Urgent: Not set
            ...0 .... = Acknowledge: Not set
            .... 0... = Push: Not set
            .... .0.. = Reset: Not set
            .... ..1. = Syn: Set
            .... ...0 = Fin: Not set
         Window size: 64240
         Checksum: 0xb965 [correct]
        >Options: (8 bytes)
          Maximum segment size: 1460 bytes
          NOP
          NOP
          SACK permitted
```

How is the first datagram in a TCP session identified?

_____

_____

Figure 4-5 shows a TCP datagram.

Figure 4-5   TCP Packet Fields for Lab 4-2

An explanation of each field is provided to refresh your memory:

- **TCP source port number:** Belongs to the TCP session host that opened a connection. The value is normally a random value above 1023.

- **TCP destination port number:** Is used to identify the upper-layer protocol or application on the remote site. The values in the range of 0 to 1023 represent the so-called well-known ports and are associated with popular services and applications (as described in RFC 1700, such as Telnet, FTP, HTTP, and so on). The quadruple field combination (Source IP Address, Source Port, Destination IP Address, Destination Port) uniquely identifies the session to both sender and receiver.

- **Sequence number:** Specifies the number of the last octet in a segment.

- **Acknowledgment number:** Specifies the next octet expected by the receiver.

- **Code bits:** Have a special meaning in session management and in the treatment of segments. Among interesting values are

  - **ACK:** Acknowledgment of a segment receipt

  - **SYN:** Synchronize, which is only set when a new TCP session is negotiated during the TCP three-way handshake

  - **FIN:** Finish, which is the request to close the TCP session

- **Window size:** Is the value of the sliding window (that is, how many octets can be sent before waiting for an acknowledgment).

- **Urgent pointer:** Is only used with an URG (Urgent) flag (when the sender needs to send urgent data to the receiver).

- **Options:** The only option currently defined is the maximum TCP segment size (optional value).

    Using the Wireshark capture of the first TCP session start-up (SYN bit set to 1), fill in information about the TCP header in Table 4-10.

Table 4-10   TCP Header: SYN Bit Set to 1

Characteristics	Answers
Source IP address	
Destination IP address	
Source port number	
Destination port number	
Sequence number	
Acknowledgment number	
Header length	
Window size	

Using the Wireshark capture of the first TCP session start-up (SYN and ACK bits are set to 1), fill in information about the TCP header in Table 4-11.

Table 4–11   TCP Header: SYN and ACK Bits Set to 1

Characteristics	Answers
Source IP address	
Destination IP address	
Source port number	
Destination port number	
Sequence number	
Acknowledgment number	
Header length	
Window size	

Using the Wireshark capture of the first TCP session start-up (only ACK bit is set to 1), fill in information about the TCP header in Table 4-12.

Table 4–12   TCP Header: ACK Bits Set to 1

Characteristics	Answers
Source IP address	__ 172.16.__.__
Destination IP address	
Source port number	
Destination port number	
Sequence number	
Acknowledgment number	
Header length	
Window size	

Ignoring the TCP session started when a data transfer occurred, how many other TCP datagrams contained a SYN bit?

Attackers take advantage of the three-way handshake by initiating a "half-open" connection. In this sequence, the opening TCP session sends a TCP datagram with the SYN bit set, and the receiver sends a related TCP datagram with the SYN ACK bits set. A final ACK bit is never sent to finish the TCP handshake. Instead, a new TCP connection is started in half-open fashion. With sufficient TCP sessions in the half-open state, the receiving computer may exhaust resources and crash. A crash could involve a loss of networking services or could corrupt the operating system. In either case, the attacker has won; networking service has been stopped on the receiver. This is one example of a denial-of-service (DoS) attack.

The FTP client and server communicate with each other, unaware and uncaring that TCP has control and management over the session. When the FTP server sends a Response: 220 to the FTP client, the TCP session on the FTP client sends an acknowledgment to the TCP session on Eagle Server. This sequence, visible in the Wireshark capture, is shown in Figure 4-6.

Figure 4-6   TCP Session Management

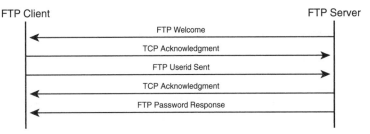

When the FTP session has finished, the FTP client sends a command to "quit." The FTP server acknowledges the FTP termination with a Response: 221 Goodbye. At this time, the FTP server TCP session sends a TCP datagram to the FTP client, announcing the termination of the TCP session. The FTP client TCP session acknowledges receipt of the termination datagram, and then sends its own TCP session termination. When the originator of the TCP termination, FTP server, receives a duplicate termination, an ACK datagram is sent to acknowledge the termination, and the TCP session is closed. This sequence, visible in the Wireshark capture, is shown in Figure 4-7.

Figure 4-7   Orderly TCP Session Termination

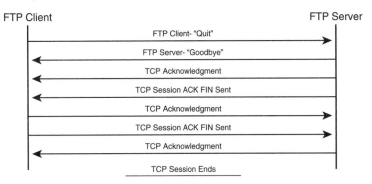

Without an orderly termination, such as when the connection is broken, the TCP sessions will wait a certain period of time until closing. The default timeout value varies, but is normally 5 minutes.

Task 2: Identify UDP Header Fields and Operation Using a Wireshark TFTP Session Capture

Step 1.   Capture a TFTP session.

Following the procedure in Task 1, open a command-line window. The TFTP command has a different syntax than FTP. For example, there is no authentication. Also, there are only two commands, **GET**, to retrieve a file, and **PUT**, to send a file.

Example 4-4 contains Windows TFTP client syntax. The TFTP server has its own directory on Eagle Server, /tftpboot, which is different from the directory structure supported by the FTP server. No authentication is supported.

Example 4-4   TFTP Syntax for a Windows TFTP Client

```
>tftp -help


Transfers files to and from a remote computer running the TFTP service.


TFTP [-i] host [GET ¦ PUT] source [destination]


  -i        Specifies binary image transfer mode (also called

            octet). In binary image mode the file is moved

            literally, byte by byte. Use this mode when

            transferring binary files.

  host      Specifies the local or remote host.

  GET       Transfers the file destination on the remote host to

            the file source on the local host.

  PUT       Transfers the file source on the local host to

            the file destination on the remote host.

  source    Specifies the file to transfer.

  Destination    Specifies where to transfer the file.
```

Start a Wireshark capture, and then download the s1-central configuration file from Eagle Server with the Windows TFTP client. The command and syntax to perform this follows:

`>tftp eagle-server.example.com get s1-central`

Step 2.   Analyze the UDP fields.

Switch to the Wireshark capture windows. Student capture should be similar to the capture shown in Figure 4-8. A TFTP transfer will be used to analyze transport layer UDP operation.

Figure 4-8   UDP Session Capture

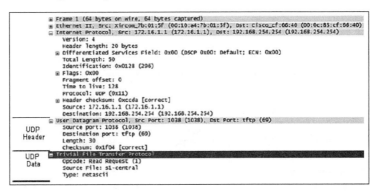

In Wireshark, detailed UDP information is available in the middle window. Highlight the first UDP datagram from the host computer, and move the cursor to the middle window. You might have to adjust the middle window and expand the UDP record by clicking the protocol expand box. The expanded UDP datagram should look similar to Figure 4-9.

Figure 4–9   UDP Datagram Capture

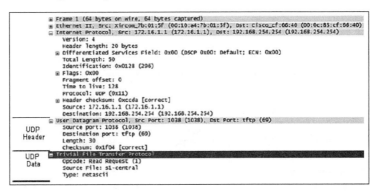

See Figure 4-10, a UDP datagram diagram. Header information is sparse, compared to the TCP datagram. There are similarities, however. Each UDP datagram is identified by the UDP source port and UDP destination port.

Figure 4–10   UDP Format

UDP Segment

0		16	31
UDP Source Port		UDP Destination Port	
UDP Message Length		UDP Checksum	
Data			
Data...			

Using the Wireshark capture of the first UDP datagram, fill in information about the UDP header in Table 4-13. The checksum value is a hexadecimal (base 16) value, denoted by the preceding 0x code.

Table 4-13   UDP Header Table

Characteristics	Answers
Source IP address	__ 172.16.__.__
Destination IP address	
Source port number	
Destination port number	
UDP message length	
UDP checksum	

How does UDP verify datagram integrity?

_____

_____

_____

Examine the first packet returned from Eagle Server. Fill in information about the UDP header in Table 4-14.

Table 4-14   UDP Header Information

Characteristics	Answers
Source IP address	
Destination IP address:	___172.16.___.___
Source port number	
Destination port number	
UDP message length	
UDP checksum: 0x	Ox_____

Notice that the return UDP datagram has a different UDP source port, but this source port is used for the remainder of the TFTP transfer. Because there is no reliable connection, only the original source port used to begin the TFTP session is used to maintain the TFTP transfer.

Task 3: Reflection

This lab provided you with the opportunity to analyze TCP and UDP protocol operations from captured FTP and TFTP sessions. TCP manages communication much differently from UDP, but reliability and guaranteed delivery requires additional control over the communication channel. UDP has less overhead and control, and the upper-layer protocol must provide some type of acknowledgment control. Both protocols, however, transport data between clients and servers using application layer protocols and are appropriate for the upper-layer protocol each supports. Both protocols have advantages and disadvantages. Applications are designed to use one protocol or another based on maximizing the advantages while minimizing the disadvantages. Consider how you would determine which protocol to use if you were designing an application.

Task 4: Challenge

Because neither FTP nor TFTP are secure protocols, all data transferred is sent in clear text. This includes any user IDs, passwords, or clear-text file contents. Analysis of the upper-layer FTP session will quickly identify the user ID, password, and configuration file passwords. Upper-layer TFTP data examination is a bit more complicated, but the data field can be examined and configuration user ID and password information extracted.

Task 5: Cleanup

During this lab, several files were transferred to the host computer and should be removed.

Unless directed otherwise by the instructor, turn off power to the host computers. Remove anything that was brought into the lab, and leave the room ready for the next class.

Lab 4-3: Application and Transport Layer Protocols (4.5.3.1)

Upon completion of this lab, you will be able to do the following:

- Configure the host computer to capture application layer protocols.

- Capture and analyze HTTP communication between the pod host computer and a web server.

- Capture and analyze FTP communication between the pod host computer and an FTP server.

- Observe TCP establish and manage communication channels with HTTP and FTP connections.

Background

The primary function of the transport layer is to keep track of multiple application conversations on the same host. However, different applications have different requirements for their data, and therefore different transport protocols have been developed to meet these requirements.

Application layer protocols define the communication between network services, such as a web server and client, and an FTP server and client. Clients initiate communication to the appropriate server, and the server responds to the client. For each network service, a different server is listening on a different port for client connections. There may be several servers on the same end device. A user may open several client applications to the same server, yet each client communicates exclusively with a session established between the client and server.

Application layer protocols rely on lower-level TCP/IP protocols, such as TCP and UDP. This lab examines two popular application layer protocols, HTTP and FTP, and how transport layer protocols TCP and UDP manage the communication channel. Also examined are popular client requests and corresponding server responses.

Scenario

In this lab, you use client applications to connect to Eagle Server network services. You monitor the communication with Wireshark and analyze the captured packets.

A web browser such as Internet Explorer or Firefox will be used to connect to the Eagle Server network service. Eagle Server has several network services preconfigured, such as HTTP, waiting to respond to client requests.

The web browser will also be used to examine the FTP protocol, as will the FTP command-line client. This exercise demonstrates that although clients may differ, the underlying communication to the server remains the same.

The lab should be configured as shown in Figure 4-11 and Table 4-15. If it is not, ask the instructor for assistance before proceeding.

Figure 4–11   Topology for Lab 4-3

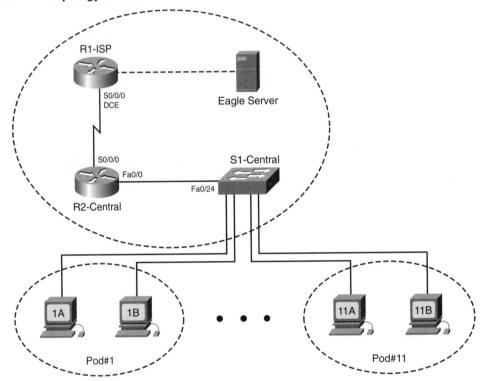

Table 4–15   Addressing Table

Device	Interface	IP Address	Subnet Mask	Default Gateway
R1-ISP	S0/0/0	10.10.10.6	255.255.255.252	N/A
	Fa0/0	192.168.254.253	255.255.255.0	N/A
R2-Central	S0/0/0	10.10.10.5	255.255.255.252	10.10.10.4
	Fa0/0	172.16.255.254	255.255.0.0	N/A
Eagle Server	N/A	192.168.254.254	255.255.255.0	192.168.254.253
	N/A	172.31.24.254	255.255.255.0	N/A
Host Pod#A	N/A	172.16.Pod#.1	255.255.0.0	172.16.255.254
Host Pod#B	N/A	172.16.Pod#.2	255.255.0.0	172.16.255.254
S1-Central	N/A	172.16.254.1	255.255.0.0	172.16.255.254

Task 1: Configure the Pod Host Computer to Capture Application Layer Protocols

Step 1.   Download and install Wireshark.

If Wireshark is not installed on the pod host computer, you can download it from eagle-server.example.com. See Figure 4-12. The download URL is ftp://eagle-server.example.com/pub/eagle_labs/eagle1/chapter3. Right-click the Wireshark filename, and then save the file to the host pod computer.

Figure 4-12   Wireshark Interface Capture

After the file has downloaded, double-click the filename and install Wireshark with the default settings.

Step 2.   Start Wireshark and configure the capture interface.

Start Wireshark from **Start** > **All Programs** > **Wireshark** > **Wireshark**.

When the opening screen appears, set the correct capture interface. The interface with the IP address of the pod host computer is the correct interface.

Wireshark can be started by clicking the interface **Start** button. Thereafter, the interface is used as the default and does not need to be changed.

Wireshark should begin to log data.

Step 3.   Stop Wireshark for the moment. Wireshark will be used in upcoming tasks.

Task 2: Capture and Analyze HTTP Communication Between the Pod Host Computer and a Web Server

HTTP is an application layer protocol, relying on lower-level protocols such as TCP to establish and manage the communication channel. HTTP version 1.1 is defined in RFC 2616, dated 1999. This part of the lab demonstrates how sessions between multiple web clients and the web server are kept separate.

Step 1.   Start Wireshark captures.

Wireshark will display captures based on packet type.

Step 2.   Start the pod host web browser.

Using a web browser such as Internet Explorer or Firefox, connect to URL http://eagle-server.example.com. A web page similar to Figure 4-13 will display. Do not close this web browser until instructed to do so.

Figure 4-13   Web Server Screen

Click the web browser **Refresh** button. There should be no change to the display in the web client.

Open a second web browser, and connect to URL http://eagle-server.example.com/page2.html. This will display a different web page.

Do not close either browser until Wireshark capture is stopped.

Step 3.   Stop Wireshark captures and analyze the captured data.

Close the web browsers.

The resulting Wireshark data will display. There were actually at least three HTTP sessions created in Step 2. The first HTTP session started with a connection to http://eagle-server.example.com. The second session occurred with a refresh action. The third session occurred when the second web browser accessed http://eagle-server.example.com/page2.html.

Figure 4-15 shows a sample captured HTTP session. Before HTTP can begin, the TCP session must be created. This is seen in the first three session lines, numbers 10, 11, and 12.

Figure 4-14   Captured HTTP Session

No. ▾	Time	Source	Destination	Protocol	Info
10	10.168217	172.16.1.2	192.168.254.254	TCP	1056 > http [SYN] Seq=0 Len=0 MSS=1460
11	10.170734	192.168.254.254	172.16.1.2	TCP	http > 1056 [SYN, ACK] Seq=0 Ack=1 Win=5840 Len=0 MSS=1460
12	10.170787	172.16.1.2	192.168.254.254	TCP	1056 > http [ACK] Seq=1 Ack=1 Win=64240 Len=0
13	10.171086	172.16.1.2	192.168.254.254	HTTP	GET / HTTP/1.1
14	10.171625	192.168.254.254	172.16.1.2	TCP	http > 1056 [ACK] Seq=1 Ack=208 Win=6432 Len=0
15	10.172518	192.168.254.254	172.16.1.2	HTTP	HTTP/1.1 200 OK (text/html)
16	10.172540	192.168.254.254	172.16.1.2	TCP	http > 1056 [FIN, ACK] Seq=448 Ack=208 Win=6432 Len=0
17	10.172567	172.16.1.2	192.168.254.254	TCP	1056 > http [ACK] Seq=208 Ack=449 Win=63793 Len=0
18	10.174196	172.16.1.2	192.168.254.254	TCP	1056 > http [FIN, ACK] Seq=208 Ack=449 Win=63793 Len=0
19	10.174661	192.168.254.254	172.16.1.2	TCP	http > 1056 [ACK] Seq=449 Ack=209 Win=6432 Len=0

Fill in Table 4-16 from the information presented in the HTTP session.

Table 4-16   HTTP Session Table

Characteristics	Answers
Web browser IP address	
Web server IP address	
Transport layer protocol (UDP/TCP)	
Web browser port number	
Web server port number	

Which computer initiated the HTTP session, and how?

Which computer initially signaled an end to the HTTP session, and how?

Highlight the first line of the HTTP protocol, a **GET** request from the web browser. In Figure 4-14, the **GET** request is on line 13.

Move into the second (middle) Wireshark window to examine the layered protocols. If necessary, expand the fields.

Which protocol is carried (encapsulated) inside the TCP segment?

Expand the last protocol record and any subfields. This is the actual information sent to the web server. Complete Table 4-17 using information from the protocol.

Table 4–17   HTTP Session Table

Characteristics	Answer
Protocol version	
Request Method	
* Request URI	
Language	

*Request URI is the path to the requested document. In the first browser, the path is the root directory of the web server. Although no page was requested, some web servers are configured to display a default file if one is available.

The web server responds with the next HTTP packet. In Figure 4-14, this is on line 15. A response to the web browser is possible because the web server understands the type of request and has a file to return. Crackers sometimes send unknown or garbled requests to web servers in an attempt to stop the server or gain access to the server command line. Also, a request for an unknown web page will result in an error message.

Highlight the web server response, and then move into the second (middle) window. Open all collapsed subfields of HTTP. Notice the information returned from the server. In this reply, there are only a few lines of text (web server responses can contain thousands or millions of bytes). The web browser understands and correctly formats the data in the browser window.

What is the web server response to the web client **GET** request?

____

What does this response mean?

____

____

Scroll down the top window of Wireshark until the second HTTP session, refresh, is visible. Figure 4-15 shows a sample capture.

Figure 4-15 Captured HTTP Session

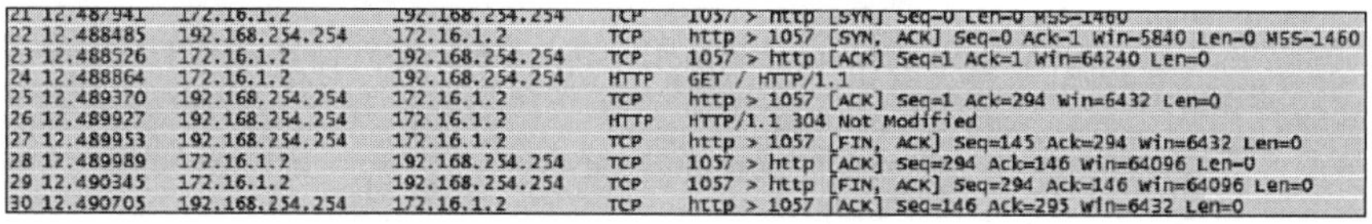

21	12.487941	172.16.1.2	192.168.254.254	TCP	1057 > http [SYN] Seq=0 Len=0 MSS=1460
22	12.488485	192.168.254.254	172.16.1.2	TCP	http > 1057 [SYN, ACK] Seq=0 Ack=1 Win=5840 Len=0 MSS=1460
23	12.488526	172.16.1.2	192.168.254.254	TCP	1057 > http [ACK] Seq=1 Ack=1 Win=64240 Len=0
24	12.488864	172.16.1.2	192.168.254.254	HTTP	GET / HTTP/1.1
25	12.489370	192.168.254.254	172.16.1.2	TCP	http > 1057 [ACK] Seq=1 Ack=294 Win=6432 Len=0
26	12.489927	192.168.254.254	172.16.1.2	HTTP	HTTP/1.1 304 Not Modified
27	12.489953	192.168.254.254	172.16.1.2	TCP	http > 1057 [FIN, ACK] Seq=145 Ack=294 Win=6432 Len=0
28	12.489989	172.16.1.2	192.168.254.254	TCP	1057 > http [ACK] Seq=294 Ack=146 Win=64096 Len=0
29	12.490345	172.16.1.2	192.168.254.254	TCP	1057 > http [FIN, ACK] Seq=294 Ack=146 Win=64096 Len=0
30	12.490705	192.168.254.254	172.16.1.2	TCP	http > 1057 [ACK] Seq=146 Ack=295 Win=6432 Len=0

The significance of the refresh action is in the server response, 304 Not Modified. With a single packet returned for both the initial **GET** request and refresh, the bandwidth used is minimal. However, for an initial response that contains millions of bytes, a single reply packet can save significant bandwidth.

Because this web page was saved in the web client's cache, the **GET** request contained the following additional instructions to the web server:

```
If-modified-since: Fri, 26 Jan 2007 06:19:33 GMT\r\n
If-None-Match: "98072-b8-82da8740"\r\n  <- page tag number (ETAG)
```

What is the ETAG response from the web server?

____

Task 3: Capture and Analyze FTP Communication Between the Pod Host Computer and a Web Server

The application layer protocol FTP has undergone significant revision since it first appeared in RFC 114, in 1971. FTP version 5.1 is defined in RFC 959, dated October 1985.

The familiar web browser can be used to communicate with more than just the HTTP server. In this task, the web browser and a command-line FTP utility are used to download data from an FTP server.

In preparation for this task, open a command line on the host pod computer. To do so, click **Start > Run**, enter **cmd**, and then click **OK**. A screen similar to Figure 4-16 will display.

Figure 4-16   Windows Command Line

Step 1.   Start Wireshark captures.

If necessary, refer to Task 1, Step 2, to open Wireshark.

Step 2.   Start the pod host command-line FTP client.

Start a pod host computer FTP session with the FTP server, using the Windows FTP client utility. To authenticate, use user ID **anonymous**. In response to the password prompt, press **Enter**, as shown in Example 4-5.

Example 4-5   FTP Eagle Server Example

```
>ftp eagle-server.example.com
Connected to eagle-server.example.com.
220 Welcome to the eagle-server FTP service.
User (eagle-server.example.com:(none)): anonymous
331 Please specify the password.
Password: <ENTER>
230 Login successful.
```

The FTP client prompt is ftp>. This means that the FTP client is waiting for a command to send to the FTP server. To view a list of FTP client commands, type **help** and press **Enter,** as shown in Example 4-6.

Example 4-6   FTP Client Commands

```
ftp> help
Commands may be abbreviated.   Commands are:

!           delete      literal     prompt        send
?           debug       ls          put           status
append      dir         mdelete     pwd           trace
ascii       disconnect  mdir        quit          type
bell        get         mget        quote         user
binary      glob        mkdir       recv          verbose
bye         hash        mls         remotehelp
cd          help        mput        rename
close       lcd         open        rmdir
```

Unfortunately, the large number of FTP client commands makes using the command-line utility difficult for a novice. We will only use a few commands for Wireshark evaluation.

Enter the command **dir** to display the current directory contents, as shown in Example 4-7.

Example 4-7   FTP Directory Output

```
ftp> dir
200 PORT command successful. Consider using PASV.
150 Here comes the directory listing.
drwxr-xr-x    3 0        0           4096 Jan 12 04:32 pub
```

The FTP client is at the root directory of the FTP server. This is not the real root directory of the server, but only the highest point that user anonymous can access. User anonymous has been placed into a root jail, prohibiting access outside of the current directory.

Subdirectories can be traversed, however, and files transferred to the pod host computer. Move into directory pub/eagle_labs/eagle1/chapter2, download a file, and exit. See Example 4-8.

Example 4-8   FTP Subdirectory Example

```
ftp> cd pub/eagle_labs/eagle1/chapter2
250 Directory successfully changed.
ftp> dir
200 PORT command successful. Consider using PASV.
150 Here comes the directory listing.
-rw-r—r—  1 0 100      5853 Jan 12 04:26 ftptoeagle-server.pcap
-rw-r—r—  1 0 100      4493 Jan 12 04:27 http to eagle-server.pcap
-rw-r—r—  1 0 100      1486 Jan 12 04:27 ping to 192.168.254.254.pcap
-rw-r—r—  1 0 100 15163750 Jan 12 04:30 wireshark-setup-0.99.4.exe
226 Directory send OK.
ftp: 333 bytes received in 0.04Seconds 8.12Kbytes/sec.
ftp> get "ftptoeagle-server.pcap"
200 PORT command successful. Consider using PASV.
150 Opening BINARY mode data connection for ftptoeagle-server.pcap (5853
bytes).
226 File send OK.
ftp: 5853 bytes received in 0.34Seconds 17.21Kbytes/sec.
ftp> quit
221 Goodbye.
```

Close the command-line window with the **exit** command.

Stop Wireshark captures, and save the captures as FTP_Command_Line_Client.

Step 3.   Start the pod host web browser.

Start Wireshark captures again.

Open a web browser as shown in Figure 4-17, and enter the URL **ftp://eagle-server. example.com**. A browser window opens with the pub directory displayed. Also, the web browser logged in to the FTP server as user anonymous, as shown on the bottom of the Figure 4-17.

Figure 4-17   Web Browser FTP Client

Using the browser, go down the directories until the URL path is pub/eagle-labs/eagle1/chapter2. Double-click the file ftptoeagle-server.pcap and save the file.

When finished, close the web browser.

Stop Wireshark captures, and save the captures as FTP_Web_Browser_Client.

Step 4.   Analyze the captured data.

If not already opened, open the Wireshark capture FTP_Web_Browser_Client.

On the top Wireshark window, select the FTP capture that is the first FTP protocol transmission, Response: 220. In Figure 4-18, this is line 23.

Figure 4-18   Wireshark FTP Capture

Move into the middle Wireshark window and expand the FTP protocol. FTP communicates using codes, similar to HTTP.

What is the FTP server response 220?

When the FTP server issued a Response: 331 Please specify the password, what was the web browser reply?

Which port number does the FTP client use to connect to the FTP server port 21?

When data is transferred or with simple directory listings, a new port is opened. This is called the *transfer mode*. The transfer mode can be either active or passive. In active mode, the server opens a TCP session to the FTP client and transfers data across that port. The FTP server source port number is 20, and the FTP client port number is some number above 1023. In passive mode, however, the client opens a new port to the server for data transfer. Both port numbers are above 1023.

What is the FTP data port number used by the FTP server?

Open the Wireshark capture FTP_Web_Browser_Client, and observe the FTP communication. Although the clients are different, the commands are similar.

Step 5.   Compare FTP active and passive transfer modes.

The implications between the two modes are important from an information security perspective. The transfer mode sets how the data port is configured.

In active transfer mode, a client initiates an FTP session with the server on well-known TCP port 21. For data transfer, the server initiates a connection from well-known TCP port 20 to a client's high port, a port number above 1023. See Figure 4-19.

Figure 4-19   Active FTP

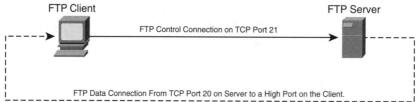

Unless the FTP client firewall is configured to permit connections from the outside, data transfer may fail. To establish connectivity for data transfer, the FTP client must permit either FTP-related connections (implying stateful packet filtering) or disable blocking.

In passive transfer mode, a client initiates an FTP session with the server on well-known TCP port 21, the same connection used in the active transfer mode. For data transfer, however, there are two significant changes. First, the client initiates the data connection to the server. Second, high ports are used on both ends of the connection. See Figure 4-20.

Figure 4-20   Passive FTP

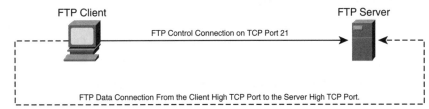

Unless the FTP server is configured to permit a connection to a random high port, data transfer will fail. Not all FTP client applications support changes to the transfer mode.

Task 4: Reflection

Both HTTP and FTP protocols rely on TCP to communicate. TCP manages the connection between client and server to ensure datagram delivery.

A client application may be either a web browser or command-line utility, but each must send and receive messages that can be correctly interpreted. The communication protocol is normally defined in an RFC.

The FTP client must authenticate to the FTP server, even if the authentication is open to the world. User anonymous normally has restricted access to the FTP server and cannot upload files.

An HTTP session begins when a request is made to the HTTP server and ends when the response has been acknowledged by the HTTP client. An FTP session, however, lasts until the client signals that it is leaving with the **quit** command.

HTTP uses a single protocol to communicate with the HTTP server. The server listens on port 80 for client connections. FTP, however, uses two protocols. The FTP server listens on TCP port 21, as the command line. Depending on the transfer mode, the server or client may initiate the data connection.

Multiple application layer protocols can be accessed through a simple web browser. Although only HTTP and FTP were examined here, Telnet and Gopher may also be supported on the browser. The browser acts as a client to the server, sending requests and processing replies. All of these services use TCP. Think about the differences between TCP and UDP, and consider why UDP is inappropriate for HTTP, FTP, Telnet, and Gopher.

Task 5: Challenge

Enabling Wireshark capture, use a web browser or command-line Telnet client to connect to a Cisco device such as S1-Central or R2-Central. Observe the Telnet protocol behavior. Issue a **GET** request and observe the results.

How is the application layer protocol Telnet similar to HTTP and FTP? How does Telnet differ?

_____

_____

Task 6: Clean Up

If Wireshark was installed on the pod host computer for this lab, the instructor may want the application removed. To remove Wireshark, click **Start > Control Panel > Add or Remove Programs**. Scroll to the bottom of the list, right-click **Wireshark**, and then click **Remove**.

If downloaded files need to be removed from the host pod computer, delete all files retrieved from the FTP server.

Unless directed otherwise by the instructor, turn off power to the host computers. Remove anything that was brought into the lab, and leave the room ready for the next class.

Packet Tracer Companion: Application and Transport Layer Protocols Examination (4.5.3.2)

You can now open the file LSG01-Lab4532.pka on the CD-ROM that accompanies this book to repeat this hands-on lab using Packet Tracer. Remember, however, that Packet Tracer is not a substitute for a hands-on lab experience with real equipment. A summary of the instructions is provided within the activity.

Skills Integration Challenge: Analyzing the Application and Transport Layers (4.6.1.3)

Open the file LSG01-PTSkills4.pka on the CD-ROM that accompanies this book to perform this exercise using Packet Tracer.

Upon completion of this activity, you will be able to do the following:

- Configure hosts and services.
- Connect and configure hosts and services on the model of the lab network.
- Explore How DNS, UDP, HTTP, and UDP work together.
- Use simulation mode to visualize the operation of DNS, UDP, HTTP, and TCP on the model of the lab network.

Background

Throughout the course, you will be using a standard lab setup created from actual PCs, servers, routers, and switches to learn networking concepts. At the end of each chapter, you will build increasingly larger parts of this topology in Packet Tracer, and analyze increasingly more complex protocol interactions.

You will use the topology in Figure 4-21 and the addressing table in Table 4-18 to document your design.

Figure 4-21   Topology for Challenge

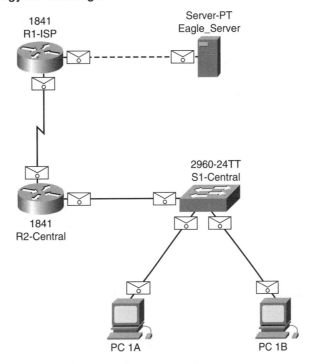

Table 4-18   Addressing Table

Device	Interface	IP Address	Subnet Mask	Default Gateway
R1-ISP	Fa0/0	192.168.254.253	255.255.255.0	N/A
	S0/0/0	10.10.10.6	255.255.255.252	N/A
R2-Central	Fa0/0	172.16.255.254	255.255.0.0	10.10.10.6
	S0/0/0	10.10.10.5	255.255.255.252	10.10.10.6
S1-Central	VLAN 1	172.16.254.1	255.255.0.0	172.16.255.254
PC 1A	NIC	172.16.1.1	255.255.0.0	172.16.255.254
PC 1B	NIC	172.16.1.2	255.255.0.0	172.16.255.254
Eagle Server	NIC	192.168.254.254	255.255.255.0	192.168.254.253

Task 1: Repair and Test the Topology

The server has been replaced. It must be powered on. Then configure it with the following settings:

- IP address 192.168.254.254

- Subnet mask 255.255.255.0

- Default gateway 192.168.254.253

- DNS enabled, with the association of eagle-server.example.com with the server's IP address

- HTTP enabled

Connect the Eagle Server to the Fa0/0 port on the R1-ISP router using a crossover cable.

PC 1A has lost its IP address information. Configure it with the following settings:

- IP address 172.16.1.1

- Subnet mask 255.255.0.0

- Default gateway 172.16.255.254

- DNS server 192.168.254.254

Connect PC 1A to the Fa0/1 port of the S1-Central switch using a straight-through cable. Verify your work using feedback from the Check Results button and the Assessment Items tab. Test connectivity, in real time, by using the Add Simple PDU to test connectivity between PC 1A and the Eagle Server.

Note that when you add a simple PDU, it appears in the PDU List window as part of Scenario 0. The first time you issue this one-shot ping message, it will show as Failed; this is because of the Address Resolution Protocol (ARP) process, which is explained later in Chapter 9, "Ethernet." Double-clicking the Fire button in the PDU List window, send this single test ping a second time. This time it will succeed. In Packet Tracer, the term *scenario* means a specific configuration of one or more test packets. You can create different test packet scenarios by using the New button (for example, Scenario 0 might have one test packet from PC 1A to Eagle Server, Scenario 1 might have test packets between PC 1B and the routers). You can remove all test packets in a particular scenario by using the Delete button. For example, if you use the Delete button for Scenario 0, the test packet you just created between PC 1A and Eagle Server will be removed; please do this before the next task.

Task 2: Explore How DNS, UDP, HTTP, and TCP Work Together

Switch from real time to simulation mode. Make sure Event Filter is set to display DNS, UDP, HTTP, TCP, and ICMP. Open a web browser from the desktop of 1A. Type the URL **eagle-server.example.com**, press **Enter**, and then use the **Capture / Forward** button in the event List to capture the interaction of DNS, UDP, HTTP, and TCP.

You can examine the packet in two ways: by clicking the packet envelope as it is displayed in the animation, or by clicking the Info column for that packet instance as it is listed in the Event List. Play this animation and examine the packet contents (PDU Information window, Inbound PDU Details, Outbound PDU Details) for each event in the event list, especially when the packets are at PC 1A or at the Eagle Server. If you receive a Buffer Full message, click the **View Previous Events** button. Although the processing of the packets at the switch and the routers might not make sense to you yet, you should be able to see how DNS, UDP, HTTP, and TCP work together by studying tracing the packets and using the PDU Information window to look "inside" them.

Task 3: Reflection

Can you make a diagram of the sequence of protocol events involved in requesting a web page using a URL? Where might things go wrong? Compare and contrast DNS and HTTP, and UDP and TCP.

The Study Guide portion of this chapter uses a combination of matching, fill-in-the-blank, multiple-choice, and open-ended questions to test your knowledge of the importance of data networks and the major components and characteristics of network architectures.

The Labs and Activities portion of this chapter includes all the online curriculum activities and labs to ensure you have mastered the practical, hands-on skills needed to understand the opportunities and challenges associated with modern networks.

As you work through this chapter, use Chapter 5 in the Network Fundamentals CCNA Exploration online curriculum or use the corresponding Chapter 5 in the *Network Fundamentals CCNA Exploration Companion Guide* for assistance.

Study Guide

IPv4

The network layer provides services to exchange the individual pieces of data over the network between end devices.

The most significant network layer protocol is the Internet Protocol (IP). IP version 4 (IPv4) is the network layer protocol used as an example throughout this study guide. IPv4 defines many different fields in the packet header. These fields contain binary values that the IPv4 services reference as they forward packets across the network.

Concept Questions

1. What are the four basic processes used in the network layer to accomplish end-to-end transport?

   _____

   _____

   _____

   _____

   _____

2. List three protocols implemented at the network layer that carry user data.

   _____

   _____

   _____

3. IPv4 is going to be replaced by IPv6. What is the most significant difference between the two?

   _____

   _____

4. List three basic characteristics of IPv4.

_____

5. If out-of-order or missing packets create problems for the application using the data, which services have to resolve these issues?

_____

6. In some cases, an intermediary device, usually a router, will need to split up a packet when forwarding it from one media to a media with a smaller maximum transmission unit (MTU). What is this process called?

_____

Vocabulary Exercise: Completion

Fill in the blanks for the following questions.

1. Each route that a packet takes to reach the next device is called a _____.

2. Intermediary devices that connect the networks are called _____.

3. Any individual IP packet can be communicated electrically over _____, as optical signals over _____, or wirelessly as _____.

4. The header of an IPv4 packet does not include fields required for _____ data delivery. There are no _____ of packet delivery. There is no _____ for data.

Vocabulary Exercise: Define

Table 5-1 lists the six key fields in a typical IPv4 header. Fill in the purpose of each field.

Table 5-1   Key Fields of IPv4 Header

Field	Purpose
IP source address	
IP destination address	
Time-to-Live (TTL)	
Type-of-Service (ToS)	
Protocol	
Fragment offset	

Networks: Dividing Hosts into Groups

As networks get larger, it is a good idea to break the network into groups. Dividing large networks so that hosts who need to communicate are grouped together reduces the unnecessary overhead of all hosts needing to know all addresses.

Separating networks is relatively simple if you use hierarchical addressing. Using a hierarchical addressing scheme means that the higher levels of the address can be retained, with the middle level denoting the network addresses and the lower level the individual hosts.

Internet Research Exercise

Use your favorite Internet search engine to find a website that describes the advantages to using hierarchical addressing. Be prepared to discuss and present your findings in class.

Vocabulary Exercise: Completion

Fill in the blanks for the following questions.

1. As networks grow larger, they present problems that can be at least partially alleviated by

   _____.

2. To support data communications between networks over internetworks, network layer addressing schemes are _____.

3. A _____ uniquely identifies each host.

4. A _____ is a message sent from one host to all other hosts on the network.

5. Broadcasts are contained within a _____.

6. The _____ function performed by an intermediary permits only known, trusted data to access the network.

7. The default _____ is a router on a network that serves as an exit from that network.

Routing: How Our Data Packets Are Handled

Within a network or a subnetwork, hosts communicate with each other without the need for any network layer intermediary device. When a host needs to communicate with another network, an intermediary device, or router, acts as a gateway to the other network. The gateway, also known as the default gateway, is needed to send a packet out of the local network.

Routing is done packet by packet and hop by hop. A router will do one of the following with a packet:

- Forward it to the next-hop router
- Forward it to the destination host
- Drop it

Concept Questions

1. On a Windows computer, what graphical user interface (GUI) tool do you use to configure the default gateway IPv4 address?

2. What piece of addressing information should both the IPv4 host address and its default gateway share?

_____

_____

3. Can a packet be forwarded without a route?

_____

4. Routes must have which three main features in a routing table?

_____

_____

5. When forwarding a packet, which route will a router select?

_____

6. Why is Layer 3 addressing hierarchical?

_____

_____

7. What is a default route?

_____

8. When should you use a default route?

_____

_____

_____

_____

Vocabulary Exercise: Define

Table 5-2 lists some terms about routing. Define each term and write your responses in the definition column.

Table 5-2   Routing Terms Definitions

Terms	Definition
Next hop	
Default route	
Gateway	

Routing Processes: How Routes Are Learned

Routing requires that every hop, or router, along the path to a packet's destination have a route to forward the packet. Otherwise, the packet is dropped at that hop. Each router in a path does not need a route to all networks. It only needs to know the next hop on the path to the packet's destination network.

The routing table contains the information that a router uses in its packet-forwarding decisions. For the routing decisions, the routing table needs to represent the most accurate state of network pathways that the router can access.

To ensure that packets are routed to use the best possible next hops, each known destination network needs to either have a route or a default route configured. Because packets are forwarded at every hop, every router must be configured with static routes to next hops that reflect its location in the internetwork.

Routing protocols are the set of rules by which routers dynamically share their routing information. As routers become aware of changes to the networks for which they act as the gateway, or changes to links between routers, this information is passed on to other routers. When a router receives information about new or changed routes, it updates its own routing table and, in turn, passes the information to other routers.

Vocabulary Exercise: Completion

Fill in the blanks for the following questions.

1. Out-of-date routing information means that packets might not be forwarded to the most appropriate _____, causing delays or packet loss.

2. Static routing is routing that depends on _____ routes in the routing table.

3. Routing is the process of finding _____ to a destination host.

Labs and Activities

 ## Lab 5-1: Examining a Device's Gateway (5.5.1.1)

Upon completion of this lab, you will be able to do the following:

- Understand and explain the purpose of a gateway address.

- Understand how network information is configured on a Windows computer.

- Troubleshoot a hidden gateway address problem.

Background

An IP address is composed of a network portion and a host portion. A computer that communicates with another device must first know how to reach the device. For devices on the same LAN, the host portion of the IP address is used as the host identifier. The network portion of the destination device is the same as the network portion of the host device.

However, devices on different networks have different source and destination network numbers. The network portion of the IP address is used to identify when a packet must be sent to a gateway address, which is assigned to a network device that forwards packets between distant networks.

A router is assigned the gateway address for all the devices on the LAN. One purpose of a router is to serve as an entry point for packets coming into the network and exit point for packets leaving the network.

Gateway addresses are important to users. Cisco estimates that 80 percent of network traffic will be destined to devices on other networks, and only 20 percent of network traffic will go to local devices. This is called the 80/20 rule. Therefore, if a gateway cannot be reached by the LAN devices, users will not be able to perform their job.

Scenario

Pod host computers must communicate with Eagle Server, but Eagle Server is located on a different network. If the pod host computer gateway address is not configured properly, connectivity with Eagle Server will fail.

By the use of several common utilities, network configuration on a pod host computer will be verified.

Figure 5-1 shows the topology for this lab, and Table 5-3 shows the corresponding addressing table.

Figure 5-1   Topology for Lab 5-1

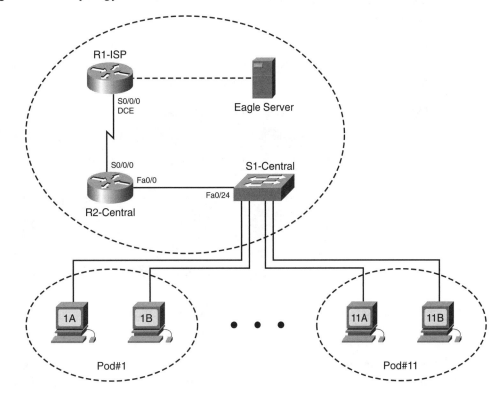

Table 5-3   Addressing Table

Device	Interface	IP Address	Subnet Mask	Default Gateway
R1-ISP	S0/0/0	10.10.10.6	255.255.255.252	N/A
	Fa0/0	192.168.254.253	255.255.255.0	N/A
R2-Central	S0/0/0	10.10.10.5	255.255.255.252	10.10.10.6
	Fa0/0	172.16.255.254	255.255.0.0	N/A
Eagle Server	N/A	192.168.254.254	255.255.255.0	192.168.254.253
	N/A	172.31.24.254	255.255.255.0	N/A
Host *Pod#*A	N/A	172.16.*Pod#*.1	255.255.0.0	172.16.255.254
Host *Pod#*B	N/A	172.16.*Pod#*.2	255.255.0.0	172.16.255.254
S1-Central	N/A	172.16.254.1	255.255.0.0	172.16.255.254

Task 1: Understand and Explain the Purpose of a Gateway Address

For LAN traffic, the gateway address is the address of the Ethernet device. Figure 5-2 shows two devices on the same network communicating with the **ping** command. Any device that has the same network address (in this example, 172.16.0.0) is on the same LAN.

Figure 5-2   Communication Between LAN Devices

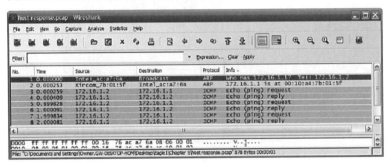

Referring to Figure 5-2, what is the MAC address of the network device on IP address 172.16.1.1?

Several Windows commands will display a network gateway address. One popular command is **netstat –r**. In Example 5-1, the **netstat –r** command is used to view the gateway addresses for this computer.

The first highlighted line shows what gateway address is used to forward all network packets destined outside of the LAN. The "quad-zero" Network Destination and Netmask values, 0.0.0.0 and 0.0.0.0, refer to *any* network not specifically known. For any nonlocal network, this computer will use 172.16.255.254 as the default gateway. The fourth highlighted line displays the information in human-readable form. More specific networks are reached through other gateway addresses. A local interface, called the *loopback interface*, is automatically assigned to the 127.0.0.0 network. This interface is used to identify the local host to local network services. See the second highlighted entry. Finally, any device on network 172.16.0.0 is accessed through gateway 172.16.1.2, the IP address for this Ethernet interface. This entry is the third highlighted line.

Example 5-1   Output of the netstat Command

```
C:\>netstat -r


Route Table

=======================================================================
Interface List
0x1 ........................ MS TCP Loopback interface
0x20005 ...00 16 76 ac a7 6a  Intel(R) 82562V 10/100 Network Connection
=======================================================================


=======================================================================
Active Routes:
Network Destination        Netmask          Gateway    Interface  Metric
          0.0.0.0          0.0.0.0   172.16.255.254   172.16.1.2    1
        127.0.0.0        255.0.0.0        127.0.0.1    127.0.0.1    1
       172.16.0.0      255.255.0.0       172.16.1.2   172.16.1.2   20
       172.16.1.2  255.255.255.255        127.0.0.1    127.0.0.1   20
   172.16.255.255  255.255.255.255       172.16.1.2   172.16.1.2   20
  255.255.255.255  255.255.255.255       172.16.1.2   172.16.1.2    1
Default Gateway:       172.16.255.254
=======================================================================
Persistent Routes:
  None
C:\>
```

Step 1.   Open a terminal window on a pod host computer.

What is the default gateway address?

_____

Step 2.   Use the **ping** command to verify connectivity with IP address 127.0.0.1.

Was the ping successful?

_____

Step 3.   Use the **ping** command to ping different IP addresses on the 127.0.0.0 network, 127.10.1.1, and 127.255.255.255.

Were responses successful? If not, why?

_____

_____

_____

A default gateway address permits a network device to communicate with other devices on different networks. In essence, it is the door to other networks. All traffic destined to different networks must go through the network device that has the default gateway address.

As shown in Figure 5-3, communication between devices on different networks is different than on a LAN. Pod host computer 2, IP address 172.16.1.2, initiates a ping to IP address 192.168.254.254. Because network 172.16.0.0 differs from 192.168.254.0, the pod host computer requests the MAC address of the default gateway device. This gateway device, a router, responds with its MAC address. The computer composes the Layer 2 header with the destination MAC address of the router and places frames on the wire to the gateway device.

Figure 5-3   Communication Between Devices on Different Networks

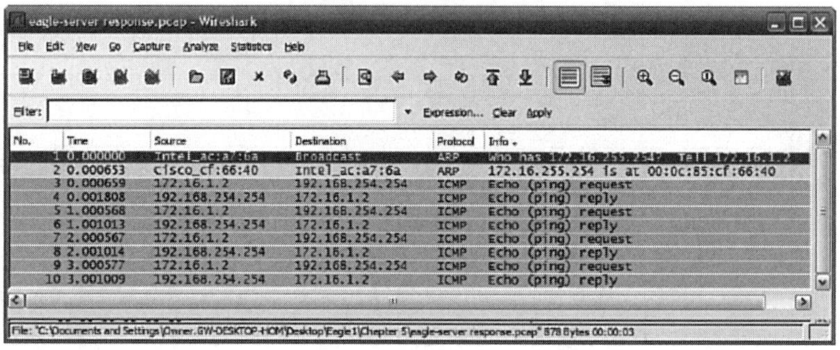

Referring to Figure 5-3, what is the MAC address of the gateway device?

_____

Referring to Figure 5-3, for which IP can you not find a MAC address?

_____

_____

_____

_____

Task 2: Understand How Network Information Is Configured on a Windows Computer

Many times connectivity issues are attributed to incorrect network settings. For troubleshooting connectivity issues, several tools are available to quickly determine the network configuration for any Windows computer.

Step 1.   Examine network properties settings.

One method that might prove useful to determine the network interface IP properties is to examine the pod host computer's Network Properties settings. To access this window, Click **Start** > **Control Panel** > **Network Connections**.

Right-click **Local Area Connection**, and choose **Properties**.

On the General tab, scroll down the list of items in the pane, select **Internet Protocol (TCP/IP)**, and click the **Properties** button. A window similar to the one in Figure 5-4 will display.

Figure 5-4   Network Interface with Static IP Address

However, a dynamic IP address may be configured, as shown in Figure 5-5. In this case, the Network Properties settings window is not very useful for determining IP address information.

Figure 5-5   Network Interface with Dynamic IP Address

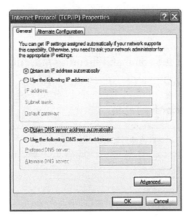

A more consistently reliable method for determining network settings on a Windows computer is to use the **ipconfig** command, as shown in Example 5-2.

Example 5-2   Output of the ipconfig Command

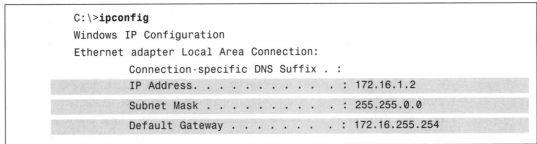

```
C:\>ipconfig
Windows IP Configuration
Ethernet adapter Local Area Connection:
        Connection-specific DNS Suffix . :
        IP Address. . . . . . . . . . . : 172.16.1.2
        Subnet Mask . . . . . . . . . . : 255.255.0.0
        Default Gateway . . . . . . . . : 172.16.255.254
```

The first highlight shows the IP address for this pod host computer. The second highlight shows the subnet mask. The third highlight shows the default gateway address.

Several options are available with the **ipconfig** command, accessible with the command **ipconfig /?**. To show the most information about the network connections, use the command **ipconfig /all**, as shown in Example 5-3. The highlighted line shows the domain name server IP address.

Example 5-3   Output of the ipconfig /all Command

```
C:\>ipconfig /all
Windows IP Configuration
        Host Name . . . . . . . . . . . . : GW-desktop-hom
        Primary Dns Suffix  . . . . . . . :
        Node Type . . . . . . . . . . . . : Unknown
        IP Routing Enabled  . . . . . . . : No
        WINS Proxy Enabled  . . . . . . . : No
Ethernet adapter Local Area Connection:
        Connection-specific DNS Suffix  . :
        Description . . . . . . . . . . . : Intel (R) 82562V 10/100
Network Connection
        Physical Address. . . . . . . . . : 00-16-76-AC-A7-6A
        Dhcp Enabled. . . . . . . . . . . : No
        IP Address. . . . . . . . . . . . : 172.16.1.2
        Subnet Mask . . . . . . . . . . . : 255.255.0.0
        Default Gateway . . . . . . . . . : 172.16.255.254
        DNS Servers . . . . . . . . . . . : 192.168.254.254
```

Step 2.   Using the command **ipconfig /all**, fill in the Table 5-4 with information from your pod host computer.

Table 5-4   ipconfig Table

Description	Address
IP address	
Subnet mask	
Default gateway	
DNS server	

Task 3: Troubleshoot a Hidden Gateway Address Problem

When troubleshooting network issues, a thorough understanding of the network can often assist in identifying the real problem. Refer to the network topology in Figure 5-1 and the logical IP address assignments in Table 5-3.

As the third-shift help desk Cisco engineer, you are asked for assistance from the help desk technician. The technician received a trouble ticket from a user on computer host 1A, complaining that computer host 11B, host-11B.example.com, does not respond to pings. The technician verified the cables and network settings on both computers, but nothing unusual was found. You check with the corporate network engineer, who reports that R2-Central has been temporarily brought down for a hardware upgrade.

Nodding your head in understanding, you ask the technician to ping the IP address for host 11B, 172.16.11.2 from host 1A. The pings succeed. Then, you ask the technician to ping the gateway IP address, 172.16.255.254, and the pings fail.

What is wrong?

_____

_____

_____

You instruct the help desk technician to tell the user to use the IP address for host 11B temporarily; after that, the user is able to establish connectivity with the computer. Within the hour, the gateway router is back on line and normal network operation resumes.

Task 4: Reflection

A gateway address is critical to network connectivity, and in some instances LAN devices require a default gateway to communicate with other devices on the LAN.

Windows command-line utilities such as **netstat –r** and **ipconfig /all** will report gateway settings on host computers.

Task 5: Challenge

Use Wireshark to capture a ping between two pod host computers. You might have to restart the host computer to flush the DNS cache. First, use the hostname of the destination pod computer for DNS to reply with the destination IP address. Observe the communication sequence between network devices, especially the gateway. Next, capture a ping between network devices using only IP addresses. The gateway address should not be needed.

Task 6: Clean Up

Unless directed otherwise by the instructor, turn off power to the host computers. Remove anything that was brought into the lab, and leave the room ready for the next class.

Packet Tracer Companion: Examining a Device's Gateway (5.5.1.2)

You can now open the file LSG01-Lab5512.pka on the CD-ROM that accompanies this book to repeat this hands-on lab using Packet Tracer. Remember, however, that Packet Tracer is not a substitute for a hands-on lab experience with real equipment. A summary of the instructions is provided within the activity.

Lab 5-2: Examining a Route (5.5.2.1)

Learning Objectives

Upon completion of this lab, you will be able to do the following:

- Use the **route** command to modify a Windows computer routing table.

- Use a Windows Telnet client command **telnet** to connect to a Cisco router.

- Examine router routes using basic Cisco IOS commands.

Background

For packets to travel across a network, a device must know the route to the destination network. This lab compares how routes are used in Windows computers and the Cisco router.

Some routes are added to routing tables automatically, based upon configuration information on the network interface. The device considers a network directly connected when it has an IP address and network mask configured, and the network route is automatically entered into the routing table. For networks that are not directly connected, a default gateway IP address is configured that will send traffic to a device that should know about the network.

Scenario

Using a pod host computer, examine the routing table with the **route** command and identify the different routes and gateway IP address for the route. Delete the default gateway route, test the connection, and then add the default gateway route back to the host table.

Use a pod host computer to telnet into R2-Central, and examine the routing table.

Figure 5-6 shows the topology for this lab, and Table 5-5 shows the corresponding addressing table.

Figure 5-6   Topology for Lab 5-2

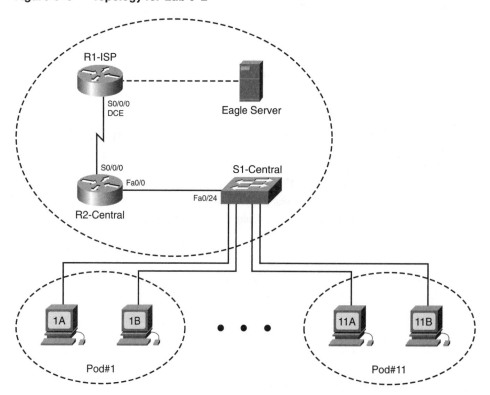

Table 5-5   Addressing Table

Device	Interface	IP Address	Subnet Mask	Default Gateway
R1-ISP	S0/0/0	10.10.10.6	255.255.255.252	N/A
	Fa0/0	192.168.254.253	255.255.255.0	N/A
R2-Central	S0/0/0	10.10.10.5	255.255.255.252	10.10.10.6
	Fa0/0	172.16.255.254	255.255.0.0	N/A
Eagle Server	N/A	192.168.254.254	255.255.255.0	192.168.254.253
	N/A	172.31.24.254	255.255.255.0	N/A
Host *Pod#*A	N/A	172.16.*Pod#*.1	255.255.0.0	172.16.255.254
Host *Pod#*B	N/A	172.16.*Pod#*.2	255.255.0.0	172.16.255.254
S1-Central	N/A	172.16.254.1	255.255.0.0	172.16.255.254

Task 1: Use the route Command to Modify a Windows Computer Routing Table

Shown in Example 5-4, output from the **netstat –r** command is useful to determine route and gateway information.

Example 5-4   Output of the netstat Command

```
C:\>netstat -r
Route Table
=====================================================================
Interface List
0x1 ...................... MS TCP Loopback interface
0x20005 ...00 16 76 ac a7 6a  Intel(R) 82562V 10/100 Network Connection
=====================================================================

=====================================================================
Active Routes:
Network Destination        Netmask          Gateway    Interface  Metric
          0.0.0.0          0.0.0.0  172.16.255.254   172.16.1.2       1
        127.0.0.0        255.0.0.0       127.0.0.1    127.0.0.1       1
       172.16.0.0      255.255.0.0      172.16.1.2   172.16.1.2      20
       172.16.1.2  255.255.255.255       127.0.0.1    127.0.0.1      20
   172.16.255.255  255.255.255.255      172.16.1.2   172.16.1.2      20
  255.255.255.255  255.255.255.255      172.16.1.2   172.16.1.2       1
Default Gateway:      172.16.255.254
=====================================================================
Persistent Routes:
  None
C:\>
```

Step 1.   Examine the active routes on a Windows computer.

A useful command to modify the routing table is the **route** command. Unlike the **netstat –r** command, the **route** command can be used to view, add, delete, or change routing table entries. To view detailed information about the **route** command, use the option **route /?**, as shown in Example 5-5.

Example 5-5   Output of the route Command

```
C:\>route /?
An abbreviated option list for the route command is shown below:
route PRINT    Prints active routes
route ADD      Adds a route:
        route ADD network MASK mask gateway
route DELETE   Deletes a route:
        route DELETE network
route CHANGE   Modifies an existing route
```

To view active routes, issue the command **route PRINT**, as shown in Example 5-6.

Example 5-6   Output of the route PRINT Command

```
C:\ >route PRINT
=====================================================================
Interface List
0x1 ......................... MS TCP Loopback interface
0x70003 ...00 16 76 ac a7 6a .Intel(R) 82562V 10/100 Network Connection
=====================================================================
Active Routes:
  Network Destination        Netmask          Gateway   Interface  Metric
          0.0.0.0          0.0.0.0  172.16.255.254   172.16.1.2      1
        127.0.0.0        255.0.0.0       127.0.0.1    127.0.0.1      1
       172.16.0.0      255.255.0.0      172.16.1.2   172.16.1.2     20
       172.16.1.2  255.255.255.255       127.0.0.1    127.0.0.1     20
   172.16.255.255  255.255.255.255      172.16.1.2   172.16.1.2     20
  255.255.255.255  255.255.255.255      172.16.1.2   172.16.1.2      1
Default Gateway:      172.16.255.254
=====================================================================
Persistent Routes:
  None
C:\>
```

Verify network connectivity to Eagle Server, as shown in Example 5-7.

Example 5-7   Output of the ping Command

```
C:\> ping eagle-server.example.com
Pinging eagle-server.example.com [192.168.254.254] with 32 bytes of
data:

Reply from 192.168.254.254: bytes=32 time<1ms TTL=63
Reply from 192.168.254.254: bytes=32 time<1ms TTL=63
Reply from 192.168.254.254: bytes=32 time<1ms TTL=63
Reply from 192.168.254.254: bytes=32 time<1ms TTL=63

Ping statistics for 192.168.254.254:
    Packets: Sent = 4, Received = 4, Lost = 0 (0% loss),
Approximate round trip times in milli-seconds:
    Minimum = 0ms, Maximum = 0ms, Average = 0ms
C:\>
```

What is the gateway address to eagle-server.example.com?

Step 2.   Delete a route from the Windows computer routing table.

How important is the default gateway route? Delete the gateway route, and try to ping Eagle Server. The syntax to remove the default gateway route is this:

route DELETE *network*

The full command is as follows:

C:/> **route DELETE 0.0.0.0**

Examine the active routing table, and verify that the default gateway route has been removed:

What is the default gateway IP address?

_____

_____

_____

_____

_____

_____

_____

_____

_____

_____

_____

_____

_____

_____

_____

_____

_____

_____

_____

_____

Try to ping Eagle Server. What are the results?

_____

If the default gateway IP address is removed, how can the DNS server be reached to resolve eagle-server.example.com?

_____

_____

_____

Can other LAN devices be reached, such as 172.16.255.254?

_____

Step 3.   Insert a route into the Windows computer routing table.

In the following configuration, use the IP address assigned to your host pod interface. The syntax to add a route to the Windows computer routing table is this:

`route ADD` *network* `MASK` *mask gateway-IP address*

The full command appears is as follows:

`C:/> route ADD 0.0.0.0 MASK 0.0.0.0 172.16.255.254`

Examine the active routing table. Has the default gateway route been restored?

_____

_____

_____

_____

_____

_____

_____

_____

_____

_____

_____

_____

_____

_____

_____

_____

_____

_____

_____

Try to ping Eagle Server. What are the results?

_____

_____

_____

_____

_____

_____

_____

_____

_____

_____

_____

_____

_____

Task 2: Use a Windows Telnet Client Command telnet to Connect to a Cisco Router

In this task, you telnet into the R2-Central router and use common Cisco IOS commands to examine the router routing table. Cisco devices have a Telnet server and, if properly configured, will permit remote logins. Access to the router is restricted, however, and requires a username and password. The password for all usernames is cisco. The username depends on the pod. Username ccna1 is for users on pod 1 computers, ccna2 is for students on pod 2 computers, and so on.

Step 1.   Using the Windows Telnet client, log in to a Cisco router.

Open a terminal window by clicking **Start** > **Run**. Type **cmd**, and then click **OK**. A terminal window and prompt should be available. The Telnet utility has several options and can be viewed with the **telnet /?** command. A username and password will be required to log in to the router. For all usernames, the corresponding password is cisco. Table 5-6 shows the pod numbers and the corresponding usernames.

Table 5-6   Pod Number Table

Pod Number	Username
1	ccna1
2	ccna2
3	ccna3
4	ccna4
5	ccna5
6	ccna6
7	ccna7
8	ccna8
9	ccna9
10	ccna10
11	ccna11

To start a Telnet session with router R2-Central, enter the following command:

```
C:/> telnet 172.16.255.254 <ENTER>
```

A login window will prompt for a username, as shown in Example 5-8. Enter the applicable username, and press **Enter**. Type the password, **cisco**, and press **Enter**. The router prompt should be visible after a successful login.

Example 5-8   Output for R2-Central

```
         ************************************************************
                      This is Eagle 1 lab router R2-Central.
                      Authorized access only.
         ************************************************************


         User Access Verification


         Username: ccna1
         Password: cisco
         !The password is hidden when typed in
         R2-Central>
```

At the prompt, R2-Central#, a successful Telnet login has been created. Only limited permissions for ccnax usernames are available; therefore, it is not possible to modify router settings or view the configuration. The purpose of this task was to establish a Telnet session, which has been accomplished. In the next task, the router routing table is examined.

Task 3: Examine Router Routes Using Basic Cisco IOS Commands

As with any network device, gateway addresses instruct the device about how to reach other networks when no other information is available. Similar to the host computer default gateway IP address, a router may also employ a default gateway. Also similar to a host computer, a router is knowledgeable about directly connected networks.

This task does not examine Cisco IOS commands in detail, but instead uses a common IOS command to view the routing table. The syntax to view the routing table is this:

```
show ip route <ENTER>
```

Enter the command to display the router routing table.

The route information displayed is much more detailed than the route information on a host computer. This is to be expected, because the job of a router is to route traffic between networks. The information required of this task, however, is not difficult to glean. Example 5-9 shows the routing table for R2-Central.

Example 5-9   Output of the show ip route Command

```
R2-Central#show ip route
Codes: C - connected, S - Static, R - RIP, M - mobile, B - BGP
       D - EIGRP, EX - EIGRP external, O - OSPF, IA - OSPF inter area
       N1 - OSPF NSSA external type 1, N2 - OSPF NSSA external type 2
       E1 - OSPF external type 1, E2 - OSPF external type 2
       i - IS-IS, su - IS-IS summary, L1 - IS-IS level-1, L2 - IS-IS level-2
       ia - IS-IS inter area, * - candidate default, U - per-user static route
```

Example 5-9   Output of the show ip route Command   *continued*

```
        o - ODR, P - periodic downloaded static route


Gateway of last resort is 10.10.10.6 to network 0.0.0.0


C     172.16.0.0/16 is directly connected, FastEthernet0/0
      10.0.0.0/30 is subnetted, 1 subnets
C     10.10.10.4 is directly connected, Serial0/2/0
S*    0.0.0.0/0 [1/0] via 10.10.10.6
R2-Central#
```

The Codes section shown in Example 5-10 explains the symbols to the left of each route entry.

Example 5-10   Explanation of Codes

```
R2-Central#show ip route
Codes:?C - connected, S - Static, R - RIP, M - mobile, B - BGP
       D - EIGRP, EX - EIGRP external, O - OSPF, IA - OSPF inter area
       N1 - OSPF NSSA external type 1, N2 - OSPF NSSA external type 2
       E1 - OSPF external type 1, E2 - OSPF external type 2
       i - IS-IS, su - IS-IS summary, L1 - IS-IS level-1, L2 - IS-IS level-2
       ia - IS-IS inter area, * - candidate default, U - per-user static route
       o - ODR, P - periodic downloaded static route


Gateway of last resort is 10.10.10.6 to network 0.0.0.0


C     172.16.0.0/16 is directly connected, FastEthernet0/0
       10.0.0.0/30 is subnetted, 1 subnets
C     10.10.10.4 is directly connected, Serial0/2/0
S*    0.0.0.0/0 [1/0] via 10.10.10.6
R2-Central#
```

Two highlighted lines in the example show C, which denotes directly connected networks and the interface that supports the connection. One highlighted line shows S, denoting a static route, which is manually entered by the network administrator. The asterisk shows the example is a candidate default route, because the route is "quad-zero"(0.0.0.0). If there is no other route in the routing table, use the gateway of last resort IP address to forward packets.

How is IP mask information displayed in a router routing table?

_____

_____

What would the router do with packets destined to 192.168.254.254?

_____

When finished examining the routing table, exit the router with the command **exit**. The Telnet client will also close the connection with the Telnet escape sequence Ctrl+] and **quit**. Close the terminal window.

Task 4: Reflection

Two new Windows commands were used in this lab. The **route** command was used to view, delete, and add route information on the pod host computer.

The Windows Telnet client, **telnet**, was used to connect to a lab router, R2-Central. This technique will be used in other labs to connect to Cisco network devices.

The router routing table was examined with the Cisco IOS command **show ip route**. Routes for directly connected networks, statically assigned routes, and gateway of last resort information are displayed.

Task 5: Challenge

You can use other Cisco IOS commands to view IP address information on a router. Similar to the Windows **ipconfig** command, the Cisco IOS command **show ip interface brief** shown in Example 5-11 will display IP address assignments.

Example 5-11   Output of the show ip interface brief Command

```
R2-Central#show ip interface brief
Interface        IP-Address       OK? Method Status                 Protocol
FastEthernet0/0  172.16.255.254   YES manual up                     up
FastEthernet0/1  unassigned       YES unset  administratively down  down
Serial0/2/0      10.10.10.5       YES manual up                     up
Serial0/2/1      unassigned       YES unset  administratively down  down
R2-Central#
```

Using Windows commands and the Cisco IOS commands in this lab, compare network information output. What was missing? What critical network information was similar?

_____

_____

_____

_____

_____

_____

_____

_____

_____

Task 6: Clean Up

Unless directed otherwise by the instructor, turn off power to the host computers. Remove anything that was brought into the lab, and leave the room ready for the next class.

Packet Tracer Companion: Examining a Route (5.5.2.2)

You can now open the file LSG01-Lab5522.pka on the CD-ROM that accompanies this book to repeat this hands-on lab using Packet Tracer. Remember, however, that Packet Tracer is not a substitute for a hands-on lab experience with real equipment. A summary of the instructions is provided within the activity.

Skills Integration Challenge: Routing IP Packets (5.6.1.3)

Open the file LSG01-PTSkills5.pka on the CD-ROM that accompanies this book to perform this exercise using Packet Tracer.

Upon completion of this activity, you will be able to do the following:

- Configure a router interface using a GUI.

- Explore a routing table.

- Configure a static route using a GUI.

- Explore the routing of IP packets.

Background

Throughout the course, you will be using a standard lab setup created from actual PCs, servers, routers, and switches to learn networking concepts. At the end of each chapter, you will build increasingly larger parts of this topology in Packet Tracer, and analyze increasingly more complex protocol interactions.

You have already studied a variety of application protocols, such as DNS, HTTP, TFTP, DHCP, and Telnet, and two transport layer protocols, TCP and UDP. You may have noticed that regardless of what application and transport protocols were involved, in Inbound and Outbound PDU Details view they were always encapsulated in IP packets. In this activity, you will examine how IP, the dominant network layer protocol of the Internet, works in the context of a simple example of IP routing.

Figure 5-7 shows the topology for this skills integration challenge, and Table 5-7 shows the corresponding addressing table.

Table 5-7   Addressing Table

Device	Interface	IP Address	Subnet Mask	Default Gateway
R1-ISP	Fa0/0	192.168.254.253	255.255.255.0	N/A
	S0/0/0	10.10.10.6	255.255.255.252	N/A
R2-Central	Fa0/0	172.16.255.254	255.255.0.0	10.10.10.6
	S0/0/0	10.10.10.5	255.255.255.252	10.10.10.6
S1-Central	VLAN 1	172.16.254.1	255.255.0.0	172.16.255.254
PC 1A	NIC	172.16.1.1	255.255.0.0	172.16.255.254
PC 1B	NIC	172.16.1.2	255.255.0.0	172.16.255.254
Eagle Server	NIC	192.168.254.254	255.255.255.0	192.168.254.253

Figure 5-7   Topology for Challenge

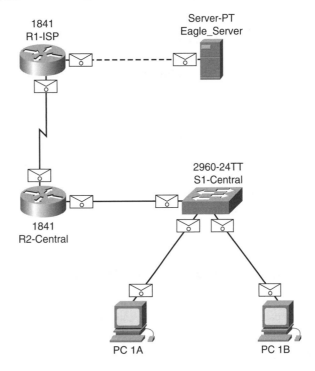

Task 1: Configure a Router Interface

There is a problem on the LAN: PC 1A cannot reach the Eagle Server (verify this in real-time mode). It appears there is a problem with the router. Move your cursor over the R2-Central router, and note the condition of the Fa0/0 interface (to which switch is connected). This interface must have an IP address, subnet mask, and be turned on to act as the default gateway for the LAN.

Click router R2-Central and go to the Config tab. At the end of the course, you will learn how to use the Cisco IOS command-line interface (CLI) to perform this task. For now, the Config tab is easier and will allow you to focus on the basic idea of IP routing.

In the list shown, find INTERFACE, FastEthernet0/0. Add the IP address **172.16.255.254** with subnet mask **255.255.0.0**, and turn the port on. Close the router window. Verify that the router interface (port) is now working by using the mouse over.

Try reaching Eagle Server. The request still fails. What are some possible reasons why?

_____

_____

Task 2: Examining Routes

Use the Inspect tool (magnifying glass) to examine the routing table of R2-Central. You will see the router's directly connected networks, but there is no way to reach the Eagle Server network.

Task 3: Configure a Route Using a GUI

Click router R2-Central and go to the Config tab. In the list shown, find ROUTING, Static. Configure what is known as a default static route, using the address **0.0.0.0**, mask **0.0.0.0**, and the next hop of **10.10.10.6** (the S0/0/0 interface on the R1-ISP router) and click the **Add** button. This route is configured so that wherever packets from the 172.16.0.0 /16 LAN are destined, they will go to the R1-ISP router.

Under GLOBAL, Settings, click the **Save** button to save the interface and route configuration you have just done to NVRAM (in case the router is power cycled). Use the Inspect tool (magnifying glass) to examine the routing table of R2-Central again. You should now see the route you configured in the routing table.

Verify your work using feedback from the Check Results button and the Assessment Items tab. Test connectivity, in real time, by using Add Simple PDU to test connectivity between PC 1A and the Eagle Server. The PDU, a one-shot ping, will appear in the User Created PDU list for future use, too.

Task 4: Examine the Routing of the IP Packet

Switch to simulation mode. Using the PDU you created in Task 3, double-click **Fire** to send it again. Trace the packet's journey from PC 1A to Eagle Server and back using the **Capture / Forward** button and examining the packet's contents by either clicking the envelope or clicking the colored square in the Info column of the event list.

Task 5: Reflection

What data can an IP packet contain? What is meant by the phrase "the IP packet is routed"? What is a route? Where might things go wrong?

CHAPTER 6

Addressing the Network: IPv4

The Study Guide portion of this chapter uses a combination of matching, fill-in-the-blank, multiple-choice, and open-ended questions to test your knowledge of network addressing.

The Labs and Activities portion of this chapter includes all the online curriculum activities and labs to ensure you have mastered the practical, hands-on skills needed to understand the opportunities and challenges associated with IPv4.

As you work through this chapter, use Chapter 6 in the Network Fundamentals CCNA Exploration online curriculum, or use the corresponding Chapter 6 in the *Network Fundamentals CCNA Exploration Companion Guide*, for assistance.

Study Guide

IPv4 Addresses

With IPv4, each packet has a 32-bit source address and a 32-bit destination address in the Layer 3 header. These addresses are used in the data network as binary patterns.

Data that appears in binary may represent many different forms of data to the human network. In this chapter, we refer to binary as it relates to IPv4 addressing. This means that we look at each byte as a decimal number in the range of 0 to 255.

For each IPv4 address, some portion of the high-order bits represents the network address. At Layer 3, we define a network as a group of hosts that have identical bit patterns in the network address portion of their addresses.

Concept Questions

1. What is another name for digital logic?

   Binary Pattern is

2. What is the format used for IP addresses called?

   is dotted decimal format

3. What is another way to refer to 1 byte or 8 bits?

   Another is octet.

4. What does IPv4 provide for packets that carry data?

   IPv4 provide heirarchical addressing for packets that carry data.

Binary-to-Decimal Conversion Exercise

Convert the following 32-bit binary number into an IP address, keeping in mind the following:

- Divide the 32 bits into four octets.
- Convert each octet to decimal.
- Add a "dot" between each decimal.

Binary number:

10101100000100000000010000010100

IP address: _____

Decimal-to-Binary Conversion Exercise

Convert the following IP address into a 32-bit binary number.

IP address: 172.16.5.20

Binary number: _____

Addresses for Different Purposes

Within the address range of each IPv4 network are three types of addresses:

- Network addresses
- Broadcast addresses
- Host addresses

Vocabulary Exercise: Matching

In Table 6-1, match the type of network address on the left to its definition on the right.

Table 6-1   Network Address Type Matching Exercise

Address Type	Definition
A. Network address	__ A special address used to send data to all hosts in the network
B. Broadcast address	__ An address assigned to an end device in the network
C. Host address	__ The address by which we refer to the network

In Table 6-2, match the type of communication on the left to its definition on the right.

Table 6-2   Communication Type Matching Exercise

Communication Type	Definition
A. Unicast	__ The process of sending a packet from one host to all hosts in the network
B. Broadcast	__ The process of sending a packet from one host to a selected group of hosts
C. Multicast	__ The process of sending a packet from one host to an individual host

Internet Research Exercise

Using any search engine available on the Internet, look up a website detailing the utility of calculating addresses by hand, or find a calculator for the three address types.

Vocabulary: Completion

Fill in the blanks in the following sentences.

1. Expressed in dotted-decimal format, the IPv4 address range is _____ to _____.

2. One major block of addresses reserved for special purposes is the IPv4 experimental address range _____ to _____. Currently, these addresses are listed as _____.

3. Another major block of addresses reserved for special purposes is the IPv4 _____ range 224.0.0.0 to 239.255.255.255.

4. The globally scoped multicast addresses are _____ to 238.255.255.255.

Concept Questions

1. How do you know how many bits represent the network portion and how many bits represent the host portion?

2. What is the prefix length?

3. What are the private address blocks?

4. Which addresses in a network cannot be assigned to hosts?

5. What is the reserved block for default routing?

6. What is the loopback address, and what block is reserved for loopback?

7. What block of addresses is designated "link-local"?

8. What block of addresses is designated "TEST-NET"?

9. Define classless addressing.

_____

_____

Assigning Addresses

The allocation of network layer address space within the corporate network needs to be well designed. Network administrators should not randomly select the addresses used in their networks. Nor should address assignment within the network be random.

The allocation of these addresses inside the networks should be planned and documented for the following reasons:

- Preventing duplication of addresses
- Providing and controlling access
- Monitoring security and performance

Internet Research Exercises

Using your favorite search engine, search for an example of an IPv4 addressing scheme or an article about IPv4's addressing. Be prepared to present your findings.

Go to the IANA website at http://www.iana.org, and spend a few minutes familiarizing yourself with the site. Be prepared to discuss your opinions of the IANA with the class.

Concept Questions

1. Describe the pros and cons of static addressing.

_____

_____

_____

_____

2. Describe the pros and cons of using DHCP for addressing.

_____

_____

_____

_____

_____

3. List four types of devices that work best using static IP addresses.

_____

_____

4. What is the primary focus of each of the three tiers of ISPs?

Tier 1:

_____

Tier 2:

_____

Tier 3:

_____

5. List some improvements that IPv6 will provide.

_____

_____

_____

_____

Is It on My Network?

To define the network and host portions of an address, the devices use a separate 32-bit pattern called a subnet mask. We express the subnet mask in the same dotted-decimal format as the IPv4 address. The prefix and the subnet mask are different ways of representing the same thing—the network portion of an address.

Binary Matching Exercise

There are a limited number of subnet mask octets. In Table 6-3, match the binary number to its numeric value.

Table 6-3   IPv4 Binary Matching Exercise

Binary Number	Numeric Value
a. 00000000	__ 192
b. 10000000	__ 224
c. 11000000	__ 248
d. 11100000	__ 240
e. 11110000	__ 0
f. 11111000	__ 255
g. 11111100	__ 252
h. 11111110	__ 254
i. 11111111	__ 128

Concept Questions

1. How is a subnet mask created?

_____

_____

2. Why do routers use ANDing?

_____

3. How does ANDing help an originating host?

_____

_____

4. If the routers and end devices calculate these processes without your intervention, why do you need to learn how to AND?

_____

_____

Internet Research Exercise

Using your favorite search engine, research ANDing (be sure to specify that you mean in IPv4 networks). Be prepared to present your findings.

_____

Calculating Addresses

Subnetting lets you create multiple logical networks from a single address block. Because we use a router to connect these networks, each interface on a router must have a unique network ID. Every node on that link is on the same network.

Concept Questions

1. What is the formula to calculate the number of subnets?

_____

2. What are the two most useful tools in designing a network?

_____

3. Using VLSM makes it easier to group networks around what commonalities?

_____

_____

Multiple-Choice Questions

1. Why would you use a VLSM chart?

   a. This method helps prevent assigning addresses that have already been allocated.

   b. This method lets you assign addresses that have already been allocated.

   c. This method prevents addresses from being allocated.

   d. Using a chart makes calculating VLSM easier.

2. For what is VLSM an acronym?

   a. Very Long String of Marbles

   b. Variant Language Superior Model

   c. Variable-Length Subsidiary Mode

   d. Variable-Length Subnet Mask

3. What utility attempts to trace the path that a packet takes through the network?

   a. ping

   b. SNMP

   c. traceroute

   d. Configmaker

Testing the Network Layer

Ping is a utility for testing IP connectivity between hosts. Ping sends out requests for responses from a specified host address. Ping uses a Layer 3 protocol that is a part of the TCP/IP suite called Internet Control Message Protocol (ICMP).

Concept Questions

1. How does ping work? Be as specific as you can.

   _____

   _____

   _____

   _____

   _____

   _____

   _____

   _____

   _____

   _____

2. What does a response from 127.0.0.1 indicate?

   _____

3. Assume that you ping your gateway. If the gateway does not respond, but another host does, what sort of problem could this indicate?

_____

_____

_____

_____

_____

_____

4. Why is ping not always the most reliable test for connectivity on a network?

_____

_____

_____

5. What does traceroute do?

_____

6. What does RTT stand for?

_____

7. What does TTL stand for?

_____

8. Name the different ICMP message types.

_____

_____

Vocabulary Exercise: Completion

Fill in the blanks in the following statements.

1. What do the first four Destination Unreachable codes mean?

    0 = _____

    1 = _____

    2 = _____

    3 = _____

2. If a router does not have enough _____ to receive incoming packets, the router discards these _____. A destination host may also send a _____ message if datagrams arrive too fast to be processed.

Labs and Activities

 ## Lab 6-1: Ping and Traceroute (6.7.1.1)

Upon completion of this lab, you will be able to

- Use the **ping** command to verify simple TCP/IP network connectivity.

- Use the **tracert/traceroute** command to verify TCP/IP connectivity.

Background

Two tools that are indispensable when testing TCP/IP network connectivity are ping and tracert. The ping utility is available on Windows, Linux, and Cisco IOS; it tests network connectivity. The tracert utility is available on Windows, and a similar utility, traceroute, is available on Linux and Cisco IOS. In addition to testing for connectivity, tracert can be used to check for network latency.

For example, when a web browser fails to connect to a web server, the problem can be anywhere between the client and the server. A network engineer may use the **ping** command to test for local network connectivity or connections where there are few devices. In a complex network, the **tracert** command would be used. Where to begin connectivity tests has been the subject of much debate; it usually depends on the experience of the network engineer and familiarity with the network.

Both ping and tracert use Internet Control Message Protocol (ICMP) to send messages between devices. ICMP is a TCP/IP network layer protocol, first defined in RFC 792 in September 1981. ICMP message types were later expanded in RFC 1700.

Scenario

This lab examines the **ping** and **tracert** commands. Command options will be used to modify the command behavior. To familiarize you with the use of the commands, devices in the Cisco lab will be tested.

Measured delay time will probably be less than that on a production network. This is because the Eagle Server lab has little network traffic.

Figure 6-1 shows the topology for this lab, and Table 6-4 is the corresponding addressing table.

Table 6-4   Addressing Table

Device	Interface	IP Address	Subnet Mask	Default Gateway
R1-ISP	S0/0/0	10.10.10.6	255.255.255.252	—
	Fa0/0	192.168.254.253	255.255.255.0	—
R2-Central	S0/0/0	10.10.10.5	255.255.255.252	10.10.10.6
	Fa0/0	172.16.255.254	255.255.0.0	—
Eagle Server	—	192.168.254.254	255.255.255.0	192.168.254.253
	—	172.31.24.254	255.255.255.0	—
Host Pod#A	—	172.16.Pod#.1	255.255.0.0	172.16.255.254
Host Pod#B	—	172.16.Pod#.2	255.255.0.0	172.16.255.254
S1-Central	—	172.16.254.1	255.255.0.0	172.16.255.254

Figure 6-1   Topology for Lab 6-1

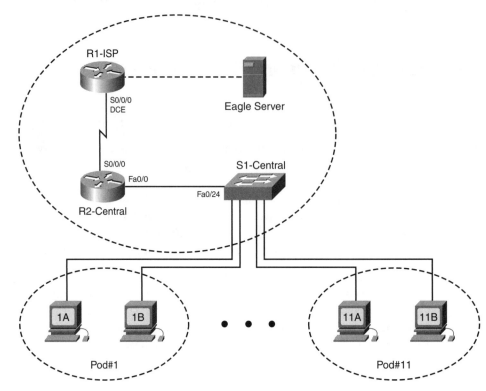

Task 1: Use the ping Command to Verify Simple TCP/IP Network Connectivity

The **ping** command is used to verify TCP/IP network layer connectivity on the local host computer or another device in the network. This command can be used with a destination IP address or qualified name, such as eagle-server.example.com, to test Domain Name System (DNS) functionality. For this lab, only IP addresses are used.

The ping operation is straightforward. The source computer sends an ICMP echo request to the destination. The destination responds with an echo reply. If there is a break between the source and destination, a router may respond with an ICMP message that the host is unknown or the destination network is unknown.

Step 1.   Verify TCP/IP network layer connectivity on the local host computer.

Open a Windows terminal and determine the IP address of the pod host computer with the **ipconfig** command, as shown in Example 6-1.

Example 6-1   Output of the ipconfig Command

```
C:\> ipconfig
Windows IP Configuration
Ethernet adapter Local Area Connection:
        Connection-specific DNS Suffix  . :
        IP Address. . . . . . . . . . . : 172.16.1.2
        Subnet Mask . . . . . . . . . . : 255.255.0.0
        Default Gateway . . . . . . . . : 172.16.255.254
C:\>
```

The output should look the same except for the IP address. Each pod host computer should have the same network mask and default gateway address; only the IP address may differ. If the information is missing or if the subnet mask and default gateway are different, reconfigure the TCP/IP settings to match the settings for this pod host computer.

Record local TCP/IP network information in Table 6-5.

Table 6-5   TCP/IP Information

TCP/IP Information	Value
IP address	
Subnet mask	
Default gateway	

Use the **ping** command to verify TCP/IP network layer connectivity on the local host computer.

By default, four ping requests are sent to the destination, and reply information is received. The output should look similar to that shown in Example 6-2.

Example 6-2   Output of the ping Command on the Local TCP/IP Stack

```
C:\> ping 172.16.1.2
Pinging 172.16.1.1 with 32 bytes of data:
Reply from 172.16.1.2: bytes=32 time<1ms TTL=128
Reply from 172.16.1.2: bytes=32 time<1ms TTL=128
Reply from 172.16.1.2: bytes=32 time<1ms TTL=128
Reply from 172.16.1.2: bytes=32 time<1ms TTL=128
```

Example 6-2   Output of the ping Command on the Local TCP/IP Stack *continued*

```
Ping statistics for 172.16.1.2:
       Packets: Sent = 4, Received = 4, Lost = 0 (0% loss),
Approximate round trip times in milli-seconds:
       Minimum = 0ms, Maximum = 0ms, Average = 0ms
C:\>
```

The first highlighted line shows the destination address, set to the IP address of the local computer. The second highlighted entry shows the following reply information:

- Bytes: Size of the ICMP packet.

- Time: Elapsed time between transmission and reply.

- TTL: Default TTL value of the destination device, minus the number of routers in the path. The maximum TTL value is 255. For newer Windows machines the default value is 128.

The third highlighted line shows summary information about the replies:

- Packets sent: The number of packets transmitted. By default, four packets are sent.

- Packets received: The number of packets received.

- Packets lost: The difference between the number of packets sent and received.

Example 6-2 also shows information about the delay in replies, measured in milliseconds. Lower round-trip times indicate faster links. A computer timer is set to 10 milliseconds. Values faster than 10 milliseconds display 0.

In Table 6-6, fill in the results of the **ping** command on your computer.

Table 6-6   Field Information

Field	Value
Size of packet	
Number of packets sent	
Number of replies	
Number of lost packets	
Minimum delay	
Maximum delay	
Average delay	

Step 2.   Verify TCP/IP network layer connectivity on the LAN.

Use the **ping** command to verify TCP/IP network layer connectivity to the default gateway. The results should be similar to those shown in Example 6-3.

Example 6-3   Output of the ping Command to the Default Gateway

```
C:\> ping 172.16.255.254
Pinging 172.16.255.254 with 32 bytes of data:
Reply from 172.16.255.254: bytes=32 time=1ms TTL=255
Reply from 172.16.255.254: bytes=32 time<1ms TTL=255
Reply from 172.16.255.254: bytes=32 time<1ms TTL=255
Reply from 172.16.255.254: bytes=32 time<1ms TTL=255
Ping statistics for 172.16.255.254:
    Packets: Sent = 4, Received = 4, Lost = 0 (0% loss),
Approximate round trip times in milli-seconds:
    Minimum = 0ms, Maximum = 1ms, Average = 0ms
C:\>
```

The Cisco IOS default TTL value is set to 255. Because the router was not crossed, the TTL value returned is 255.

In Table 6-7, fill in the results of the **ping** command to the default gateway.

Table 6-7   Field Information

Field	Value
Size of packet	
Number of packets sent	
Number of replies	
Number of lost packets	
Minimum delay	
Maximum delay	
Average delay	

What would be the result of a loss of connectivity to the default gateway?

_____

_____

_____

Step 3.   Verify TCP/IP network layer connectivity to a remote network.

Use the **ping** command to verify TCP/IP network layer connectivity to a device on a remote network. In this case, Eagle Server is used. The results should be similar to those shown in Example 6-4.

Example 6-4   Output of the ping Command to Eagle Server

```
C:\> ping 192.168.254.254
Pinging 192.168.254.254 with 32 bytes of data:
Reply from 192.168.254.254: bytes=32 time<1ms TTL=62
Reply from 192.168.254.254: bytes=32 time<1ms TTL=62
Reply from 192.168.254.254: bytes=32 time<1ms TTL=62
```

Example 6-4   Output of the ping Command to Eagle Server   *continued*

```
Reply from 192.168.254.254: bytes=32 time<1ms TTL=62
Ping statistics for 192.168.254.254:
    Packets: Sent = 4, Received = 4, Lost = 0 (0% loss),
Approximate round trip times in milli-seconds:
    Minimum = 0ms, Maximum = 0ms, Average = 0ms
C:\>
```

The Linux default TTL value is set to 64. Two routers were crossed to reach Eagle Server; therefore, the returned TTL value is 62.

Step 4: In Table 6-8, fill in the results of the **ping** command on your computer.

Table 6-8   Field Information

Field	Value
Size of packet	
Number of packets sent	
Number of replies	
Number of lost packets	
Minimum delay	
Maximum delay	
Average delay	

The **ping** command is extremely useful when you're troubleshooting network connectivity. However, there are limitations. In Example 6-5, the output shows that a user cannot reach Eagle Server. Is the problem with Eagle Server or a device in the path? The **tracert** command, examined next, can display network latency and path information.

Example 6-5   Output of the ping Command to the Lost Packets

```
C:\> ping 192.168.254.254
Pinging 192.168.254.254 with 32 bytes of data:
Request timed out.
Request timed out.
Request timed out.
Request timed out.
Ping statistics for 192.168.254.254:
    Packets: Sent = 4, Received = 0, Lost = 4 (100% loss),
C:\>
```

Task 2: Use the tracert Command to Verify TCP/IP Connectivity

The **tracert** command is useful for learning about network latency and path information. Instead of using the **ping** command to test the connectivity of each device to the destination, one by one, you can use the **tracert** command.

On Linux and Cisco IOS devices, the equivalent command is **traceroute**.

Step 1.   Verify TCP/IP network layer connectivity with the **tracert** command.

Open a Windows terminal, and issue the following command:

C:\> **tracert 192.168.254.254**

The output from the **tracert** command should be similar to that shown in Example 6-6.

Example 6-6   Output of the tracert Command to Eagle Server

```
C:\> tracert 192.168.254.254
Tracing route to 192.168.254.254 over a maximum of 30 hops
   1    <1 ms    <1 ms    <1 ms   172.16.255.254
   2    <1 ms    <1 ms    <1 ms   10.10.10.6
   3    <1 ms    <1 ms    <1 ms   192.168.254.254
Trace complete.
C:\>
```

Record your results in Table 6-9.

Table 6-9   Field Information

Field	Value
Maximum number of hops	
First router IP address	
Second router IP address	
Destination reached?	

Step 2.   Observe **tracert** output to a host that lost network connectivity.

If there is a loss of connectivity to an end device such as Eagle Server, the **tracert** command can give you valuable clues about the source of the problem. The **ping** command would show the failure but not any other kind of information about the devices in the path. Referring to the topology diagram shown in Figure 6-1, both R2-Central and R1-ISP are used for connectivity between the pod host computers and Eagle Server.

Refer to Example 6-7. Options are used with the **tracert** command to reduce wait time (in milliseconds), **-w 5**, and maximum hop count, **-h 4**. If Eagle Server were disconnected from the network, the default gateway would respond correctly, as well as R1-ISP. The problem must be on the 192.168.254.0/24 network. In this example, Eagle Server has been turned off.

Example 6-7   Output of the tracert Command

```
C:\> tracert -w 5 -h 4 192.168.254.254
Tracing route to 192.168.254.254 over a maximum of 4 hops
   1    <1 ms    <1 ms    <1 ms   172.16.255.254
   2    <1 ms    <1 ms    <1 ms   10.10.10.6
```

Example 6-7   Output of the tracert Command   *continued*

```
3    *         *         *         Request timed out.
4    *         *         *         Request timed out.


Trace complete.
C:\>
```

What would the tracert output be if R1-ISP failed?

_____

What would the tracert output be if R2-Central failed?

_____

Task 3: Challenge

The default values for the **ping** command normally work for most troubleshooting scenarios. There are times, however, when fine-tuning **ping** options may be useful. Issuing the **ping** command without any destination address displays the options shown in Example 6-8.

Example 6-8   Output of a ping Command with No Destination Address

```
C:\> ping

Usage: ping [-t] [-a] [-n count] [-l size] [-f] [-i TTL] [-v TOS]
            [-r count] [-s count] [[-j host-list] ¦ [-k host-list]]
            [-w timeout] target_name

Options:
    -t              Ping the specified host until stopped.
                    To see statistics and continue - type Control-Break;
                    To stop - type Control-C.
    -a              Resolve addresses to hostnames.
    -n count        Number of echo requests to send.
    -l size         Send buffer size.
    -f              Set Don't Fragment flag in packet.
    -i TTL          Time To Live.
    -v TOS          Type Of Service.
    -r count        Record route for count hops.
    -s count        Timestamp for count hops.
    -j host-list    Loose source route along host-list.
    -k host-list    Strict source route along host-list.
    -w timeout      Timeout in milliseconds to wait for each reply.
C:\>
```

The most useful options are highlighted. Some options do not work together, such as the **-t** and **-n** options. Other options can be used together. Experiment with those described in this section.

To ping the destination address until stopped, use the **-t** option, as shown in Example 6-9. To stop the output, press Ctrl-C.

Example 6-9   Output of a ping Command Using the -t Option

```
C:\> ping -t 192.168.254.254
Pinging 192.168.254.254 with 32 bytes of data:
Reply from 192.168.254.254: bytes=32 time<1ms TTL=63
Reply from 192.168.254.254: bytes=32 time<1ms TTL=63
Reply from 192.168.254.254: bytes=32 time<1ms TTL=63
Reply from 192.168.254.254: bytes=32 time<1ms TTL=63
Reply from 192.168.254.254: bytes=32 time<1ms TTL=63
Reply from 192.168.254.254: bytes=32 time<1ms TTL=63
Ping statistics for 192.168.254.254:
    Packets: Sent = 6, Received = 6, Lost = 0 (0% loss),
Approximate round trip times in milli-seconds:
    Minimum = 0ms, Maximum = 0ms, Average = 0ms
Control-C
^C
C:\>
```

To **ping** the destination once and record router hops, use the **-n** and **-r** options, as shown in Example 6-10.

Note: Not all devices honor the **-r** option.

Example 6-10   Output of a ping Command Using the -n and -r Options

```
C:\> ping -n 1 -r 9 192.168.254.254
Pinging 192.168.254.254 with 32 bytes of data:
Reply from 192.168.254.254: bytes=32 time=1ms TTL=63
    Route:      10.10.10.5 ->
           192.168.254.253 ->
           192.168.254.254 ->
              10.10.10.6 ->
            172.16.255.254
Ping statistics for 192.168.254.254:
    Packets: Sent = 1, Received = 1, Lost = 0 (0% loss),
Approximate round trip times in milli-seconds:
    Minimum = 1ms, Maximum = 1ms, Average = 1ms
C:\>
```

Task 4: Reflection

Network engineers use both ping and tracert to test network connectivity. For basic network connectivity, the **ping** command works best. To test latency and the network path, the **tracert** command is preferred.

The ability to accurately and quickly diagnose network connectivity issues is a skill expected from a network engineer. Knowledge about the TCP/IP protocols and practice with troubleshooting commands will build that skill.

Task 5: Clean Up

Unless directed otherwise by the instructor, turn off power to the host computers. Remove anything that was brought into the lab, and leave the room ready for the next class.

Packet Tracer Companion: ping and traceroute (6.7.1.2)

You can now open the file LSG01-Lab6712.pka on the CD-ROM that accompanies this book to repeat this hands-on lab using Packet Tracer. Remember, however, that Packet Tracer is not a substitute for a hands-on lab experience with real equipment. The instructions are summarized within the activity.

Lab 6-2: Examining ICMP Packets (6.7.2.1)

Upon completion of this lab, you will be able to

- Understand the format of ICMP packets.

- Use Wireshark to capture and examine ICMP messages.

Background

Internet Control Message Protocol (ICMP) was first defined in RFC 792 in September 1981. ICMP message types were later expanded in RFC 1700. ICMP operates at the TCP/IP network layer and is used to exchange information between devices.

ICMP packets serve many uses in today's computer networks. When a router cannot deliver a packet to a destination network or host, an informational message is returned to the source. Also, the **ping** and **tracert** commands send ICMP messages to destinations, and destinations respond with ICMP messages.

Scenario

Using Eagle Server, Wireshark captures will be made of ICMP packets between network devices.

Figure 6-2 shows the topology for this lab, and Table 6-10 is the corresponding addressing table.

Figure 6-2   Topology for Lab 6-2

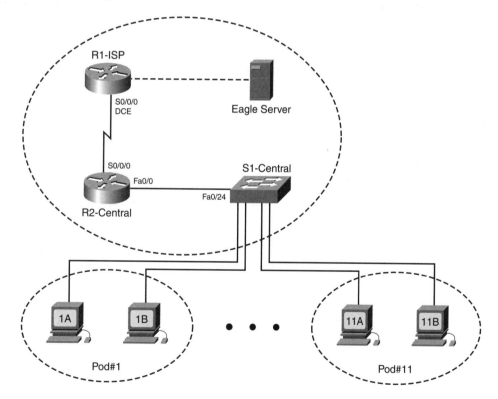

Table 6-10   Addressing Table

Device	Interface	IP Address	Subnet Mask	Default Gateway
R1-ISP	S0/0/0	10.10.10.6	255.255.255.252	—
	Fa0/0	192.168.254.253	255.255.255.0	—
R2-Central	S0/0/0	10.10.10.5	255.255.255.252	10.10.10.6
	Fa0/0	172.16.255.254	255.255.0.0	—
Eagle Server	—	192.168.254.254	255.255.255.0	192.168.254.253
	—	172.31.24.254	255.255.255.0	—
Host *Pod#*A	—	172.16.*Pod#*.1	255.255.0.0	172.16.255.254
Host *Pod#*B	—	172.16.*Pod#*.2	255.255.0.0	172.16.255.254
S1-Central	—	172.16.254.1	255.255.0.0	172.16.255.254

Task 1: Understand the Format of ICMP Packets

Refer to Figure 6-3, which shows the ICMP header fields common to all ICMP message types. Each ICMP message starts with an 8-bit Type field, an 8-bit Code field, and a computed 16-bit Checksum. The ICMP message type describes the remaining ICMP fields. Table 6-11 shows ICMP message types from RFC 792.

Figure 6-3   ICMP Message Header

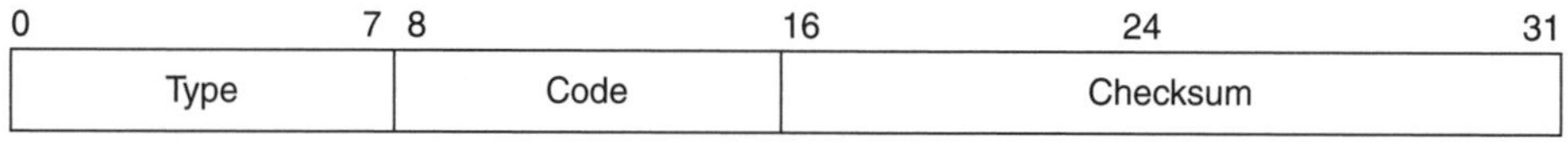

0	7 8	16	24	31
Type	Code	Checksum		

Table 6-11   ICMP Message Types

Value	Meaning
0	Echo Reply
3	Destination Unreachable
4	Source Quench
5	Redirect
8	Echo
11	Time Exceeded
12	Parameter Problem
13	Timestamp
14	Timestamp Reply
15	Information Request
16	Information Reply

Codes provide additional information to the Type field. For example, if the Type field is 3, Destination Unreachable, additional information about the problem is returned in the Code field. Table 6-12 shows message codes for an ICMP Type 3 message, Destination Unreachable, from RFC 1700.

Table 6-12   ICMP Type 3 Message Codes

Code Value	Meaning
0	Net Unreachable
1	Host Unreachable
2	Protocol Unreachable
3	Port Unreachable
4	Fragmentation Needed and Don't Fragment Was Set
5	Source Route Failed
6	Destination Network Unknown
7	Destination Host Unknown
8	Source Host Isolated
9	Communication with Destination Network Is Administratively Prohibited
10	Communication with Destination Host Is Administratively Prohibited
11	Destination Network Unreachable for Type of Service
12	Destination Host Unreachable for Type of Service

Using the ICMP message capture shown in Example 6-11, fill in the fields in Figure 6-4 for the ICMP packet echo request. Values beginning with 0x are hexadecimal numbers.

Example 6-11   ICMP Packet Echo Request

```
Internet Control Message Protocol
        Type: 8 (Echo (Ping) request)
        Code: 0
        Checksum: 0x365c [correct]
        Identifier: 0x0200
        Sequence number: 0x1500
        Data (32 bytes)
```

Figure 6-4   ICMP Packet Echo Request

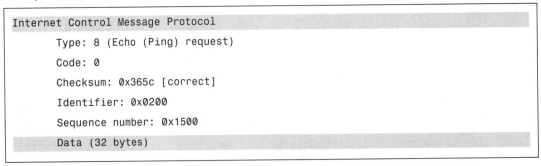
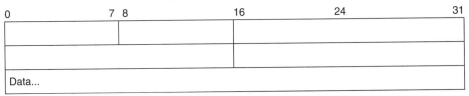

Using the ICMP message capture shown in Example 6-12, fill in the fields in Figure 6-5 for the ICMP packet echo reply.

Example 6-12   ICMP Packet Echo Reply

```
Internet Control Message Protocol
        Type: 0 (Echo (Ping) reply)
        Code: 0
        Checksum: 0x3e5c [correct]
        Identifier: 0x0200
        Sequence number: 0x1500
        Data (32 bytes)
```

Figure 6-5   ICMP Packet Echo Reply

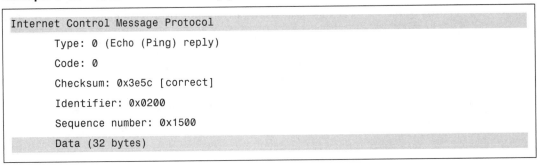
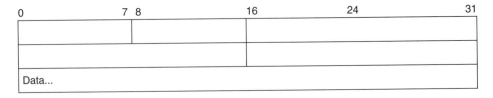

At the TCP/IP network layer, communication between devices is not guaranteed. However, ICMP does provide minimal checks for a reply to match the request. From the information provided in the ICMP messages just shown, how does the sender know that the reply is to a specific echo?

Task 2: Use Wireshark to Capture and Examine ICMP Messages

If Wireshark has not been loaded on the pod host computer, you can download it from Eagle Server:

1. Open a web browser and go to ftp://eagle-server.example.com/pub/eagle_labs/eagle1/chapter6.

2. Right-click the Wireshark filename, choose **Save Link As**, and save the file to the pod host computer.

3. When the file has been downloaded, open and install Wireshark.

Step 1.   Capture and evaluate ICMP echo messages to Eagle Server.

In this step, you use Wireshark to examine ICMP echo messages.

Open a Windows terminal on the pod host computer.

When ready, start the Wireshark capture.

From the Windows terminal, ping Eagle Server. You should receive four successful replies, as shown in Example 6-13.

Example 6-13   Successful ping Replies from Eagle Server

```
C:\> ping eagle-server.example.com
Pinging eagle-server.example.com [192.168.254.254] with 32 bytes of data:
Reply from 192.168.254.254: bytes=32 time<1ms TTL=63
Reply from 192.168.254.254: bytes=32 time<1ms TTL=63
Reply from 192.168.254.254: bytes=32 time<1ms TTL=63
Reply from 192.168.254.254: bytes=32 time<1ms TTL=63
Ping statistics for 192.168.254.254:
    Packets: Sent = 4, Received = 4, Lost = 0 (0% loss),
Approximate round trip times in milli-seconds:
    Minimum = 0ms, Maximum = 0ms, Average = 0ms
C:\>
```

Stop the Wireshark capture. There should be a total of four ICMP echo requests and matching echo replies, similar to those shown in Figure 6-6.

Figure 6-6   Wireshark Capture of ping Requests and Replies

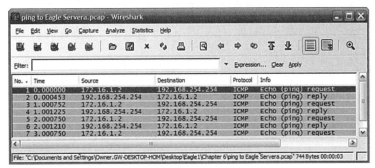

Which network device responds to the ICMP echo request?

Expand the middle window in Wireshark, and expand the Internet Control Message Protocol record until all fields are visible. The bottom window also is needed to examine the Data field.

In Table 6-13, record information from the *first* echo request packet to Eagle Server.

Table 6-13   Ping Echo Request Fields

Field	Value
Type	
Code	
Checksum	
Identifier	
Sequence number	
Data	

Are there 32 bytes of data?

In Table 6-14, record information from the *first* echo reply packet from Eagle Server.

Table 6-14   Ping Echo Reply Fields

Field	Value
Type	
Code	
Checksum	
Identifier	
Sequence number	
Data	

Which fields, if any, changed from the echo request?

Note: The Identifier field may change for subsequent echo request messages, depending on the operating system. For example, Cisco IOS increments the Identifier field by 1, but Windows keeps the Identifier field the same.

Continue to evaluate the remaining echo requests and replies. In Table 6-15, fill in information from each new ping.

Table 6-15   Ping Echo Requests and Replies

Packet	Checksum	Identifier	Sequence Number
Request #2			
Reply #2			
Request #3			
Reply #3			
Request #4			
Reply #4			

Why do the Checksum values change with each new request?

Step 2.   Capture and evaluate ICMP echo messages to 192.168.253.1.

In this step, pings are sent to a fictitious network and host. The results from the Wireshark capture are evaluated.

Try to ping IP address 192.168.253.1.

`C:\> ping 192.168.253.1`

See Example 6-14. Instead of a request timeout, an echo response occurs.

Example 6-14   Ping Results from a Fictitious Destination

```
C:\> ping 192.168.253.1
Pinging 192.168.253.1 with 32 bytes of data:
Reply from 172.16.255.254: Destination host unreachable.
Reply from 172.16.255.254: Destination host unreachable.
Reply from 172.16.255.254: Destination host unreachable.
Reply from 172.16.255.254: Destination host unreachable.
Ping statistics for 192.168.253.1:
    Packets: Sent = 4, Received = 4, Lost = 0 (0% loss),
Approximate round trip times in milli-seconds:
    Minimum = 0ms, Maximum = 0ms, Average = 0ms
C:\>
```

What network device responds to pings to a fictitious destination?

Figure 6-7 shows Wireshark captures to a fictitious destination. Expand the middle Wireshark window and the Internet Control Message Protocol record.

Figure 6-7   Wireshark Capture from a Fictitious Destination

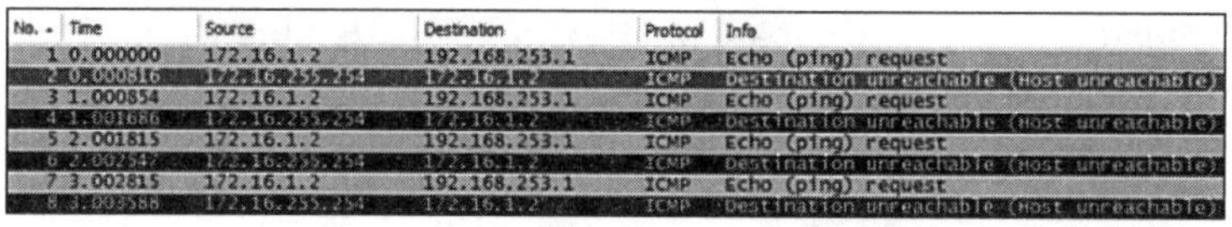

Which ICMP message type is used to return information to the sender?

_____

What code is associated with the message type?

_____

Step 3. Capture and evaluate ICMP echo messages that exceed the TTL value.

In this step, pings are sent with a low TTL value, simulating an unreachable destination. Ping Eagle Server, and set the TTL value to **1**:

```
C:\> ping -i 1 192.168.254.254
```

Example 6-15 shows ping replies when the TTL value has been exceeded.

Example 6-15   Ping Results for an Exceeded TTL

```
C:\> ping -i 1 192.168.254.254

Pinging 192.168.254.254 with 32 bytes of data:

Reply from 172.16.255.254: TTL expired in transit.

Reply from 172.16.255.254: TTL expired in transit.

Reply from 172.16.255.254: TTL expired in transit.

Reply from 172.16.255.254: TTL expired in transit.

Ping statistics for 192.168.254.254:

    Packets: Sent = 4, Received = 4, Lost = 0 (0% loss),

Approximate round trip times in milli-seconds:

    Minimum = 0ms, Maximum = 0ms, Average = 0ms

C:\>
```

What network device responds to pings that exceed the TTL value?

_____

Figure 6-8 shows Wireshark captures to a fictitious destination. Expand the middle Wireshark window and the Internet Control Message Protocol record.

Figure 6-8   Wireshark Capture of TTL Value Exceeded

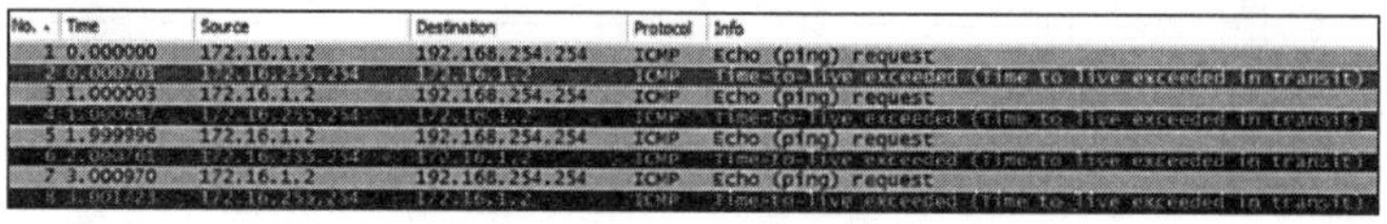

Which ICMP message type is used to return information to the sender?

_____

What code is associated with the message type?

_____

Which network device is responsible for decrementing the TTL value?

_____

Task 3: Challenge

Use Wireshark to capture a **tracert** session to Eagle Server and then to 192.168.254.251. Examine the ICMP TTL exceeded message. This demonstrates how the **tracert** command traces the network path to the destination.

Task 4: Reflection

The ICMP protocol is very useful when troubleshooting network connectivity issues. Without ICMP messages, a sender has no way to tell why a destination connection failed. Using the **ping** command, you can capture and evaluate different ICMP message type values.

Task 5: Clean Up

Wireshark may have been loaded on the pod host computer. If the program must be removed, choose **Start > Control Panel > Add or Remove Programs**, and scroll down to Wireshark. Click the filename, click **Remove**, and follow the uninstall instructions.

Remove any Wireshark pcap files that were created on the pod host computer.

Unless directed otherwise by the instructor, turn off power to the host computers. Remove anything that was brought into the lab, and leave the room ready for the next class.

Packet Tracer Companion: Examining ICMP Packets (6.7.2.2)

You can now open the file LSG01-Lab6722.pka on the CD-ROM that accompanies this book to repeat this hands-on lab using Packet Tracer. Remember, however, that Packet Tracer is not a substitute for a hands-on lab experience with real equipment. The instructions are summarized within the activity.

Activity 6-1: IPv4 Address Subnetting, Part 1 (6.7.3.1)

Upon completion of this activity, you will be able to determine network information for a given IP address and network mask.

Background

This activity is designed to teach you how to compute network IP address information from a given IP address.

Scenario

When given an IP address and network mask, you will be able to determine other information about the IP address, such as

- Network address
- Network broadcast address
- Total number of host bits
- Number of hosts

Task 1: For a Given IP Address, Determine Network Information

Given the following information:

- Host IP address: 172.25.114.250
- Network mask: 255.255.0.0 (/16)

you will determine the following information in this task:

- Network address
- Network broadcast address
- Total number of host bits
- Number of hosts

Step 1. Translate the host IP address and network mask into binary notation.

In Table 6-16, convert the host IP address and network mask into binary.

Table 6-16   Decimal-to-Binary Conversion

	172	25	114	250
IP address				
Network mask				
	255	255	0	0

Step 2.   Determine the network address.

In Table 6-17, perform the following tasks:

- Draw a line under the mask.

- Perform a bitwise AND operation on the IP address and subnet mask.

Note: 1 AND 1 results in a 1; 0 AND anything results in a 0.

- Express the result in dotted-decimal notation. The result is the network address for this host IP address, which is 172.25.0.0.

Table 6-17   AND Operation

	172	25	114	250
IP address				
Subnet mask				
Network address				
	172	25	0	0

Step 3.   In Table 6-18, determine the broadcast address for the network address.

The network mask separates the network portion of the address from the host portion. The network address has all 0s in the host portion of the address, and the broadcast address has all 1s in the host portion of the address.

Table 6-18   Broadcast Information

	172	25	0	0
Network address				
Subnet mask				
Broadcast address				
	172	25	255	255

By counting the number of host bits, you can determine the total number of usable hosts for this network.

Host bits: 16

Total number of hosts:

$2^{16} = 65,536$

$65,536 - 2 = 65,534$ (addresses that cannot use the *all-0s* address [the network address] or the *all-1s* address [the broadcast address])

Add this information to Table 6-19.

Table 6-19   Host Bits: Information on the Number of Hosts

Field	Value
Host IP address	172.25.114.250
Network mask	255.255.0.0 (/16)
Network address	
Network broadcast address	
Total number of host bits	
Number of hosts	

Task 2: Challenge

For all problems, create a subnetting worksheet to show and record all work for each problem.

Table 6-20 shows Problem 1.

Table 6-20   Problem 1

Field	Value
Host IP address	172.30.1.33
Network mask	255.255.0.0
Network address	
Network broadcast address	
Total number of host bits	
Number of hosts	

Table 6-21 shows Problem 2.

Table 6-21   Problem 2

Field	Value
Host IP address	172.30.1.33
Network mask	255.255.255.0
Network address	
Network broadcast address	
Total number of host bits	
Number of hosts	

Table 6-22 shows Problem 3.

Table 6-22   Problem 3

Field	Value
Host IP address	192.168.10.234
Network mask	255.255.255.0
Network address	
Network broadcast address	
Total number of host bits	
Number of hosts	

Table 6-23 shows Problem 4.

Table 6-23   Problem 4

Field	Value
Host IP address	172.17.99.71
Network mask	255.255.0.0
Network address	
Network broadcast address	
Total number of host bits	
Number of hosts	

Table 6-24 shows Problem 5.

Table 6-24   Problem 5

Field	Value
Host IP address	192.168.3.219
Network mask	255.255.0.0
Network address	
Network broadcast address	
Total number of host bits	
Number of hosts	

Table 6-25 shows Problem 6.

Table 6-25   Problem 6

Field	Value
Host IP address	192.168.3.219
Network mask	255.255.255.224
Network address	
Network broadcast address	
Total number of host bits	
Number of hosts	

Task 3: Clean Up

Remove anything that was brought into the lab, and leave the room ready for the next class.

Activity 6-2: IPv4 Address Subnetting, Part 2 (6.7.4.1)

In this activity, you learn how to determine subnet information for a given IP address and subnetwork mask.

Background

Determine how many bits must be allocated to create a certain number of subnets or a certain number of hosts per subnet.

Using the chart shown in Table 6-26, it is easy to determine how many bits must be borrowed.

Table 6-26   Hosts or Subnets

2^{10}	2^9	2^8	2^7	2^6	2^5	2^4	2^3	2^2	2^1	2^0
1,024	512	256	128	64	32	16	8	4	2	1

Number of bits borrowed:

10	9	8	7	6	5	4	3	2	1	1
1,024	512	256	128	64	32	16	8	4	2	1

Remember, subtract 2 for the usable number of hosts per subnet—one for the subnet address and one for the subnet's broadcast address.

Because subnet masks must be contiguous 1s followed by contiguous 0s, the converted dotted-decimal notation can contain one of a certain number of values, as shown in Table 6-27.

Table 6-27   Decimal-to-Binary Conversion

Decimal	Binary
255	11111111
254	11111110
252	11111100
248	11111000
240	11110000
224	11100000
192	11000000
128	10000000
0	00000000

Scenario

When given an IP address, network mask, and subnetwork mask, you will be able to determine other information about the IP address:

- The subnet address of this subnet

- The broadcast address of this subnet

- The range of host addresses for this subnet

- The maximum number of subnets for this subnet mask

- The number of hosts for each subnet

- The number of subnet bits

- The number of this subnet

Task 1: For a Given IP Address and Subnet Mask, Determine Subnet Information

Given the following information:

- Host IP address: 172.25.114.250

- Network mask: 255.255.0.0 (/16)

- Subnet mask: 255.255.255.192 (/26)

you will determine the following information in this task:

- Number of subnet bits

- Number of subnets

- Number of host bits per subnet

- Number of usable hosts per subnet

- Subnet address for this IP address

- IP address of the first host on this subnet

- IP address of the last host on this subnet

- Broadcast address for this subnet

Step 1.   Translate the host IP address and subnet mask into binary notation in Table 6-28.

Table 6-28   Translate Host IP Addresses

Field	Value			
IP address	**172**	**25**	**114**	**250**
Subnet mask				
	255	**255**	**255**	**192**

Step 2. In Table 6-29, determine the network (or subnet) where this host address belongs.

Draw a line under the mask.

Perform a bitwise AND operation on the IP address and subnet mask.

Table 6-29   Determine the Network

	172	25	114	250
IP address	10101100	11001000	01110010	11111010
Subnet mask	11111111	11111111	11111111	11000000
Subnet address	10101100	11001000	01110010	11000000

Note: 1 AND 1 results in a 1; 0 AND anything else results in a 0.

Express the result in dotted-decimal notation. The result is the subnet address of this subnet, which is 172.25.114.192.

Step 3. Determine which bits in the address contain network information and which contain host information.

As shown in Figure 6-9, draw the *major divide* (M.D.) as a wavy line where the 1s in the major network mask end (also the mask if there was no subnetting). In this example, the major network mask is 255.255.0.0, or the first 16 leftmost bits.

Figure 6-9   Major Divide/Subnet Divide

		M.D.	S.D.	
IP Address	10101110	11001000	01110010	11 111010
Subnet Mask	11111111	11111111	11111111	11 000000
Subnet Add.	10001010	11001000	01110010	11 000000

10 Bits

Draw the *subnet divide* (S.D.) as a straight line where the 1s in the given subnet mask end. The network information ends where the 1s in the mask end.

The result is the number of subnet bits, which can be determined by simply counting the number of bits between the M.D. and S.D., which in this case is 10 bits.

Step 4. Determine the bit ranges for subnets and hosts.

As shown in Figure 6-10, label the *subnet counting range* between the M.D. and the S.D. This range contains the bits that are being incremented to create the subnet numbers or addresses.

Figure 6-10   Bit Ranges for Subnets and Hosts

		M.D.	S.D.	
IP Address	10101110	11001000	01110010	11 111010
Subnet Mask	11111111	11111111	11111111	11 000000
Subnet Add.	10001010	11001000	01110010	11 000000
			← Subnet Counting Range →	← Host Counting Range →

Label the *host counting range* between the S.D. and the last bits at the end on the right. This range contains the bits that are being incremented to create the host numbers or addresses.

Step 5.   Use Figure 6-11 to determine the range of host addresses available on this subnet and the broadcast address on this subnet.

Figure 6-11   Subnet Counting Range and Host Counting Range

		M.D.	S.D.	
IP Address	10101100	11001000	01110010	11 111010
Subnet Mask	11111111	11111111	11111111	11 000000
Subnet Add.	10101100	11001000	01110010	11 000000
			← Subnet Counting Range →	← Host Counting Range →
First Host	10101100	11001000	01110010	11 000001
	172	25	114	193
Last Host	10101100	11001000	01110010	11 111110
	172	25	114	254
Broadcast	10101100	11001000	01110010	11 111111
	172	25	114	255

Write down all the network/subnet bits of the network address (that is, all bits before the S.D.).

In the host portion (to the right of the S.D.), make the host bits all 0s except for the right-most bit (or least-significant bit), which you make a 1. This gives us the *first* host IP address on this subnet, which is the *first part* of the result for Range of Host Addresses for This Subnet, which in the example is 172.25.114.193.

Next, in the host portion (to the right of the S.D.), make the host bits all 1s except for the rightmost bit (or least-significant bit), which you make a 0. This gives us the *last* host IP address on this subnet, which is the last part of the result for Range of Host Addresses for This Subnet, which in the example is 172.25.114.254.

In the host portion (to the right of the S.D.), make the host bits all 1s. This gives us the broadcast IP address on this subnet. This is the result for Broadcast Address of This Subnet, which in the example is 172.25.114.255.

Add the missing information to Table 6-30.

Table 6-30   Fill in the Missing Information

Field	Value
Host IP address	172.25.114.250
Major network mask	255.255.0.0 (/16)
Major (base) network address	172.25.0.0
Major network broadcast address	172.25.255.255
Total number of host bits	
Number of hosts	16 bits or 2^{16} or 65,536 total hosts
	65,536 – 2 = 65,534 usable hosts
Subnet mask	255.255.255.192 (/26)
Number of subnet bits	
Number of subnets	
Number of host bits per subnet	
Number of usable hosts per subnet	
Subnet address for this IP address	
IP address of the first host on this subnet	
IP address of the last host on this subnet	
Broadcast address for this subnet	

Step 6. Determine the number of subnets.

The number of subnets is determined by how many bits are in the *subnet counting range* (in this example, 10 bits).

Use the formula 2^n, where *n* is the number of bits in the *subnet counting range*.

$2^{10} = 1024$

Number of subnet bits: 10 bits

Number of subnets (all 0s used, all 1s not used): $2^{10} = 1024$ subnets

Step 7. Determine the number of usable hosts per subnet.

The number of hosts per subnet is determined by the number of host bits (in this example, 6 bits) minus 2 (1 for the subnet address and 1 for the broadcast address of the subnet).

$2^6 - 2 = 64 - 2 = 62$ hosts per subnet

Number of host bits per subnet: 6 bits

Number of usable hosts per subnet: $2^6 - 2 = 64 - 2 = 62$ hosts per subnet

Step 8.   Review the final answers in Table 6-31.

Table 6-31   Final Answers

Field	Value
Host IP address	172.25.114.250
Subnet mask	255.255.255.192 (/26)
Number of subnet bits	26 bits
Number of subnets	$2^{10} = 1024$ subnets
Number of host bits per subnet	6 bits
Number of usable hosts per subnet	$2^6 - 2 = 64 - 2 = 62$ hosts per subnet
Subnet address for this IP address	172.25.114.192
IP address of the first host on this subnet	172.25.114.193
IP address of the last host on this subnet	172.25.114.254
Broadcast address for this subnet	172.25.114.255

Task 2: Challenge

For all problems, create a subnetting worksheet to show and record all work for each problem.

Table 6-32 shows Problem 1.

Table 6-32   Problem 1

Field	Value
Host IP address	172.30.1.33
Subnet mask	255.255.255.0
Number of subnet bits	
Number of subnets	
Number of host bits per subnet	
Number of usable hosts per subnet	
Subnet address for this IP address	
IP address of the first host on this subnet	
IP address of the last host on this subnet	
Broadcast address for this subnet	

Table 6-33 shows Problem 2.

Table 6-33   Problem 2

Field	Value
Host IP address	172.30.1.33
Subnet mask	255.255.255.252
Number of subnet bits	
Number of subnets	
Number of host bits per subnet	
Number of usable hosts per subnet	
Subnet address for this IP address	
IP address of the first host on this subnet	
IP address of the last host on this subnet	
Broadcast address for this subnet	

Table 6-34 shows Problem 3.

Table 6-34   Problem 3

Field	Value
Host IP address	192.192.10.234
Subnet mask	255.255.255.0
Number of subnet bits	
Number of subnets	
Number of host bits per subnet	
Number of usable hosts per subnet	
Subnet address for this IP address	
IP address of the first host on this subnet	
IP address of the last host on this subnet	
Broadcast address for this subnet	

Table 6-35 shows Problem 4.

Table 6-35   Problem 4

Field	Value
Host IP address	172.17.99.71
Subnet mask	255.255.0.0
Number of subnet bits	
Number of subnets	
Number of host bits per subnet	
Number of usable hosts per subnet	
Subnet address for this IP address	
IP address of the first host on this subnet	
IP address of the last host on this subnet	
Broadcast address for this subnet	

Table 6-36 shows Problem 5.

Table 6-36   Problem 5

Field	Value
Host IP address	192.168.3.219
Subnet mask	255.255.255.0
Number of subnet bits	
Number of subnets	
Number of host bits per subnet	
Number of usable hosts per subnet	
Subnet address for this IP address	
IP address of the first host on this subnet	
IP address of the last host on this subnet	
Broadcast address for this subnet	

Table 6-37 shows Problem 6.

Table 6-37   Problem 6

Field	Value
Host IP address	192.168.3.218
Subnet mask	255.255.255.252
Number of subnet bits	
Number of subnets	
Number of host bits per subnet	
Number of usable hosts per subnet	
Subnet address for this IP address	
IP address of the first host on this subnet	
IP address of the last host on this subnet	
Broadcast address for this subnet	

Task 3: Clean Up

Remove anything that was brought into the lab, and leave the room ready for the next class.

Lab 6-3: Subnet and Router Configuration (6.7.5.1)

Upon completion of this lab, you will be able to

- Subnet an address space given requirements.

- Assign appropriate addresses to interfaces and document them.

- Configure and activate serial and FastEthernet interfaces.

- Test and verify configurations.

- Reflect on and document the network implementation.

Scenario

In this lab activity, you design and apply an IP addressing scheme for the topology shown in Figure 6-12. You are given one address block that you must subnet to provide a logical addressing scheme for the network. The routers then will be ready for interface address configuration according to your IP addressing scheme. When the configuration is complete, verify that the network is working properly.

Figure 6-12   Topology for Lab 6-3

Task 1: Subnet the Address Space

Step 1.   Examine the network requirements. Use the smallest subnet sizes that will accomodate the appropriate number of hosts.

You have been given the 192.168.1.0/24 address space to use in your network design. The network consists of the following segments:

- The network connected to router R1 requires enough IP addresses to support 15 hosts.

- The network connected to router R2 requires enough IP addresses to support 30 hosts.

- The link between router R1 and router R2 requires IP addresses at each end of the link.

Step 2.   Consider the following questions when creating your network design:

- How many subnets are needed for this network? _____

- What is the subnet mask for this network in dotted-decimal format?

  _____

- What is the subnet mask for the network in slash format? _____

- How many usable hosts are there per subnet? _____

Step 3.   Assign subnetwork addresses to the topology diagram shown in Figure 6-12:

- Assign subnet 1 to the network attached to R1.

- Assign subnet 2 to the link between R1 and R2.

- Assign subnet 3 to the network attached to R2.

Task 2: Determine Interface Addresses

Step 1.   Assign appropriate addresses to the device interfaces:

- Assign the first valid host address in subnet 1 to the LAN interface on R1.

- Assign the last valid host address in subnet 1 to PC1.

- Assign the first valid host address in subnet 2 to the WAN interface on R1.

- Assign the last valid host address in subnet 2 to the WAN interface on R2.

- Assign the first valid host address in subnet 3 to the LAN interface on R2.

- Assign the last valid host address in subnet 3 to PC2.

Step 2.   In Table 6-38, document the addresses to be used.

Table 6-38   Addressing Table

Device	Interface	IP Address	Subnet Mask	Default Gateway
R1	Fa0/0			—
	S0/0/0			—
R2	Fa0/0			—
	S0/0/0			—
PC1	NIC			
PC2	NIC			

Task 3: Configure the Serial and FastEthernet Addresses

Step 1.   Configure the router interfaces.

Configure the interfaces on the R1 and R2 routers with the IP addresses from your network design. Note that to complete the activity in Packet Tracer, you will use the Config tab. When you have finished, be sure to save the running configuration to the router's NVRAM.

Step 2.   Configure the PC interfaces.

Configure the Ethernet interfaces of PC1 and PC2 with the IP addresses and default gateways from your network design.

Task 4: Verify the Configurations

Answer the following questions to verify that the network is operating as expected:

- From the host attached to R1, can you ping the default gateway? _____

- From the host attached to R2, can you ping the default gateway? _____

- From the router R1, can you ping the Serial 0/0/0 interface of R2? _____

- From the router R2, can you ping the Serial 0/0/0 interface of R1? _____

Note: The answers to the preceding questions should be yes. If any of the pings failed, check the physical connections and configurations.

Task 5: Reflection

Are there any devices on the network that cannot ping each other?

_____

What is missing from the network that is preventing communication between these devices?

_____

Packet Tracer Companion: Subnet and Router Configuration (6.7.5.2)

You can now open the file LSG01-Lab6752.pka on the CD-ROM that accompanies this book to repeat this hands-on lab using Packet Tracer. Remember, however, that Packet Tracer is not a substitute for a hands-on lab experience with real equipment. The instructions are summarized within the activity.

Skills Integration Challenge: Planning Subnets and Configuring IP Addresses (6.8.1.3)

Open the file LSG01-PTSkills6.pka on the CD-ROM that accompanies this book to perform this exercise using Packet Tracer.

Upon completion of this lab, you will be able to

- Do IP subnet planning: Practice your subnetting skills.

- Build the network: Connect devices with Ethernet and serial cables.

- Configure the network: Apply your subnetting scheme to servers, PCs, and router interfaces; configure services and static routing.

- Test the network: Using ping, trace, web traffic, and Inspect tools.

Background

You have been asked to implement the standard lab topology, but with a new IP addressing scheme. You will use many of the skills you have learned to this point in the course. Figure 6-13 shows the topology for this lab.

Figure 6-13   Topology for Challenge

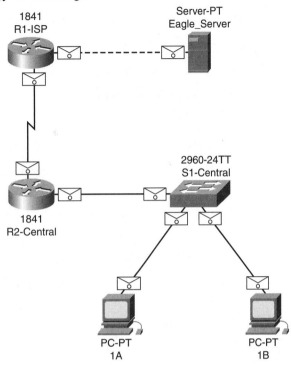

Task 1: IP Subnet Planning

You have been given an IP address block of 192.168.23.0 /24. You must provide for existing networks as well as future growth. Fill in your answers in Table 6-39.

Table 6-39   Addressing Table

Device	Interface	IP Address	Subnet Mask	Default Gateway
R1-ISP	Fa0/0			—
	S0/0/0			—
R2-Central	Fa0/0			
	S0/0/0			
PC 1A	NIC			
PC 1B	NIC			
Eagle Server	NIC			

Subnet assignments:

- First subnet, existing student LAN (off of router R2-Central), up to 60 hosts

- Second subnet, future student LAN, up to 28 hosts

- Third subnet, existing ISP LAN, up to 12 hosts

- Fourth subnet, future ISP LAN, up to 8 hosts

- Fifth subnet, existing WAN, point-to-point link

- Sixth subnet, future WAN, point-to-point link

- Seventh subnet, future WAN, point-to-point link

Interface IP addresses:

- For the server, configure the second-highest usable IP address on the existing ISP LAN subnet.

- For R1-ISP's Fa0/0 interface, configure the highest usable IP address on the existing ISP LAN subnet.

- For R1-ISP's S0/0/0 interface, configure the highest usable address on the existing WAN subnet.

- For R2-Central's S0/0/0 interface, use the lowest usable address on the existing WAN subnet.

- For R2-Central's Fa0/0 interface, use the highest usable address on the existing student LAN subnet.

- For hosts 1A and 1B, use the first two IP addresses (the two lowest usable addresses) on the existing student LAN subnet.

Additional configurations:

- For PCs 1A and 1B, in addition to IP configuration, configure them to use DNS services.

- For the server, enable DNS services, use the domain name eagle-server.example.com, and enable HTTP services.

- For the R1-ISP router serial interface, you need to set the clock rate (a timing mechanism required on the DCE end of serial links) to 64000.

- No clock rate is needed on the DTE side—in this case, R2-Central's serial interface.

Task 2: Finish Building the Network in Packet Tracer

Add cables where they are missing:

- Connect a serial DCE cable to R1-ISP S0/0/0, with the other end to R2-Central S0/0/0.

- Connect PC 1A to the first FastEthernet port on switch S1-Central.

- Connect PC 1B to the second FastEthernet port on switch S1-Central.

- Connect interface Fa0/0 on router R2-Central to the highest FastEthernet port on switch S1-Central.

- For all devices, make sure the power is on to the device and the interfaces.

Task 3: Configure the Network

You need to configure the server, both routers, and the two PCs. You do not need to configure the switch, nor do you need the IOS CLI to configure the routers. Part of the router configuration has already been done for you. All you must do is configure the static routes and the interfaces via the GUI. The static route on R1-ISP should point to the existing student LAN subnet via R2-Central's serial interface IP address. The static route on R2-Central should be a default static route that points to R1-ISP's serial interface IP address. These procedures were explained in the Chapter 5 Skills Integration Challenge.

Task 4: Test the Network

Use ping, trace, web traffic, and the Inspect tool. Trace packet flow in simulation mode, with HTTP, DNS, TCP, UDP, and ICMP viewable, to test your understanding of how the network is operating.

Task 5: Reflection

Reflect on how much you have learned so far! Practicing IP subnetting skills and network building, configuration, and testing skills will serve you well throughout your networking courses.

OSI Data Link Layer

The Study Guide portion of this chapter uses a combination of matching, fill-in-the-blank, and open-ended questions to test your knowledge of the data link layer.

The Labs and Activities portion of this chapter includes all the online curriculum activities and labs to ensure that you have mastered the practical, hands-on skills you need to work with the data link layer.

As you work through this chapter, use Chapter 7 in the Network Fundamentals CCNA Exploration online curriculum, or use the corresponding Chapter 7 in the *Network Fundamentals CCNA Exploration Companion Guide*, for assistance.

Study Guide

Data Link Layer: Accessing the Media

The data link layer plays a major role in networks, because it is the layer that accesses the physical medium and causes network traffic to traverse different physical media. The media can consist of many different types, including copper cabling, optical fibers, and the air in the case of wireless. The data link layer hides the details of these media from the upper layers and takes on the job of transmitting data across each network segment.

Vocabulary Exercise: Matching

In Table 7-1, match the term on the left to its definition on the right.

Table 7-1   Data Link Layer Terms

Term	Definition
a. Frame	__ Two or more devices connected to a common medium
b. Node	__ A layer of the Open Systems Interconnection (OSI) model that frames upper-layer data and controls how data is placed on a medium
c. Media	__ A device on a network
d. Network	__ The physical means used to carry data signals
e. Data link	__ The protocol data unit (PDU) used in Layer 2 of the OSI model

Concept Questions

1. What are the two main jobs of the data link layer?

   _____

   _____

2. What is the difference between a logical network and a physical network?

   _____

   _____

3. If the data link layer didn't exist, what changes would be required of a network layer protocol such as Internet Protocol (IP)?

_____

_____

_____

_____

Vocabulary Exercise: Completion

Fill in the blanks in the following statements.

1. The technique for getting a frame on and off a medium is called the _____ method.

2. To connect to a network, a _____ uses an adapter, such as a _____ on a local-area network (LAN). The adapter manages the _____ and _____.

3. An intermediary device, such as a _____, has physical interfaces that can _____ a packet into the appropriate _____ and handle the _____ method to access each link.

4. A router uses _____ layer services to receive a _____ from one medium, _____ the frame to the Layer 3 PDU, _____ the Layer 3 PDU into a new frame, and place the frame on the _____ of the next link in the network.

Media Access Control Techniques

Media access control regulates the placement of data frames on a medium. There are different ways to accomplish this regulation, depending on the medium and the data link layer protocols in use. Some methods are complicated and add overhead to the process. Other methods are less complicated but may not scale as well.

Concept Questions

1. Compare and contrast controlled media access control and contention-based media access control.

_____

_____

_____

_____

_____

_____

_____

_____

2. List the steps in the carrier sense multiple access collision detect (CSMA/CD) process. At this point, you can keep the list simple. You will learn more about CSMA/CD in Chapter 9, "Ethernet."

_____

_____

_____

_____

_____

_____

3. What is the difference between full-duplex communication and half-duplex communication?

_____

_____

_____

_____

Vocabulary Exercise: Completion

Fill in the blanks in the following statements.

1. A logical _____ topology enables a number of nodes to communicate by using the same shared _____.

2. Having many nodes share access to the medium requires a _____ layer media access control method to _____ the _____ of data.

3. Three media access control methods used by logical multiaccess topologies include

    _____

    _____.

4. Data link layer rules (also called _____) specify the media access control method that is used for a particular _____. For example, Ethernet uses _____.

Media Access Control: Addressing and Framing Data

A fundamental job of the data link layer is to encapsulate a Layer 3 PDU into a Layer 2 PDU. The Layer 2 PDU is called a *frame*. Although different protocols place different fields in a frame, most protocols specify that the frame should have a header, data field, and trailer. Most Layer 2 frames also have addressing fields in the header that identify the sender and receiver.

Vocabulary Exercise: Matching

Table 7-2 lists some typical fields that appear in frame headers. Match the field on the left to its definition on the right.

Table 7-2   Frame Header Fields

Field	Definition
a. Start frame	__ Used to indicate overloading on the medium
b. Address	__ Used to start and stop traffic when overloading occurs
c. Type	__ Specifies the number of bytes in the data part of the frame
d. Length	__ Indicates the upper-layer service contained in the frame
e. Priority	__ Tells other devices on the network that a frame is coming along the medium
f. Flow control	__ Identifies the sender and receiver
g. Congestion control	__ Indicates a particular type of communication service for special processing

Table 7-3 lists three major data link layer protocols. Match each protocol on the left to its specifications on the right.

Table 7-3   Data Link Layer Protocols

Protocol	Specification
a. Ethernet	__ A protocol for wireless networks that uses CSMA/CA
b. Point-to-Point Protocol	__ Defined by the IEEE 802.3 standard
c. 802.11	__ Includes specifications for operation at 10, 100, 1000, and 10,000 Mbps
	__ Establishes a logical connection (session) between two nodes
	__ Uses a preamble field at the beginning of the frame
	__ Often found on WANs
	__ Provides unacknowledged connectionless service over a shared medium using CSMA/CD
	__ Defined in a Request For Comments (RFC) document
	__ Uses a flag field at the beginning of the frame
	__ Uses an acknowledgment to confirm that a frame was received successfully

Concept Questions

1. Compare and contrast Layer 2 addresses with Layer 3 addresses.

_____

_____

_____

_____

_____

2. Why are Layer 2 addresses not needed in point-to-point topologies?

_____

_____

_____

_____

3. What is the purpose of the Frame Check Sequence (FCS) in a frame trailer?

_____

_____

_____

_____

Putting It All Together: Follow Data Through an Internetwork

When a user on a LAN wants to access a service, a number of packets are generated and encapsulated in Layer 2 frames. If you have done the reading in Chapter 7 in the Network Fundamentals CCNA Exploration online curriculum or if you have used the corresponding Chapter 7 in the *Network Fundamentals CCNA Exploration Companion Guide*, you should now be able to put together at a high level the events that take place on a network when a user accesses a service.

Vocabulary Exercise: Completion

Fill in the blanks in the following statements that describe a user accessing a web page stored on a web server that is located on a remote network. The user is on an Ethernet LAN. The user sends data to a router on that Ethernet LAN. The router sends the data to another router across a PPP WAN link. The recipient router forwards the data onto an Ethernet LAN where the server resides.

1. The user starts by clicking a _____ on a web page. A TCP _____ handshake sets up a connection with the server.

2. The user's web browser initiates a Hypertext Transfer Protocol (HTTP) _____. The _____ layer adds a Layer 7 header.

3. The _____ layer identifies the upper-layer service that the user wants to reach as the HTTP (or World Wide Web [WWW]) service. The transport layer places a destination _____ number of _____ in the TCP _____ to indicate the WWW service. The transport layer also places the source port number for this session in the segment.

4. TCP adds an _____ number that tells the web server the _____ number that TCP expects in the next _____ it receives.

5. At the _____ layer, an IP packet is constructed to identify the source and destination _____. For the _____ address, the client uses the IP address associated with the WWW server's hostname. It uses its own IPv4 address as the _____ address.

6. The _____ layer refers to the _____cache to determine the Media Access Control (MAC) address that is associated with the Ethernet interface on the client's router. The client builds an _____ frame to transport the IPv4 packet across the local medium.

7. The _____ layer frame indicates that the upper-layer data is IPv4 by placing 0x0800 in the _____ field of the Ethernet II header. The frame begins with a _____ field and ends with an _____ field for error detection. The client uses the _____ media access control method to verify that the medium is not already in use.

8. The _____ layer transmits the frame onto the medium bit by bit.

9. The router that receives the frame checks the _____ at the end of the frame to determine if the frame was received intact without any errors. The router removes the _____ header and pushes the packet up to the _____ layer.

10. At the _____ layer, the destination IPv4 address in the packet is compared to the routes in the _____. A match is found, and the router determines that the next hop for the packet is a router at the other end of a PPP WAN link.

11. The router creates a _____ frame to transport the packet across the WAN.

12. The router includes a _____ field in the PPP header with a value of 0x0021 to indicate that an IPv4 packet is encapsulated.

13. The PPP _____ has already been established, so the _____ layer begins transmitting the frame onto the WAN medium bit by bit.

14. The recipient router checks the _____ to determine if the frame was received intact without any errors. The router removes the _____ header and pushes the packet up to the _____ layer.

15. At the _____ layer, the _____ in the _____ is compared to _____ in the routing table. The router determines that the packet should be sent out an Ethernet network to the web server.

16. The router consults its _____ cache to determine the MAC address of the web server. It then builds an _____ frame to transport the IPv4 packet to the server. It uses _____ to verify that the medium is not already in use.

17. The _____ layer transmits the frame onto the medium _____ by _____.

18. The server examines the frame. It checks the _____ to determine if the frame was received intact without any _____.

19. The server compares the _____ MAC address in the frame to the MAC address of the _____ in the server. Because it matches, the server removes the _____ header and pushes the packet up to the _____ layer.

20. The server compares the _____ IPv4 address in the packet to its own IPv4 address. Because it matches, the server removes the _____ header and pushes the data to the _____ layer. Because the IP network layer header identified the upper-layer protocol as 0x06, the server pushes the data to _____.

21. The server examines the TCP _____ to determine the _____ to which the data belongs. This is done by examining the _____ and _____ ports. The TCP _____ number is used to place this segment in the proper order to be sent upward to the _____ layer.

22. At the _____ layer, the HTTP _____ is delivered to the WWW service. The service can now form a response. The 22 steps reverse themselves, and a packet flows back to the client. Eventually, as soon as all the necessary packets have been sent and received, the user sees a web page.

Labs and Activities

Lab 7-1: Frame Examination (7.5.2.1)

Upon completion of this lab, you will be able to

- Explain the header fields in an Ethernet II frame.

- Use Wireshark to capture and analyze Ethernet II frames.

Background

When upper-layer protocols communicate with each other, data flows down the OSI layers and is encapsulated in a Layer 2 frame. The frame composition depends on the media access type. For example, if the upper-layer protocol is TCP/IP and the media access is Ethernet, the Layer 2 frame encapsulation is Ethernet II.

When learning about Layer 2 concepts, it is helpful to analyze frame header information. The Ethernet II frame header is examined in this lab. Ethernet II frames can support various upper-layer protocols, such as TCP/IP.

Scenario

Wireshark will be used to capture and analyze Ethernet II frame header fields. If Wireshark has not been loaded on the host pod computer, you can download it from ftp://eagle-server.example.com/pub/eagle_labs/eagle1/chapter7/. The file is wireshark-setup-0.99.4.exe.

The Windows **ping** command will be used to generate network traffic for Wireshark to capture.

Figure 7-1 shows the topology for this lab, and Table 7-4 is the corresponding addressing table.

Figure 7-1   Topology for Lab 7-1

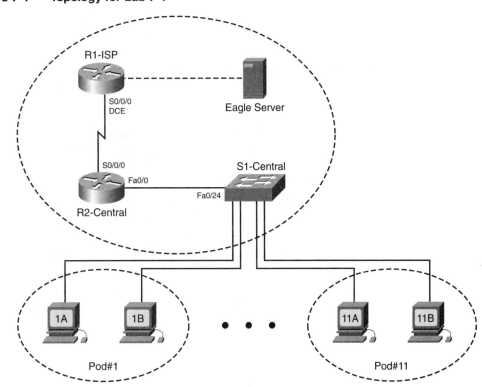

Table 7-4   Addressing Table

Device	Interface	IP Address	Subnet Mask	Default Gateway
R1-ISP	S0/0/0	10.10.10.6	255.255.255.252	—
	Fa0/0	192.168.254.253	255.255.255.0	—
R2-Central	S0/0/0	10.10.10.5	255.255.255.252	10.10.10.6
	Fa0/0	172.16.255.254	255.255.0.0	—
Eagle Server	—	192.168.254.254	255.255.255.0	192.168.254.253
	—	172.31.24.254	255.255.255.0	—
Host *Pod#*A	—	172.16.*Pod#*.1	255.255.0.0	172.16.255.254
Host *Pod#*B	—	172.16.*Pod#*.2	255.255.0.0	172.16.255.254
S1-Central	—	172.16.254.1	255.255.0.0	172.16.255.254

Task 1: Explain the Header Fields in an Ethernet II Frame

Figure 7-2 shows the format for an Ethernet II frame.

Figure 7-2   Ethernet II Frame Format

Preamble	Destination Address	Source Address	Frame Type	Data	FCS
8 Octets	6 Octets	6 Octets	2 Octets	46–1500 Octets	4 Octets

In Figure 7-3, the Panel List window shows a Wireshark capture of the **ping** command between a pod host computer and Eagle Server. The session begins with the ARP protocol querying for the MAC address of the Gateway router, followed by a DNS query. Finally, the **ping** command issues echo requests.

Figure 7-3   Wireshark Capture of the ping Command

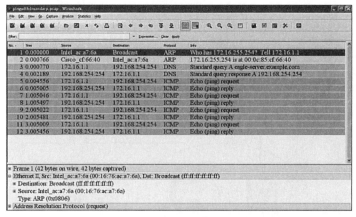

In Figure 7-3, the Packet Details window shows Frame 1 detail information. Using this window, you can obtain Ethernet II frame information. Table 7-5 shows the information you can obtain.

Table 7-5   Ethernet II Frame Header

Field	Value	Description
Preamble	Not shown in the capture	This field contains synchronizing bits, processed by the NIC hardware.
Destination Address	ff:ff:ff:ff:ff:ff	Layer 2 addresses for the frame. Each address is 48 bits long, or 6 bytes, expressed as 12 hexadecimal digits, 0 to 9, A to F. A common format is 12:34:56:78:9A:BC. The first six hex numbers indicate the manufacturer of the network interface card (NIC). Refer to http://www.neotechcc.org/forum/macid.htm for a list of vendor codes. The last six hex digits, ac:a7:6a, are the serial number of the NIC. The destination address may be a broadcast that contains all 1s, or unicast. The source address is always unicast.
Source Address	00:16:76:ac:a7:6a	
Frame Type	0x0806	For Ethernet II frames, this field contains a hexadecimal value that is used to indicate the type of upper-layer protocol in the data field. Ethernet II supports numerous upper-layer protocols. Here are two common frame types: *Value* *Description* 0x0800 IPv4 protocol 0x0806 Address Resolution Protocol (ARP)
Data	ARP	Contains the encapsulated upper-layer protocol. The Data field is between 46 and 1500 bytes.

Field	Value	Description
FCS	Not shown in the capture	Frame Check Sequence, used by the NIC to identify errors during transmission. The value is computed by the sending machine, encompassing frame addresses, type, and data field. It is verified by the receiver.

What is the significance of all 1s in the destination address field?

_____

_____

From the information contained in the Packet List window for the first frame, answer the following questions about the destination and source MAC address.

Destination Address

MAC address: _____

NIC manufacturer: _____

NIC serial number: _____

Source Address

MAC address: _____

NIC manufacturer: _____

NIC serial number: _____

From the information contained in the Packet List window for the second frame, answer the following questions about the destination and source MAC address.

Destination Address

MAC address: _____

NIC manufacturer: _____

NIC serial number: _____

Source Address

MAC address: _____

NIC manufacturer: _____

NIC serial number: _____

Figure 7-4 is an expanded view of Frame 3 from the Wireshark capture.

Figure 7-4   Frame 3 Fields

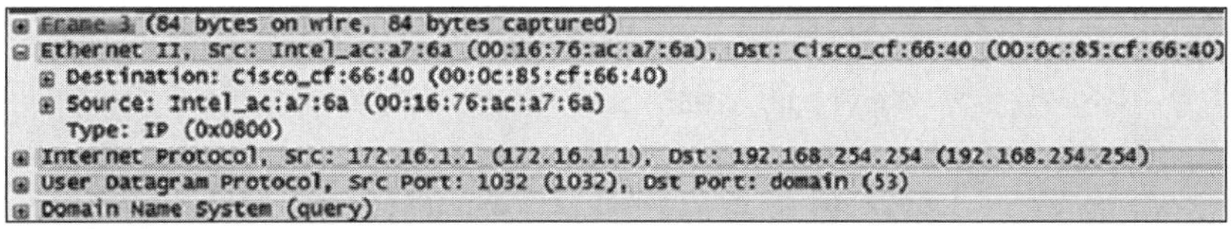

Use the information shown in Figure 7-4 to complete Table 7-6.

Table 7-6   Ethernet II Frame Header Completion

Field	Value
Preamble	
Destination Address	
Source Address	
Frame Type	
Data	
FCS	

Task 2: Use Wireshark to Capture and Analyze Ethernet II Frames

In this task, you use Wireshark to capture and analyze packets captured on the pod host computer.

Step 1.   Configure Wireshark for packet captures.

Prepare Wireshark for captures. Choose **Capture > Interfaces**, and then click the start button that corresponds to the 172.16.x.y interface IP address. This begins the packet capture.

Step 2.   Start a ping to Eagle Server, and capture the session.

Open a Windows terminal window. Choose **Start > Run**, enter **cmd**, and click **OK**.

Ping eagle-server.example.com, as shown in Example 7-1. When the command has finished executing, stop the Wireshark capture.

Example 7-1   Pinging Eagle Server

```
        Microsoft Windows XP [Version 5.1.2600]
         Copyright 1985-2001 Microsoft Corp.


        C:\> ping eagle-server.example.com


        Pinging eagle-server.example.com [192.168.254.254] with 32 bytes of
        data:


        Reply from 192.168.254.254: bytes=32 time<1ms TTL=62
        Reply from 192.168.254.254: bytes=32 time<1ms TTL=62
        Reply from 192.168.254.254: bytes=32 time<1ms TTL=62
        Reply from 192.168.254.254: bytes=32 time<1ms TTL=62


        Ping statistics for 192.168.254.254:
            Packets: Sent = 4, Received = 4, Lost = 0 (0% loss),
        Approximate round trip times in milli-seconds:
            Minimum = 0ms, Maximum = 0ms, Average = 0ms


        C:\>
```

Step 3.   Analyze the Wireshark capture.

The Wireshark Packet List window should start with an ARP request and reply for the Gateway's MAC address. Next, a DNS request is made for the IP address of eagle-server.example.com. Finally, the **ping** command is executed. Your capture should look similar to the one shown in Figure 7-3.

If you don't see an ARP exchange, you can flush the ARP cache using the **arp -d *** command, as shown in Example 7-2.

Example 7-2   Displaying and Flushing the ARP Cache

```
    C:\> arp -a
    Interface: 172.16.1.1 --- 0x30004
      Internet Address        Physical Address        Type
      172.16.255.254          00-0c-85-cf-66-40       dynamic
    C:\> arp -d *
    C:\> arp -a
    No ARP Entries Found
    C:\>
```

If you do not see a DNS query, it is because the DNS record for eagle-server.example.com is stored in the DNS cache. Use the Windows XP **ipconfig /flushdns** command to clear the DNS cache, as shown in Example 7-3.

Example 7-3   Displaying and Flushing the DNS Cache

```
C:\> ipconfig /displaydns
Windows IP Configuration
        1.0.0.127.in-addr.arpa
        ----------------------------------------
        Record Name . . . . . : 1.0.0.127.in-addr.arpa.
        Record Type . . . . . : 12
        Time To Live  . . . . : 549045
        Data Length . . . . . : 4
        Section . . . . . . . : Answer
        PTR Record  . . . . . : localhost
        eagle-server.example.com
        ----------------------------------------
        Record Name . . . . . : eagle-server.example.com
        Record Type . . . . . : 1
        Time To Live  . . . . : 86386
        Data Length . . . . . : 4
        Section . . . . . . . : Answer
        A (Host) Record . . . : 192.168.254.254
        localhost
        ----------------------------------------
        Record Name . . . . . : localhost
        Record Type . . . . . : 1
        Time To Live  . . . . : 549045
        Data Length . . . . . : 4
        Section . . . . . . . : Answer
        A (Host) Record . . . : 127.0.0.1
C:\> ipconfig /flushdns
Windows IP Configuration
Successfully flushed the DNS Resolver Cache.
C:\> ipconfig /displaydns
Windows IP Configuration
        1.0.0.127.in-addr.arpa
        ----------------------------------------
        Record Name . . . . . : 1.0.0.127.in-addr.arpa.
        Record Type . . . . . : 12
        Time To Live  . . . . : 549013
        Data Length . . . . . : 4
        Section . . . . . . . : Answer
        PTR Record  . . . . . : localhost
        localhost
        ----------------------------------------
        Record Name . . . . . : localhost
        Record Type . . . . . : 1
        Time To Live  . . . . : 549013
        Data Length . . . . . : 4
        Section . . . . . . . : Answer
        A (Host) Record . . . : 127.0.0.1
C:\>
```

Use your Wireshark capture of the **ping** command to answer the following questions.

Pod computer MAC address information

MAC address: _____

NIC manufacturer: _____

NIC serial number: _____

R2-Central MAC address information

MAC address: _____

NIC manufacturer: _____

NIC serial number: _____

A student from another school wants to know the MAC address for Eagle Server. What would you tell the student?

_____

_____

_____

What is the Ethernet II frame type value for an ARP Request?

_____

_____

What is the Ethernet II frame type value for an ARP Reply?

_____

What is the Ethernet II frame type value for a DNS query?

_____

What is the Ethernet II frame type value for a DNS query response?

_____

What is the Ethernet II frame type value for an ICMP echo?

_____

What is the Ethernet II frame type value for an ICMP echo reply?

_____

Task 3: Challenge

Use Wireshark to capture sessions from other TCP/IP protocols, such as FTP and HTTP. Analyze the captured packets, and verify that the Ethernet II frame type remains 0x0800.

Task 4: Reflection

In this lab, Ethernet II frame header information was examined. A preamble field contains 7 bytes of alternating 1010 sequences and 1 byte that signals the beginning of the frame, 10101011. Destination and source MAC addresses each contain 12 hex digits. The first six hex digits contain the manufacturer of the NIC, and the last six hex digits contain the NIC serial number. If the frame is a broadcast, the destination MAC address contains all 1s. A 2-byte frame type field contains a value that indicates the protocol in the data field. For IPv4, the value is 0x0800. The data field is variable and contains the encapsulated upper-layer protocol. At the end of a frame, a 4-byte FCS value is used to verify that there were no errors during transmission. Reflect on the necessity and formatting of each of these fields. For example, consider why the preamble field is necessary and why it consists of alternating 1s and 0s. Also reflect on the destination and source addresses, and consider why the developers of Ethernet chose to place the destination address first, before the source address.

Task 5: Clean Up

Wireshark was installed on the pod host computer. If Wireshark needs to be uninstalled, choose **Start > Control Panel**. Click **Add or Remove Programs**. Choose **Wireshark**, and click **Remove**.

Remove any files created on the pod host computer during the lab.

Unless directed otherwise by the instructor, turn off power to the host computers. Remove anything that was brought into the lab, and leave the room ready for the next class.

Skills Integration Challenge: Data Link Layer Issues (7.6.1.3)

Open file LSG01-PTSkills7.pka on the CD-ROM that accompanies this book to perform this exercise using Packet Tracer.

Upon completion of this activity, you will be able to

- Practice your IP subnet planning skills.

- Practice your subnetting skills.

- Build the network.

- Connect devices with Ethernet and serial cables.

- Configure the network.

- Apply your subnetting scheme to server, PCs, and router interfaces, and configure services and static routing.

- Test the network.

- Use ping, trace, web traffic, and the Inspect tool.

Background

Network Interface Cards (NIC) are sometimes thought of as Layer 2 and Layer 1 devices (or as Layer 2 and Layer 1 components of devices that function at all seven layers). Sometimes the NIC for a serial connection, typically used in WAN connections, is called a WAN interface card (WIC). In this challenge you must add a WIC to a device to complete the network. In addition, you have been asked to implement a new IP addressing scheme for the Exploration lab topology. Figure 7-5 shows the topology for this lab, and Table 7-7 is the corresponding addressing table.

Figure 7-5   Topology for the Challenge

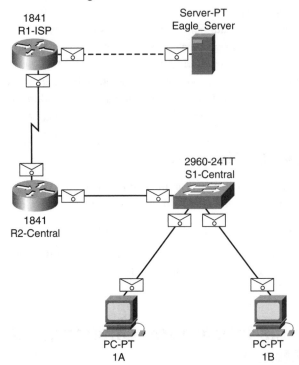

Table 7-7   Addressing Table

Device	Interface	IP Address	Subnet Mask	Default Gateway (Route)
R1-ISP	Fa0/0			—
	S0/0/0			—
R2-Central	Fa0/0			
	S0/0/0			
PC 1A	NIC			
PC 1B	NIC			
Eagle Server	NIC			

Task 1: IP Subnet Planning

You have been given an IP address block of 172.16.0.0/22. You must provide for existing networks as well as future growth.

Subnet assignments:

- First subnet, existing student LAN, up to 400 hosts (Fa0/0 on R2-Central)

- Second subnet, future student LAN, up to 180 hosts (not yet implemented)

- Third subnet, existing ISP LAN, up to 40 hosts (Fa0/0 on R1-ISP)

- Fourth subnet, future ISP LAN, up to 18 hosts (not yet implemented)

- Fifth subnet, existing WAN, point-to-point link (S0/0/0 on R1-ISP and R2-Central)

- Sixth subnet, future WAN, point-to-point link (not yet implemented)

- Seventh subnet, future WAN, point-to-point link (not yet implemented)

Interface IP addresses:

- For the server, configure the second-highest usable IP address on the existing ISP LAN subnet.

- For R1-ISP's Fa0/0 interface, configure the highest usable IP address on the existing ISP LAN subnet.

- For R1-ISP's S0/0/0 interface, configure the highest usable address on the existing WAN subnet.

- For R2-Central's S0/0/0 interface, use the lowest usable address on the existing WAN subnet.

- For R2-Central's Fa0/0 interface, use the highest usable address on the existing student LAN subnet.

- For PCs 1A and 1B, use the first two IP addresses (the two lowest usable addresses) on the existing student LAN subnet.

Additional configurations:

- For PCs 1A and 1B, in addition to IP configuration, configure them to use DNS services.

- For the server, enable DNS services, use the domain name eagle-server.example.com, and enable HTTP services.

Task 2: Finish Building the Network in Packet Tracer, Attending to Some Layer 2 Issues

On the R2-Central router, a NIC is missing for the serial connection to R1-ISP. Add a WIC-2T in the slot on the right. Also on R2-Central, Fa0/0 is shut down; turn it on. Connect a serial DCE cable to R1-ISP S0/0/0, with the other end connected to R2-Central S0/0/0. For all devices, make sure the power is on.

Task 3: Configure the Network

You need to configure the server, both routers, and the two PCs. You do not need to configure the switch, nor do you need the IOS CLI to configure the routers. Part of the router configuration has already been done for you; all you must do is configure the static routes and the interfaces via the GUI. The static route on R1-ISP should point to the existing student LAN subnet via R2-Central's serial interface IP address. The static route on R2-Central should be a default static route that points to R1-ISP's serial interface IP address. These procedures were explained in the Chapter 5 Skills Integration Challenge, and you practiced them in the Chapter 6 Skills Integration Challenge.

Task 4: Test the Network

Use ping, trace, web traffic, and the Inspect tool. Trace packet flow in simulation mode, with HTTP, DNS, TCP, UDP, and ICMP viewable, to test your understanding of how the network is operating. Note in particular what Layer 2 encapsulation is used in each step of a packet's journey, and how the headers on the Layer 2 PDUs change.

Task 5: Reflection

Consider an ICMP echo request packet sent from PC 1A to Eagle Server and the ICMP echo reply packet that results. Reflect on which addresses stay the same in this situation and which ones change.

CHAPTER 8

OSI Physical Layer

The Study Guide portion of this chapter uses a combination of multiple-choice, matching, fill-in-the-blank, and open-ended questions to test your knowledge of the OSI physical layer.

The Lab Exercises portion of this chapter includes all the online curriculum labs to further reinforce that you have mastered the practical, hands-on skills needed to understand and work with the physical layer.

As you work through this chapter, use Chapter 8 in the Network Fundamentals CCNA Exploration online curriculum or use the corresponding Chapter 8 in the *Network Fundamentals CCNA Exploration Companion Guide* for assistance.

Study Guide

The Physical Layer: Communication Signals

The role of the OSI physical layer is to encode the binary digits that represent data link layer frames into signals and to transmit and receive these signals across the physical media (copper wires, optical fiber, and wireless) that connect network devices.

Vocabulary Exercise: Completion

Fill in the blanks for the following statements.

1. The purpose of the physical layer is to create the _____, _____, or _____ signal that represents the bits in each frame.

2. _____ encoding indicates a 0 by a high-to-low voltage transition in the middle of the bit time. For a 1, there is a low-to-high voltage transition in the middle of the bit time.

Concept Questions

1. What are the three basic forms of network media on which data is represented?

    _____, _____, and _____

2. Physical layer standards cover what four areas?

    The Physical media & associated connectors
    A representation of bits on the media
    Encoding of data & control information
    Transmitter & receiver circuitry on the network device

3. What are the three fundamental functions of the physical layer?

    Physical components
    Encoding
    Signaling

Physical Signaling and Encoding: Representing Bits

Eventually, all communication from the human network becomes binary digits, which are transported individually across the physical media.

Concept Questions

1. Bits are represented on the medium by changing one or more of the following characteristics of a signal:

   _____

   _____

   _____

2. Different physical media support the transfer of bits at different speeds. Data transfer can be measured in three ways:

   _____

   _____

   _____

Vocabulary Exercise: Completion

Fill in the blanks in the following statements.

1. The capacity of a medium to carry data is described as the _____ of the media. Digital bandwidth measures the amount of _____ that can flow from one place to another in a given amount of _____.

2. _____ is the measure of the transfer of bits across the media over a given period of time.

3. _____ is the measure of usable data transferred over a given period of time, and is therefore the measure that is of most interest to network users.

Vocabulary Exercise: Matching

In Table 8-1, match the definition on the right with a term on the left.

Table 8-1   Signaling and Encoding

Term	Definition
a. NRZ signaling	__ Bit values are represented as voltage transitions.
b. Manchester encoding	__ Uses bandwidth inefficiently and is susceptible to electromagnetic interference. In addition, the boundaries between individual bits can be lost when long strings of 1s or 0s are transmitted consecutively.
c. 4B/5B	__ Each byte to be transmitted is broken into 4-bit pieces or nibbles and encoded as 5-bit values known as symbols. These symbols represent the data to be transmitted and a set of codes that help control transmission on the media.

Physical Media: Connecting Communication

The physical layer is concerned with network media and signaling. This layer produces the representation and groupings of bits as voltages, radio frequencies, or light pulses. Various standards organizations have contributed to the definition of the physical, electrical, and mechanical properties of the media available for different data communications.

Concept Questions

1. Standards for copper media are defined by what criteria?

Type of copper cabling used
Bandwidth of the communication
Type of connectors used
Pinout & color codes of connections to the media
Maximum distance of the media.

2. What can limit the susceptibility of copper cables to electronic noise?

The timing & voltage values of the signal are

Vocabulary Exercise: Matching

In Table 8-2, match a connector on the right with a media (cable) on the left.

Table 8-2   Media and Connectors

Media (Cable)	Connector
a. Unshielded twisted-pair (UTP) cabling	__ Straight-Tip (ST)
b. Coaxial cable	__ RJ-45
c. Multimode optical fiber	__ Subscriber Connector (SC)
d. Single-mode optical fiber	__ BNC

In Table 8-3, match the speed on the right with the wireless standard on the left.

Table 8-3   Wireless Media

Wireless Standard	Speed
a. Bluetooth 802.15	__ 22+ Mbps
b. 802.11(a,b,g,n), HiperLAN 2	__ < 1 Mbps
c. 802, 11, MMDS, LMDS	__ 10–384 Kbps
d. GSM, GPRS, CDMA, 2.5-3G	__ 1–54+ Mbps

Labs and Activities

Lab 8-1: Media Connectors Lab Activity (Lab 8.4.1.1)

Upon completion of this lab, you will be able to do the following:

- Test cables using a Fluke 620 LAN CableMeter and a Fluke LinkRunner.

- Become familiar with the most common functions of a cable tester.

- Test different cables for type and wiring problems.

Background

Category 5 (Cat 5) unshielded twisted-pair (UTP) cables are wired according to function. End devices, such as routers and host computers, connect to switches with Cat 5 straight-through cables. When connected together, however, a Cat 5 crossover cable must be used. This is also true of switches. When connecting one switch to another, a Cat 5 crossover cable is used again.

Problems related to cables are one of the most common causes of network failure. Basic cable tests can prove helpful in troubleshooting cabling problems with UTP. The quality of cabling components used, the routing and installation of the cable, and the quality of the connector terminations will be the main factors in determining how trouble-free the cabling will be.

The following resources are required:

- Good Cat 5 straight-through and crossover wired cables of different colors

- Cat 5 straight-through and crossover wired cables with open wire connections in the middle or one or more conductors shorted at one end that are different colors and different lengths

- Fluke 620 LAN CableMeter or equivalent (see Figure 8-1)

- Fluke LinkRunner

Figure 8-1   Fluke 620 LAN CableMeter

Scenario

First, you will visually determine whether the Cat 5 cable type is crossover or straight-through. Next, you use the cable tester to verify the cable type and common features available with the tester.

Finally, you use the cable tester to test for bad cables that cannot be determined with a visual inspection.

Task 1: Become Familiar with the Most Common Functions of a Cable Tester

Figure 8-2 shows the TIA/EIA 568B Cat 5 UTP wire positioning for a straight-through and a crossover cable. When Cat 5 connectors are held together, wire color is a quick way to determine the cable type. TIA/EIA 568B is different from TIA/EIA 568A wiring. TIA/EIA 568A straight-through cables can be identified by the color coding.

Figure 8-2   TIA/EIA 568B Cat 5 UTP

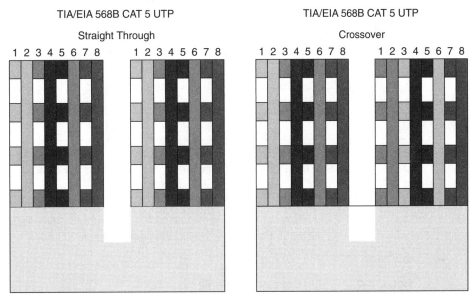

Step 1.   Visually determine cable types.

There should be two numbered cables available. Perform a visual inspection of the cables and then fill out the chart in Table 8-4 with the cable color, type, and use.

Table 8-4   Cable Types

Cable Number	Cable Color	Cable Type (Straight-Through or Crossover)	Cable Use (Circle correct device)
1			Switch to: _____ / switch
2			Switch to: host / _____

It is now time to verify the cable type and learn about the common features of the cable tester.

Step 2.   Perform initial configuration of the Fluke 620 LAN CableMeter.

Turn the rotary switch selector on the tester to the WIRE MAP position. The wire map function displays which pins on one end of the cable are connected to which pins on the other end.

Press the **Setup** button to enter the setup mode, and observe the LCD screen on the tester. The first option should be Cable. Press the **up-** or **down-arrow** buttons until the desired cable type of UTP is selected. Press **Enter** to accept that setting and go to the next one. Continue pressing the **up/down-arrow** buttons and pressing **Enter** until the tester is set to the cabling settings in Table 8-5.

Table 8-5   Cable Tester Settings for UTP

Tester Option	Desired Setting: UTP
Cable	UTP
Wiring	10Base-T or EIA/TIA 4PR
Category	Category 5
Wire size	AWG 24
CAL to Cable?	No
Beeping	On or Off
LCD contrast	From 1 through 10 (brightest)

When satisfied with the correct settings, press the **Setup** button to exit setup mode.

Step 3.   Verify the cable wire map.

Use the following procedure to test each cable with the LAN cable coupler and cable identifier, shown in Figure 8-3. The coupler and the cable identifier are accessories that come with the Fluke 620 LAN CableMeter.

Figure 8-3   Cable Coupler and Cable Identifier

cable coupler   cable identifier

Place the near end of the cable into the RJ-45 jack labeled UTP/FTP on the tester. Place the RJ-45 to RJ-45 female coupler on the far end of the cable, and then insert the cable identifier into the other side of the coupler.

The wiring of both the near and far end of the cable will be displayed. The top set of numbers displayed on the LCD screen refers to the near end, and the bottom set of numbers refers to the far end.

Perform a wire map test on each of the cables provided, and fill in Table 8-6 based on the results. For each cable, write down the number and color, and whether the cable is straight-through or crossover.

Table 8-6   Cable Tester Settings for UTP

Cable Number	Cable Color	Cable Type (Straight-Through or Crossover)
1		
2		

Note any problems encountered during this test:

Step 4.   Verify the cable length.

Move the rotary switch selector on the tester to the Length position. If power was cycled, repeat the setup steps described in Step 2. The tester Length function displays the length of the cable.

Perform a basic cable test on each of the cables, and complete Table 8-7 based on the results. For each cable, write down the number and color, the cable length, the tester screen test results, and what the problem is (if one exists).

Table 8-7   Results of Basic Cable Test

Cable Number	Cable Color	Cable Length
1		
2		

Note any problems encountered during this test:

Repeat these steps until you are comfortable using the cable tester. In the next task, unknown cables are tested.

Task 2: Test Different Cables for Type and Wiring Problems

Obtain at least five different cables from your instructor. Move the rotary switch selector on the tester to the Wire Map position. If power was cycled, repeat the setup steps described in Task 1, Step 2.

Using the cable tester Wire Map function, perform a wire map test on each of the cables provided. Then fill in Table 8-8 based on the result for each Cat 5 cable tested. For each cable, write down the number and color, whether the cable is straight-through or crossover, the tester screen test results, and any problem.

Table 8-8   Results of Wire Map Test

Cable Number	Cable Type (Visual Inspection)	Cable Color	Cable type (Straight-Through or Crossover)	*Test Results	Problem Description
1					
2					
3					
4					
5					

*Refer to the Fluke manual for a detailed description of test results for wire map.

Task 3: Perform Initial Configuration of the Fluke LinkRunner

Step 1.   Turn on the Fluke LinkRunner, which is shown in Figure 8-4.

Figure 8-4   Fluke LinkRunner

Step 2.   Press the green button on the lower right to turn it back off.

Step 3.   Place both ends of the cable into the LAN and MAP ports located on top of the LinkRunner, and press the green button on the lower right along with the blue button to the left.

If it is a correct straight-through cable, two parallel lines (as shown in Figure 8-5) will appear in the upper-left corner of the screen.

Figure 8-5   Fluke LinkRunner: Straight-Through Cable

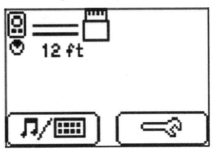

If it is a correct crossover cable, two intersecting lines (as shown in Figure 8-6) will appear in the upper-left corner of the screen.

Figure 8-6   Fluke LinkRunner: Crossover Cable

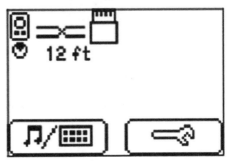

If it is a bad cable, the triangle with an exclamation mark in the center will appear and details will display, as shown in Figure 8-7.

Figure 8-7   Fluke LinkRunner: Bad Cable

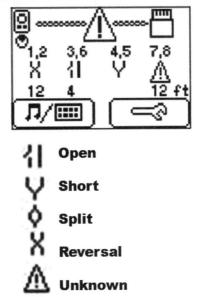

Task 4: Verify Cable Length

Note: The instructions to test a cable are the same as determining cable length.

Step 1.   Turn on the Fluke LinkRunner by pressing the green button on the lower right along with the blue button on the right.

Step 2.   Press the green button on the lower right to turn it back off.

Step 3.   Place both ends of the cable into the LAN and MAP ports located on top of the LinkRunner, and press the green button on the lower right along with the blue button to the left.

Step 4.   Locate the length of the cable below the icon indicating the type of cable (as shown in Figure 8-8).

Figure 8-8   Fluke LinkRunner: Cable Length

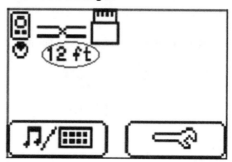

Task 5: Reflection

Problems related to cables are one of the most common causes of network failure. Network technicians should be able to determine when to use Cat 5 UTP straight-through and crossover cables.

A cable tester is used to determine cable type, length, and wire map. In a lab environment, cables are constantly moved and reconnected. A properly functioning cable today may be broken tomorrow. This isn't unusual, and is part of the learning process.

Task 6: Challenge

Look for opportunities to test other cables with the Fluke 620 LAN CableMeter. Skills learned in this lab will enable you to quickly troubleshoot wrong cable types and broken cables.

Task 7: Clean Up

The cable tester is expensive and should never be left unattended. Return the cable tester to the instructor when finished.

Ask the instructor where to return used cables. Store the cables neatly for the next class.

Skills Integration Challenge: Connecting Devices and Exploring the Physical View (8.5.1.3)

Open the file LSG01-PTSkills8.pka on the CD-ROM that accompanies this book to perform this exercise using Packet Tracer.

Upon completion of this activity, you will be able to do the following:

- Connect the devices in the standard lab setup.

- Connect the devices.

- Verify connectivity.

- View the standard lab setup in the physical workspace.

- Enter and view the physical workspace.

- View the standard lab setup at the various levels of the physical workspace.

Background

When working in Packet Tracer, in a lab environment, or in a corporate setting, it is important to know how to select the proper cable, and how to properly connect devices. This activity examines device configurations in Packet Tracer, selecting the proper cable based on the configuration, and connecting the devices. This activity also explores the physical view of the network in Packet Tracer.

Figure 8-9 shows the topology for this skills integration challenge, and Table 8-9 shows the corresponding addressing table.

Figure 8-9   Topology for Challenge

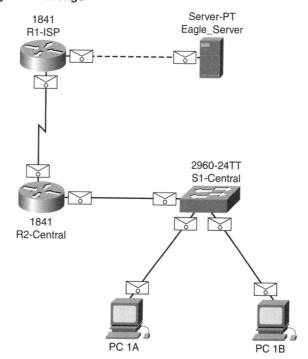

Table 8-9   Addressing Table

Device	Interface	IP Address	Subnet Mask	Default Gateway
R1-ISP	Fa0/0	192.168.254.253	255.255.255.0	N/A
	S0/0/0	10.10.10.6	255.255.255.252	N/A
R2-Central	Fa0/0	172.16.255.254	255.255.0.0	10.10.10.6
	S0/0/0	10.10.10.5	255.255.255.252	10.10.10.6
S1-Central	VLAN 1	172.16.254.1	255.255.0.0	172.16.255.254
PC 1A	NIC	172.16.1.1	255.255.0.0	172.16.255.254
PC 1B	NIC	172.16.1.2	255.255.0.0	172.168.255.254
Eagle Server	NIC	192.168.254.254	255.255.255.0	192.168.254.253

Task 1: Connect the Devices in the Standard Lab Setup

Step 1.   Connect the devices.

Connect PC 1A to the first port on switch S1-Central and PC 1B to the second port on switch S1-Central using the proper cable. Click router R2-Central and examine the configuration using the Config tab.

Connect the proper interface on the router to interface FastEthernet0/24 on switch S1-Central using the proper cable. Click both routers and examine the configuration using the Config tab.

Connect the routers together using the proper interfaces and the proper cable. Click router R1-ISP and examine the configuration using the Config tab. Connect the proper interface on the router to the proper interface on Eagle Server using the proper cable.

Step 2.   Verify connectivity.

From the command prompt on the desktop of both PCs, issue the command **ping 192.168.254.254**, the IP address of Eagle Server. If the pings fail, check your connections and troubleshoot until the pings succeed. Check your configuration by clicking the **Check Results** button.

Task 2: View the Standard Lab Setup in the Physical Workspace

Step 1.   Enter and view the physical workspace.

Most of our work in Packet Tracer has been done in the logical workspace. In an internetwork, routers may be in different sites, from across the street to across the globe. The serial link between the routers represents a dedicated leased line between two locations consisting of a DTE (data terminal equipment), such as a router, connected to a DCE (data communication equipment), such as a channel/data service unit (CSU/DSU) or modem. The DCE connects to a service provider's local loop, and the connections are repeated at the other end of the link. The physical workspace enables you to see these relationships more clearly.

Enter the physical workspace by clicking the tab in the upper-left corner of the workspace. It shows the connection between Central City and ISP City.

Step 2.   View the standard lab setup at the various levels of the physical workspace.

Click Central City. You will see the city and the location of the central office building. Click the central office building. You will see the floor plan of the building and the location of the wiring closet. Click the wiring closet. You will see a physical representation of the equipment installed in the wiring closet and the cabling that connects the equipment. Examine this view of the topology. Click Intercity on the navigation bar. Repeat the steps to view the equipment installed in ISP City.

Ethernet

The Study Guide portion of this chapter uses a combination of matching, fill-in-the-blank, multiple-choice, and open-ended questions to test your knowledge of Ethernet.

The Labs and Activities portion of this chapter includes all the online curriculum activities and labs to ensure you have mastered the practical, hands-on skills needed to work with Ethernet.

As you work through this chapter, use Chapter 9 in the Network Fundamentals CCNA Exploration online curriculum, or use the corresponding Chapter 9 in the Network Fundamentals CCNA Exploration Companion Guide, for assistance.

Study Guide

Overview of Ethernet

Ethernet is the predominant LAN technology in use today. Ethernet has been so successful because it has evolved over time to incorporate new technologies such as higher speeds and fiber-optic cabling. Ethernet's success can also be attributed to the fact that it was adopted by the Institute of Electrical and Electronics Engineers (IEEE) and standardized as IEEE 802.3. Ethernet operates at the OSI physical and data link layers. Using IEEE terminology, Ethernet operates at the physical layer and the Media Access Control (MAC) sublayer of the data link layer. The upper sublayer of the data link layer, Logical Link Control (LLC) or IEEE 802.2, can give upper-layer protocols access to Ethernet. In addition, Ethernet (without LLC) is the frame encapsulation method used for the most popular network layer protocol in use today, Internet Protocol (IP).

Vocabulary Exercise: Matching

In Table 9-1, match the function on the right with the correct IEEE sublayer of the data link layer.

Table 9-1   Data Link Layer Sublayers

Sublayer	Function
a. LLC	__ Provides an interface to the upper layers
b. MAC	__ Controls the placement of a frame on the medium
	__ Remains relatively independent of the physical equipment
	__ Adds a frame delimiter
	__ Provides a unique source and destination address

Concept Questions

1. Why has Ethernet been so successful?

_____

_____

_____

_____

_____

_____

_____

_____

2. What functions does data encapsulation provide?

_____

_____

3. How does Ethernet handle error detection?

_____

_____

_____

_____

_____

_____

Ethernet: Communication Through the LAN

The term Ethernet first appeared in 1973 when Dr. Robert M. Metcalfe of the Xerox Corporation circulated a memo to his colleagues, proposing the name for their prototype network. The name reflects the goal that Ethernet become ubiquitous, much like the ether substance that scientists in the 1800s believed filled space and matter. In 1980, Digital Equipment Corporation, Intel, and Xerox published the DIX V1.0 standard for Ethernet. DIX V2.0, also known as Ethernet II, was released in 1982. The IEEE published the 802.3 standard for Ethernet in 1985. Since 1985, Ethernet has evolved from a shared coaxial medium, to a shared hub-based network, and finally to a selective-forwarding environment with high-speed switches. Today, Ethernet forms the foundation of most industrial, educational, and government networks. Metcalfe's goal that Ethernet become ubiquitous has been achieved.

Vocabulary Exercise: Matching

In Table 9-2, match the description on the right with the correct Ethernet term on the left.

Table 9-2   Ethernet Implementations

Term	Description
a. 10BASE5	___ Only one station at a time can transmit
b. 10BASE2	___ Concentrates connections, allowing the network to see a group of nodes as a single unit
c. Hub	___ Uses 185 meters of thin coaxial cable
d. Half duplex	___ Isolates each port and sends a frame only to its proper destination (if the destination is known)
e. Full duplex	___ Both ends of a connection can send at the same time
f. Switch	___ Uses 500 meters of thick coaxial cable

Concept Questions

1. Compare and contrast half duplex and full duplex.

   _____

   _____

   _____

   _____

   _____

   _____

   _____

   _____

   _____

   _____

2. What aspects of Ethernet have remained relatively unchanged over the years, and what aspects have changed?

   _____

   _____

   _____

   _____

   _____

   _____

The Ethernet Frame

A fundamental job of the data link layer is to encapsulate a Layer 3 Protocol Data Unit (PDU) into a Layer 2 PDU. The Layer 2 PDU is called a frame. Although different protocols place different fields in a frame, most protocols specify that the frame should have a header, data field, and trailer. Most Layer 2 frames also have addressing fields in the header that identify the sender and receiver. Ethernet follows these conventions.

Vocabulary Exercise: Matching

Table 9-3 lists the fields that appear in an IEEE 802.3 header and trailer. Match the field on the left with the definition on the right.

Table 9-3   Frame Header Fields

Field	Definition
a. Preamble	__ Used for error detection
b. Start of frame delimiter	__ Used for synchronization
c. Destination address	__ Specifies the number of bytes in the data part of the frame or specifies the type of data (the upper-layer protocol)
d. Source address	__ Carries the upper-layer data
e. Length/type	__ Tells other devices on the network that a frame is coming along the medium
f. Data	__ Specifies the frame's sender
g. Frame check sequence	__ Specifies the frame's intended recipient

Multiple-Choice Questions

Choose the best answer for each of the following questions.

1. What is the maximum size of an Ethernet frame according to the IEEE 802.3ac standard?

    a. 1522 bytes

    b. 1518 bytes

    c. 1024 bytes

    d. 64 bytes

2. What is the minimum size of an Ethernet frame?

    a. 1522 bytes

    b. 128 bytes

    c. 72 bytes

    d. 64 bytes

3. What does a receiving device do if it receives a frame that is less than the allowed minimum size or greater than the allowed maximum size?

    a. The receiving device sends back a negative acknowledgment to the sender.

    b. The receiving device drops the frame.

   c. The receiving device reports a collision.

   d. The receiving device requests a retransmission.

4. How does a recipient device know if the sender used the Length/Type field to specify a length or a type?

   a. If the value is equal to or less than 1536, the field specifies a type.

   b. If the value is equal to or greater than 0x0600, the field specifies a type.

   c. The recipient sends a query to the sender to determine how the field should be interpreted.

   d. The recipient bases the decision on whether it's been configured for Ethernet II or IEEE 802.3.

5. Why is padding sometimes added to the data part of an Ethernet frame?

   a. To ensure that the frame is protected from damage.

   b. To ensure that the frame is at least 64 bytes.

   c. To provide synchronization.

   d. To specify the Portable Application Description (PAD) that describes the encapsulated data.

6. What happens if a frame arrives damaged?

   a. The recipient calculates a CRC that differs from the CRC in the FCS field and drops the frame.

   b. The recipient requests a retransmission.

   c. The sender backs off and waits a random amount of time before trying again.

   d. The sender notices the missing acknowledgment and retransmits the frame.

7. How long is a MAC address?

   a. Six hexadecimal digits

   b. 32 bits

   c. 48 bits

   d. 8 bytes

Concept Questions

1. Compare and contrast MAC addresses with IP addresses.

_____

_____

_____

_____

_____

_____

_____

_____

_____

2. Compare and contrast unicast, broadcast, and multicast communications at the MAC sublayer.

_____

_____

_____

_____

_____

_____

_____

_____

Ethernet Media Access Control

In a shared medium, all devices have guaranteed access to the medium, but they must fairly share the medium and not interfere with each other. If more than one device transmits at the same time, the physical signals collide, and the data is damaged. Both transmitters must recognize that their data has been damaged and resend it. Ethernet uses carrier sense multiple access collision detect (CSMA/CD) to detect and handle collisions and regulate use of the shared medium.

Vocabulary Exercise: Completion

Fill in the blanks for the following statements that discuss CSMA/CD.

1. Because devices using coaxial or hub-based Ethernet send their messages on a shared medium, a _____ is used to determine if the medium is already in use before a sender transmits.

2. When a device detects that no other computer is sending a frame, the device _____ if it has something to send. All devices that have messages to send must _____ before transmitting.

3. If a device detects a signal from another device, it _____ before attempting to transmit.

4. When no traffic is detected, a device _____ its message. While transmitting, the device continues to _____ for traffic from another device. If another device is sending at the same time, a _____ has occurred.

5. If a collision happens, the sending devices continue to send for the time it takes to send a _____ signal and then _____ sending. The devices invoke a _____ algorithm that causes them to wait a _____ amount of time before trying to send again.

Concept Questions

1. What is interframe spacing, and why does Ethernet use it?

_____

_____

_____

2. Why is the backoff timing random when an Ethernet collision occurs?

_____

_____

_____

_____

Ethernet Physical Layer

The many implementations of Ethernet include Classic Ethernet, Fast Ethernet, Gigabit Ethernet, and 10 Gigabit Ethernet. The differences occur at the physical layer, often called the Ethernet PHY. Four data rates are currently defined for operation over optical-fiber and twisted-pair cables:

- 10 Mbps: 10BASE-T Classic Ethernet

- 100 Mbps: Fast Ethernet

- 1000 Mbps: Gigabit Ethernet

- 10 Gbps: 10 Gigabit Ethernet

Vocabulary Exercise: Completion

Fill in the blanks for the following statements that describe Ethernet physical layer options.

1. 10BASE-T uses _____ pairs of a four-pair cable and is terminated at each end with an eight-pin _____ connector. The pair connected to _____ is used for transmitting, and the pair connected to _____ is used for receiving.

2. Replacing hubs with _____ in 10BASE-T networks has greatly increased the _____ available to these networks and has helped Ethernet maintain its _____ in the LAN market. The 10BASE-T links connected to a switch can support either half-duplex or _____ operation.

3. The most popular implementations of 100 Mbps Ethernet are _____, which uses Category 5 or later UTP cable, and _____, which uses fiber-optic cable.

4. 1000BASE-T Ethernet provides full-duplex transmission using _____ pairs of Category 5 or later UTP cable.

5. The two fiber versions of _____ are 1000BASE-SX and 1000BASE-LX. Fiber-optic cabling offers better noise _____ than UTP, a smaller _____, and higher _____ and _____.

6. A difference between 1000BASE-SX and 1000BASE-LX is the _____ of the optical signal.

7. The IEEE _____ standard was adapted to include 10-Gbps, full-duplex transmission over fiber-optic cable. 10-Gigabit Ethernet is evolving for use not only in LANs, but also in MANs and _____.

8. Although Gigabit Ethernet is now widely available and 10-Gigabit products are becoming more available, the IEEE and the _____ are working on _____, _____, and even 160-Gbps standards.

Hubs and Switches

In the 1970s and 1980s, Ethernet networks were connected in a bus topology using coaxial cable. The coaxial cable provided a shared medium. In the 1990s, administrators started connecting nodes to the shared network in a star topology using twisted-pair cabling and hubs. During the 1990s, to improve performance, administrators upgraded their hubs to switches. Switches divide collision domains into smaller domains, sometimes so small that collisions are no longer an issue. For example, in the common case where a single device is connected to a port on a switch, both ends of the communications channel can send and receive at the same time, and collisions don't occur. Switches forward broadcast and multicast traffic to all members of a LAN but provide selective forwarding for unicast traffic. The selective forwarding greatly reduces collisions and improves performance.

Vocabulary Exercise: Matching

In Table 9-4, match the characteristic on the right with the correct term on the left.

Table 9-4   Characteristics of Hubs and Switches

Term	Characteristic
a. Hub	__ Divides collision domains
b. Switch	__ Forwards received bits out every port
	__ Supports full-duplex communication
	__ Simplifies network cabling but doesn't have any performance benefits
	__ When many nodes that transmit frequently are connected to this device, latency increases, because each node must wait for an opportunity to transmit
	__ Provides an alternative to contention-based Ethernet
	__ Maintains a table that maps each MAC address to a port

Vocabulary Exercise: Completion

Fill in the blanks for the following statements that describe the selective forwarding service provided by switches.

1. A switch selectively forwards a _____ that it receives on a port to the port where the _____ is connected.

2. Switches use _____ switching, whereby the switch receives an entire frame, checks the _____ for errors, and forwards the frame to the appropriate port.

3. A switch maintains a table, called the _____ _____, that matches a MAC address with the port used to connect the node with that address.

Concept Question

List and describe the five basic operations of an Ethernet LAN switch.

_____

_____

_____

_____

_____

_____

_____

_____

_____

_____

Address Resolution Protocol (ARP)

To send an IP packet to a recipient, a sender needs to learn the recipient's MAC address. ARP provides a means for a sender to broadcast a message to find the MAC address for a known IP address.

Multiple-Choice Questions

Choose the best answer for each of the following questions.

1. What is a basic job of ARP?

   a. Resolve IPv4 addresses to MAC addresses

   b. Build a table that maps MAC addresses to ports

   c. Build a loop-free LAN from redundantly connected switches

   d. Provide a resource protocol for finding applications

2. If a node has recently sent a frame to another node, where is the mapping of IPv4 address to MAC address stored?

   a. MAC table

   b. ARP cache

   c. Routing table

   d. NVRAM

3. When a node has not recently sent a frame to another node, how does the node discover the correct MAC address to use for the IPv4 address of the destination node?

   a. The sender sends an IPv4 query to the destination node to ask the node for its MAC address.

   b. The sender broadcasts an ARP request.

   c. The sender monitors traffic until it discovers the correct MAC address to use.

   d. The sender transmits a TCP SYN to the destination node.

4. What type of header does an ARP frame contain?

   a. IP

   b. Ethernet

   c. TCP

   d. UDP

5. When an Ethernet transmitter sends to a destination not on its local network, what MAC destination address does it use, and how does it discover this address?

   a. The transmitter uses the MAC address of the destination, which it discovers with an ARP request.

   b. The transmitter uses the MAC address of the local router interface, which it discovers with an ARP request.

   c. The transmitter uses the MAC address of the destination, which it discovers with a proxy ARP request.

   d. The transmitter doesn't need a MAC address for the destination and relies on the IP destination address to provide enough information for routers to forward the frame.

6. What is the destination address in the frame when a node sends an ARP request to find the MAC address associated with a known IP address?

   a. 255.255.255.255

   b. The address of the local router interface

   c. The recipient's address

   d. FF:FF:FF:FF:FF:FF

Labs and Activities

Lab 9-1: Address Resolution Protocol (9.8.1.1)

Upon completion of this lab, you will be able to

- Use the Windows **arp** command.

- Use Wireshark to examine ARP exchanges.

Background

TCP/IP uses ARP to map a Layer 3 IP address to a Layer 2 MAC address. When a frame is placed on the network, it must have a destination MAC address. To dynamically discover the MAC address of the destination device, an ARP request is broadcast on the LAN. The device that contains the destination IP address responds, and the MAC address is recorded in the ARP cache. Every device on the LAN keeps its own ARP cache, which is a small area in RAM that holds ARP results. An ARP cache timer removes ARP entries that have not been used for a certain period of time. Depending on the device, the times differ. For example, some Windows operating systems store ARP cache entries for 2 minutes. If the entry is used again during that time, the ARP timer for that entry is extended to 10 minutes.

ARP is an excellent example of a performance trade-off. With no cache, ARP must continually request address translations each time a frame is placed on the network. This adds latency to the communication and could congest the LAN. Conversely, unlimited hold times could cause errors with devices that leave the network or change the Layer 3 address.

A network engineer needs to be aware of ARP but may not interact with the protocol on a regular basis. ARP is a protocol that enables network devices to communicate with the TCP/IP protocol. Without ARP, no efficient method exists to build the datagram Layer 2 destination address.

ARP is a potential security risk. ARP spoofing, or ARP poisoning, is a technique used by an attacker to inject the wrong MAC address association into a network. An attacker forges a device's MAC address, and frames are sent to the wrong destination. Manually configuring static ARP associations is one way to prevent ARP spoofing. In addition, an authorized MAC address list may be configured in Cisco devices to restrict network access to only approved devices.

Scenario

With a pod host computer, use the Windows **arp** utility command to examine and change ARP cache entries.

In Task 2, you will use Wireshark to capture and analyze ARP exchanges between network devices. If Wireshark has not been loaded on the host pod computer, you can download it from ftp://eagle-server.example.com/pub/eagle_labs/eagle1/chapter9/. The file is wireshark-setup-0.99.4.exe.

Figure 9-1 shows the topology for this lab, and Table 9-5 is the corresponding addressing table.

Figure 9-1   Topology for Lab 9-1

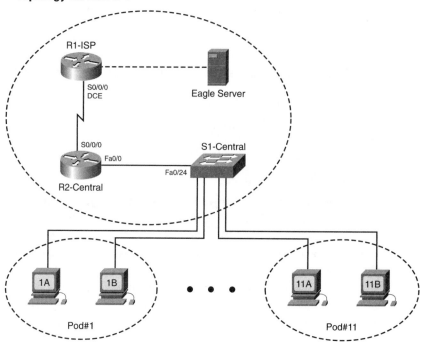

Table 9-5   Addressing Table

Device	Interface	IP Address	Subnet Mask	Default Gateway
R1-ISP	S0/0/0	10.10.10.6	255.255.255.252	—
	Fa0/0	192.168.254.253	255.255.255.0	—
R2-Central	S0/0/0	10.10.10.5	255.255.255.252	10.10.10.6
	Fa0/0	172.16.255.254	255.255.0.0	—
Eagle Server	—	192.168.254.254	255.255.255.0	192.168.254.253
	—	172.31.24.254	255.255.255.0	—
Host Pod#A	—	172.16.Pod#.1	255.255.0.0	172.16.255.254
Host Pod#B	—	172.16.Pod#.2	255.255.0.0	172.16.255.254
S1-Central	—	172.16.254.1	255.255.0.0	172.16.255.254

Task 1: Use the Windows arp Command

Step 1.   Access the Windows terminal.

Open a Windows terminal by choosing **Start > Run**. Enter **cmd**, and click **OK**.

With no options, the **arp** command displays useful help information.

Issue the **arp** command on the pod host computer, and examine the output. It should look like Example 9-1.

Example 9-1   Using the arp Command

```
C:\> arp
Displays and modifies the IP-to-Physical address translation tables used by
  address resolution protocol (ARP).
ARP -s inet_addr eth_addr [if_addr]

ARP -d inet_addr [if_addr]

ARP -a [inet_addr] [-N if_addr]

-a   Displays current ARP entries by interrogating the current protocol
data. If inet_addr is specified, the IP and Physical addresses for only
the specified computer are displayed. If more than one network interface
uses ARP, entries for each ARP table are displayed.

-g   Same as -a.

inet_addr    Specifies an internet address.

-N if_addr   Displays the ARP entries for the network interface speci-
fied by if_addr.

-d   Deletes the host specified by inet_addr. inet_addr may be wildcard-
ed with * to delete all hosts.

-s   Adds the host and associates the Internet address inet_addr with
the Physical address eth_addr.  The Physical address is given as 6 hexa-
decimal bytes separated by hyphens. The entry is permanent.

eth_addr    Specifies a physical address.

if_addr     If present, this specifies the Internet address of the
interface

whose address translation table should be modified. If not present, the

first applicable interface will be used.

Example:
 > arp -s 157.55.85.212 00-aa-00-62-c6-09  .... Adds a static entry.

 > arp -a                                  .... Displays the arp
table.

C:\>
```

Answer the following questions about the **arp** command:

■ What command is used to display all entries in the ARP cache?

_____

■ What command is used to delete all ARP cache entries (flush the ARP cache)?

_____

■ What command is used to delete the ARP cache entry for 172.16.255.254?

_____

Step 2.   Use the **arp** command to examine the local ARP cache, as shown in Example 9-2.

Example 9-2   Using the arp Command with the -a Option

```
C:\> arp -a
No ARP Entries Found
C:\>
```

Without any network communication, the ARP cache should be empty.

When you issued the command that displays ARP entries, what were the results?

_____

_____

Step 3. Use the **ping** command to dynamically add entries to the ARP cache.

The **ping** command can be used to test network connectivity. By accessing other devices, ARP associations are dynamically added to the ARP cache, as shown in Example 9-3.

Example 9-3   Using the ping Command

```
C:\> ping 172.16.1.2
Pinging 172.16.1.2 with 32 bytes of data:
Reply from 172.16.1.2: bytes=32 time<1ms TTL=128
Reply from 172.16.1.2: bytes=32 time<1ms TTL=128
Reply from 172.16.1.2: bytes=32 time<1ms TTL=128
Reply from 172.16.1.2: bytes=32 time<1ms TTL=128
Ping statistics for 172.16.1.2:
    Packets: Sent = 4, Received = 4, Lost = 0 (0% loss),
Approximate round trip times in milli-seconds:
    Minimum = 0ms, Maximum = 0ms, Average = 0ms
C:\>
C:\> arp -a
Interface: 172.16.1.1  —- 0x60004
  Internet Address       Physical Address       Type
    172.16.1.2             00-10-a4-7b-01-5f      dynamic
C:\>
```

Use the command **ipconfig /all** to verify another pod host computer's Layer 2 and Layer 3 information.

Issue the **ping** command to that pod host computer.

How was the ARP entry added to the ARP cache? Hint: Review the Type column.

_____

What is the IP address of the destination pod host computer?

_____

What is the physical address of the destination pod host computer?

_____

Do not send any traffic to the computer accessed previously. Wait between 2 and 3 minutes, and check the ARP cache again. Was the ARP cache entry cleared?

_____

If the entry was not cleared, a couple explanations are possible. First, you did not wait 2 minutes, which is how long the ARP cache stores an initial entry. Or, you accessed the destination device more than once and caused the ARP timeout for the entry to rise to 10 minutes.

Issue the **ping** command to the Gateway, R2-Central. Examine the ARP cache entry.

What is the IP address of the Gateway?

_____

What is the physical address of the Gateway?

_____

How was the address discovered?

_____

Issue the **ping** command to Eagle Server, eagle-server.example.com. Examine the ARP cache entry.

What is the physical address of Eagle Server?

_____

_____

Step 4.   Manually adjust entries in the ARP cache.

Verify that the ARP cache contains two entries: one for the Gateway and one for the destination pod host computer. It may be easier to ping both devices more than once, which will retain the cache entry for approximately 10 minutes.

Record the two ARP cache entries using Table 9-6.

Table 9-6   Initial ARP Cache Entries

Device	IP Address	Physical Address	How Is It Discovered?
Pod host computer			
Gateway			

Next, delete the entry for the pod host computer. To delete entries in the ARP cache, issue the **arp -d** {inet-addr | *} command. You can delete addresses individually by specifying the IP address, or you can delete all entries using the wildcard *.

Example 9-4 shows how to manually delete an ARP cache entry.

Example 9-4   Manually Deleting an ARP Cache Entry

```
C:\> arp -a
Interface: 172.16.1.1 —- 0x60004
  Internet Address      Physical Address      Type
  172.16.1.2            00-10-a4-7b-01-5f     dynamic
  172.16.255.254        00-0c-85-cf-66-40     dynamic
C:\>
C:\> arp -d 172.16.255.254
C:\> arp -a
Interface: 172.16.1.1 —- 0x60004
  Internet Address      Physical Address      Type
  172.16.1.2            00-10-a4-7b-01-5f     dynamic
C:\>
```

What command deletes the entry for the pod host computer?

_____

Record the remaining ARP cache entry in Table 9-7.

Table 9-7   Remaining ARP Cache Entry

Device	IP Address	Physical Address	How Is It Discovered?

Simulate removing all entries. What command deletes all entries in the ARP cache?

_____

Issue the command to remove all entries in the ARP cache on your pod host computer, and examine the ARP cache with the **arp -a** command. All entries should be removed.

Consider a secure environment where the Gateway controls access to a web server that contains top-secret information. What is one layer of security that can be applied to ARP cache entries to help counter ARP spoofing?

_____

Simulate adding a static entry for the Gateway. What command adds a static ARP entry for the Gateway to the ARP cache?

_____

Issue the command on your pod host computer, and examine the ARP cache again. Now, provide answers to these questions:

- What is the IP address of the Gateway? _____

- What is the physical address of the Gateway? _____

- What is the type of the ARP entry? _____

For the next task, Wireshark will be used to capture and examine an ARP exchange. Do not close the Windows terminal; you will use it to view the ARP cache.

Task 2: Use Wireshark to Examine ARP Exchanges

Step 1.   Configure Wireshark for packet captures.

Prepare Wireshark for captures.

Choose **Capture > Options**.

Select the interface that corresponds to the LAN.

Check the box to update the list of packets in real time.

Click **Start**.

This begins the packet capture.

Step 2.   Prepare the pod host computer for ARP captures.

If you haven't already done so, open a Windows terminal window by choosing **Start > Run**. Enter **cmd**, and click **OK**.

Flush the ARP cache; this will require ARP to rediscover address maps. What command did you use?

_____

Step 3.   Capture and evaluate ARP communication.

In this step, one ping request is sent to the Gateway, and one ping request is sent to Eagle Server. Afterward, the Wireshark capture is stopped, and the ARP communication is evaluated.

Send one ping request to the Gateway, using the command **ping -n 1 172.16.255.254**.

Send one ping request to Eagle Server, using the command **ping -n 1 192.168.254.254**.

Stop Wireshark and evaluate the communication. You should see a Wireshark screen similar to the one shown in Figure 9-2. The Wireshark Packet List window displays the number of packets captured. The Packet Details window shows ARP protocol contents.

Figure 9-2   Wireshark Screen

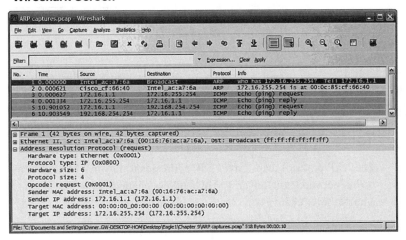

Using your Wireshark capture, answer the following questions:

- What is the first ARP packet? _____

- What is the second ARP packet?_____

Fill in Table 9-8 with information about the first ARP packet.

Table 9-8   First ARP Packet

Field	Value
Sender MAC address	
Sender IP address	
Target MAC address	
Target IP address	

Fill in Table 9-9 with information about the second ARP packet.

Table 9-9   Second ARP Packet

Field	Value
Sender MAC address	
Sender IP address	
Target MAC address	
Target IP address	

If the Ethernet II frame for an ARP request is a broadcast, why does the target MAC address contain all 0s?

Why was there no ARP request for the ping to Eagle Server?

How long should the Gateway mapping be stored in the ARP cache on the pod host computer? Why?

Task 3: Reflection

The ARP protocol maps Layer 3 IP addresses to Layer 2 MAC addresses. If a packet must move across networks, the Layer 2 MAC address changes with each hop across a router, but the Layer 3 address never changes.

The ARP cache stores ARP address mappings. If the entry was learned dynamically, it will eventually be deleted from cache. If the entry was manually inserted in the ARP cache, it is a static entry and remains until the computer is turned off or the ARP cache is manually flushed.

Task 4: Challenge

Using outside resources, perform a search on ARP spoofing. Discuss several techniques used to counter this type of attack.

Most wireless routers support a network administrator manually adding a list of MAC addresses to the router that are permitted access to the wireless network. Using outside resources, discuss the advantages of configuring MAC address restrictions for wireless networks. Discuss ways in which attackers can circumvent this security.

Task 5: Clean Up

Wireshark was installed on the pod host computer. If Wireshark needs to be uninstalled, choose **Start > Control Panel**. Click **Add or Remove Programs**. Choose **Wireshark**, and click **Remove**.

Remove any files created on the pod host computer during the lab.

Unless directed otherwise by the instructor, turn off power to the host computers. Remove anything that was brought into the lab, and leave the room ready for the next class.

Packet Tracer Companion: Address Resolution Protocol (9.8.1.2)

You can now open the file LSG01-Lab9812.pka on the CD-ROM that accompanies this book to repeat this hands-on lab using Packet Tracer. Remember, however, that Packet Tracer is not a substitute for a hands-on lab experience with real equipment. A summary of the instructions is provided within the activity.

Lab 9-2: Cisco Switch MAC Table Examination (9.8.2.1)

Upon completion of this lab, you will be able to

- Use the Telnet protocol to log into a Cisco switch.

- Use the Cisco **show mac-address-table** command to examine MAC address and port associations.

Background

Switches maintain a table of MAC addresses and associated switch ports. When a switch receives a frame, the destination MAC address is checked against the table, and the corresponding port is used to route the frame out the switch. If a switch does not know which port to use to route the frame, or the frame is a broadcast, the frame is routed out all ports except the port where it originated.

Access to Cisco devices can be accomplished through several means. A console port can be used if the Cisco router or switch is within proximity of a computer. Using the Windows hyperterm utility, a serial connection can be established. For devices physically distant from the network engineer, network connectivity can be established through two means. If the network is not secure, a modem configured on the AUX port enables telephone access. For secure networks, the Cisco device can be configured for a Telnet session. In this lab, you will connect to the switch via a Telnet session.

You will do the following:

- Telnet to S1-Central.

- Log in with your student account.

- Use the **show mac-address-table** command to examine the MAC addresses and association to ports.

Scenario

Telnet is a network service that uses a client/server model. Cisco IOS devices provide a default Telnet server, and operating systems such as Windows have built-in Telnet clients. Using Telnet, network engineers can log into network devices from anywhere across a secure network. The Cisco device must be configured for Telnet access; otherwise, it is denied. In this course, limited privileges have been configured for student use.

Figure 9-3 shows the topology for this lab, and Table 9-10 is the corresponding addressing table.

Figure 9-3   Topology for Lab 9-2

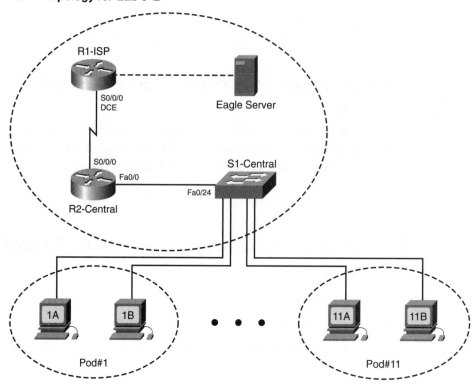

Table 9-10   Addressing Table

Device	Interface	IP Address	Subnet Mask	Default Gateway
R1-ISP	S0/0/0	10.10.10.6	255.255.255.252	—
	Fa0/0	192.168.254.253	255.255.255.0	—
R2-Central	S0/0/0	10.10.10.5	255.255.255.252	10.10.10.6
	Fa0/0	172.16.255.254	255.255.0.0	—
Eagle Server	—	192.168.254.254	255.255.255.0	192.168.254.253
	—	172.31.24.254	255.255.255.0	—
Host Pod#A	—	172.16.Pod#.1	255.255.0.0	172.16.255.254
Host Pod#B	—	172.16.Pod#.2	255.255.0.0	172.16.255.254
S1-Central	—	172.16.254.1	255.255.0.0	172.16.255.254

Task 1: Use the Telnet Protocol to Log in to a Cisco Switch

Step 1.   Access the Windows terminal.

Open a Windows terminal by choosing **Start > Run**. Enter **cmd**, and click **OK**.

Step 2.   Use the Windows Telnet client to access S1-Central.

S1-Central has been configured with 11 student accounts, ccna1 through ccna11. To provide access to each student, use the user ID corresponding to your pod. For example, for host computers on pod 1, use user ID ccna1. Unless directed otherwise by your instructor, the password is cisco.

From the Windows terminal, issue the Telnet command **telnet** destination-ip-address:

```
C:/> telnet 172.16.254.1
```

An access prompt is displayed, similar to the one shown in Example 9-5.

Example 9-5   Switch Access Prompt

```
        *****************************************************************
                        This is Lab switch S1-Central.
                        Authorized access only.
        *****************************************************************
User Access Verification
Username: ccna1
Password: cisco  (*hidden*)
S1-Central#
```

Task 2: Use the Cisco IOS show mac-address-table Command to Examine MAC Addresses and Port Associations

Step 1.   Examine the switch MAC address table.

Issue the **show mac-address-table ?** command. This outputs all options for the command.

Use Table 9-11 to fill in a description for each command option.

Table 9-11   Show Mac-Address-Table Command Options

Option	Description
address	
aging-time	
count	
dynamic	
interface	
multicast	
notification	
static	
vlan	
|	
<cr>	

Step 2.   Examine dynamic MAC address table entries.

Issue the **show mac-address-table** command. This command displays static (CPU) and dynamic, or learned, entries.

Use Table 9-12 to list the MAC addresses and corresponding switch ports.

Table 9-12   MAC Addresses and Ports

MAC Address	Switch Port

Suppose that a hub with five active hosts is connected to switch port gi0/0. How many MAC addresses are listed for switch port gi0/0?

Step 3.   Examine MAC address table aging time.

Issue the **show mac-address-table aging-time** command. This command displays the default amount of time, in seconds, that MAC address entries are stored.

What is the default aging time for VLAN 1?

Task 3: Challenge

What would be the result if the MAC address table were flushed of dynamic entries?

Task 4: Reflection

Using the Telnet protocol, network engineers can access Cisco devices remotely across secure LANs. This has the benefit of permitting access to remote devices for troubleshooting and monitoring purposes.

A switch contains a MAC address table that lists the MAC address connected to each switch port. When a frame enters the switch, the switch performs a lookup of the frame destination MAC address. If a match occurs in the MAC address table, the frame is routed out the corresponding port. Without a MAC address table, the switch would have to flood the frame out each port.

Task 5: Clean Up

Unless directed otherwise by the instructor, turn off power to the host computers. Remove anything that was brought into the lab, and leave the room ready for the next class.

Packet Tracer Companion: Cisco Switch MAC Table Examination (9.8.2.2)

You can now open the file LSG01-Lab9822.pka on the CD-ROM that accompanies this book to repeat this hands-on lab using Packet Tracer. Remember, however, that Packet Tracer is not a substitute for a hands-on lab experience with real equipment. A summary of the instructions is provided within the activity.

Lab 9-3: Intermediary Device as an End Device (9.8.3.1)

Upon completion of this lab, you will be able to

- Use Wireshark to capture and analyze frames originating from network nodes.

- Copy and paste data captured by Wireshark into Notepad for further analysis.

- Examine the origination of frames in a small network.

Background

A switch is used to forward frames between network devices. A switch normally does not originate frames to node devices. Rather, a switch efficiently passes frames from one device to another in a LAN. In this lab, however, you will see the switch originating frames, because you will use Telnet to directly access the switch.

Scenario

You will use Wireshark to capture and analyze Ethernet frames. If Wireshark has not been loaded on the host pod computer, you can download it from ftp://eagle-server.example.com/pub/eagle_labs/eagle1/chapter9/. The file is wireshark-setup-0.99.4.exe.

Figure 9-4 shows the topology for this lab, and Table 9-13 is the corresponding addressing table.

Figure 9-4   Topology for Lab 9-3

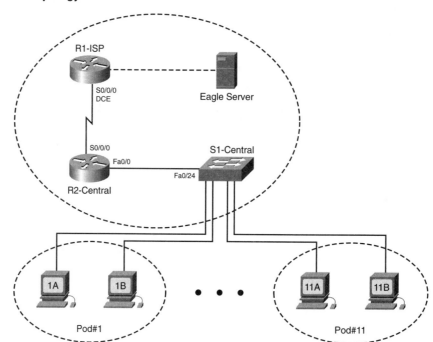

Table 9-13   Addressing Table

Device	Interface	IP Address	Subnet Mask	Default Gateway
R1-ISP	S0/0/0	10.10.10.6	255.255.255.252	—
	Fa0/0	192.168.254.253	255.255.255.0	—
R2-Central	S0/0/0	10.10.10.5	255.255.255.252	10.10.10.6
	Fa0/0	172.16.255.254	255.255.0.0	—
Eagle Server	—	192.168.254.254	255.255.255.0	192.168.254.253
	—	172.31.24.254	255.255.255.0	—
Host Pod#A	—	172.16.Pod#.1	255.255.0.0	172.16.255.254
Host Pod#B	—	172.16.Pod#.2	255.255.0.0	172.16.255.254
S1-Central	—	172.16.254.1	255.255.0.0	172.16.255.254

In this lab you will ping a neighbor's pod host computer.

Write down the IP address and port connection on S1-Central for the neighbor's pod host computer:

- IP address: _____

- S1-Central port number: _____

Task 1: Use Wireshark to Capture and Analyze Frames Originating from Network Nodes

Step 1.   Configure Wireshark for packet capture.

Choose **Capture > Options**.

Select the interface that corresponds to the LAN.

Check the box to update the list of packets in real time.

Click **Start**.

This begins the packet capture. During this capture there will probably be more than 200 packets, making analysis a bit tedious. The critical Telnet conversation between the pod host computer and S1-Central will be easy to filter, however.

Step 2.   Use the Windows Telnet client to access S1-Central.

S1-Central has been configured with 11 student accounts, ccna1 through ccna11. To provide access to each student, use the user ID corresponding to your pod. For example, for host computers on pod 1, use user ID ccna1. Unless directed otherwise by your instructor, the password is cisco.

From the Windows terminal, issue the Telnet command **telnet 172.16.254.1**.

Enter the appropriate username and password, cisco. Enter **enable** to enter privileged mode. The S1-Central prompt, S1-Central#, should be returned.

Step 3.   Examine and clear the MAC address table.

Examine the switch MAC address table with the **show mac-address-table** command. In addition to several static CPU entries, numerous dynamic address table entries should be listed. Use Table 9-14 to list the dynamic MAC address entries.

Table 9-14   Dynamic MAC Address Entries

MAC Address	Switch Port

To clear dynamic MAC address table entries, use the **clear mac-address-table dynamic** command. You can use the **show mac-address-table** command again to verify that the dynamic entries have been cleared.

Open a second terminal window. Ping your neighbor's IP address, which was recorded earlier:

```
C:>\ ping -n 1 ip-address
```

The MAC address for your neighbor's computer should be dynamically added in the S1-Central MAC address table. You can use the **show mac-address-table** command again to verify that the address is added. Use Table 9-15 to list the dynamic MAC address entries.

Table 9-15   Dynamic MAC Address Entries

MAC Address	Switch Port

What conclusion can you make about how a switch learns MAC addresses connected to switch interfaces?

_____

Stop the Wireshark capture.

You will analyze the capture in the next task.

Task 2: Examine the Origination of Frames in a Small Network

Step 1.   In Wireshark, examine the Telnet session to S1-Central.

Highlight one of the Telnet session packets.

From Wireshark, choose **Analyze > Follow TCP Stream**. A stream content window opens, using ASCII as the default display. If the username and passwords are not visible, switch to HEX Dump.

Verify the username and password that you entered:

- Username: _____

- Password: _____

Close the stream content window. To remove any display filters, click the **Filter** button at the top-left corner of the screen and remove the filter string.

Step 2.   Examine output of the **show mac-address-table** command.

Open Notepad. You will copy and paste data into Notepad for analysis.

In the top Wireshark Packet List pane, scroll down to the captured ICMP request that was generated when you pinged. Figure 9-5 shows partial output of a Wireshark capture.

Figure 9-5   Wireshark Capture of Telnet

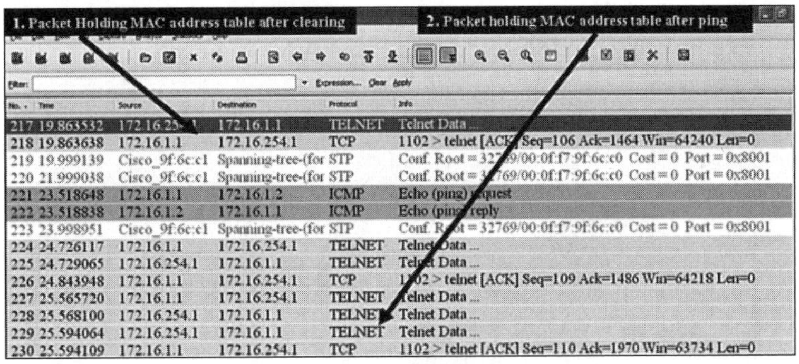

Select the last Telnet data packet from S1-Central before the **ping** command.

View the packet in the Packet Details window pane. Right-click **telnet** and choose **Copy Bytes (Printable Text Only)**. In Notepad, choose **Edit > Paste** to copy and paste the Telnet data into Notepad. You should see a dynamic mapping for your own computer similar to the output shown in Example 9-6.

Example 9-6   MAC Address Table Before the Ping

```
{_lEMaNL;RPC              Mac Address Table
— — — — — — — — — — — — — — — — — — — — — —.


Vlan    Mac Address        Type        Ports
— —     — — — — —.         — — —       — —.
All     000f.f79f.6cc0     STATIC      CPU
All     0100.0ccc.cccc     STATIC      CPU
All     0100.0ccc.cccd     STATIC      CPU
All     0100.0cdd.dddd     STATIC      CPU
  1     0010.a47b.015f     DYNAMIC     Fa0/1
Total Mac Addresses for this criterion: 5
S1-Central#
```

In Table 9-16, write down the dynamic MAC address and port number displayed in the output. Does the switch port correspond to your pod host computer?

Table 9-16   Dynamic MAC Address Entry

MAC Address	Type	Port

Why is your pod host computer mapping still in the MAC address table, despite having been cleared?

Select the last Telnet data packet following the ping reply. Next, view the packet in the Packet Details window pane. Right-click **TELNET** and choose **Copy Bytes (Printable Text Only)**. In Notepad, choose **Edit > Paste** to copy and paste the Telnet data into Notepad. The text should be similar to Example 9-7.

Example 9-7   MAC Address Table After the Ping

```
{_lEPaNM;VP           Mac Address Table
— — — — — — — — — — — — — — — — — — — — — — .

Vlan    Mac Address      Type       Ports
— —     — — — — — .      — — — —     — — -
All     000f.f79f.6cc0   STATIC     CPU
All     0100.0ccc.cccc   STATIC     CPU
All     0100.0ccc.cccd   STATIC     CPU
All     0100.0cdd.dddd   STATIC     CPU
 1      0010.a47b.015f   DYNAMIC    Fa0/1
 1      0016.76ac.a76a   DYNAMIC    Fa0/2
Total Mac Addresses for this criterion: 6
S1-Central#
```

In Table 9-17, write down the MAC address and port number for the second dynamic entry displayed in the output. Does the switch port correspond to your neighbor's pod host computer?

Table 9-17   Dynamic MAC Address Entry

MAC Address	Type	Port

Task 3: Reflection

The Wireshark capture of a Telnet session between a pod host computer and S1-Central was analyzed to show how a switch dynamically learns about nodes directly connected to it.

Task 4: Challenge

Use Wireshark to capture and analyze a Telnet session between the pod host computer and the Cisco switch. From Wireshark, choose **Analyze > Follow TCP Stream** to view the login user ID and password. How secure is the Telnet protocol? What can be done to make communication with Cisco devices more secure?

_____

_____

_____

_____

_____

Task 5: Clean Up

Wireshark was installed on the pod host computer. If Wireshark needs to be uninstalled, choose **Start > Control Panel**. Click **Add or Remove Programs**. Choose **Wireshark**, and click **Remove**.

Remove any files created on the pod host computer during the lab.

Unless directed otherwise by the instructor, turn off power to the host computers. Remove anything that was brought into the lab, and leave the room ready for the next class.

Packet Tracer Companion: An Intermediary Device as an End Device (9.8.3.2)

You can now open the file LSG01-Lab9832.pka on the CD-ROM that accompanies this book to repeat this hands-on lab using Packet Tracer. Remember, however, that Packet Tracer is not a substitute for a hands-on lab experience with real equipment. A summary of the instructions is provided within the activity.

Skills Integration Challenge: Switched Ethernet (9.9.1.3)

Open file LSG01-PTSkills9.pka on the CD-ROM that accompanies this book to perform this exercise using Packet Tracer.

Upon completion of this activity, you will be able to

- Determine IP subnet plans.

- Repair Ethernet-related network issues.

- Test the network.

Background

You have been asked to repair some problems in the network model related to the Ethernet LAN connected to R2-Central.

Figure 9-6 shows the topology for this Skills Integration Challenge, and Table 9-18 is the corresponding addressing table.

Figure 9-6   Topology for the Challenge

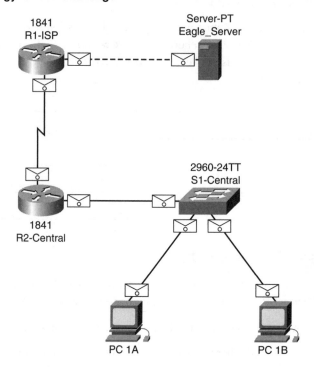

Table 9-18   Addressing Table

Device	Interface	IP Address	Subnet Mask	Default Gateway
R1-ISP	Fa0/0	192.168.111.134	255.255.255.248	—
	S0/0/0	192.168.111.138	255.255.255.252	—
R2-Central	Fa0/0	192.168.111.126	255.255.255.128	192.168.111.138
	S0/0/0	192.168.111.137	255.255.255.252	192.168.111.138
PC 1A	NIC	192.168.111.1	255.255.255.128	192.168.111.126
PC 1B	NIC	192.168.111.2	255.255.255.128	192.168.111.126
Eagle Server	NIC	192.168.111.133	255.255.255.248	192.168.111.134

Task 1: IP Subnet Planning

You have been given an IP address block of 192.168.111.0/24. You must provide for the three existing networks.

The subnet assignments are as follows:

- First subnet, existing student LAN, up to 100 hosts (Fa0/0 on R2-Central)
- Second subnet, existing ISP LAN, up to five hosts (already configured)
- Third subnet, existing WAN, point-to-point link (already configured)

Interface IP addresses:

- The server, R1-ISP, and R2-Central's serial interface have already been configured.

- For R2-Central's Fa0/0 interface, use the highest usable address on the existing student LAN subnet.

- For hosts 1A and 1B, use the first two IP addresses (the two lowest usable addresses) on the existing student LAN subnet.

- For hosts 1A and 1B, the DNS server is 192.168.111.133 /29.

- The next-hop router (to which the default route should point), R1-ISP, has an IP address of 192.168.111.138 /30.

Task 2: Repair Problems with the Ethernet Switched LAN

PC 1B has a wireless card and cannot be connected to the switch.

Remove the wireless card from PC 1B.

Add the Fast Ethernet Interface card PT-HOST-NM-1CFE to PC 1B.

Connect this newly installed Fast Ethernet NIC to the Fa0/2 interface on the switch.

Connect PC 1A to the Fa0/1 interface on the switch.

Connect the Fa0/24 interface on the switch to the R2-Central Fa0/0 interface.

Apparently the Ethernet speed and duplex settings for the R2-Central Fa0/0 interface, the S1-Central switch interfaces (Fa0/1, Fa0/2, and Fa0/24), and the PC 1A interfaces are incorrect. Set all Ethernet interfaces to autonegotiate speed and duplex (which will achieve full-duplex 100-Mbps operation if both ends of the link can support it). For all devices, make sure that the power is on to the device and to the interfaces (make sure that the Ethernet interfaces are not shut down). Add IP addresses to the router Fa0/0 interface and to the two PCs. Assign the highest usable subnet address to the gateway and the two lowest usable addresses to the PCs. The static route on R2-Central should be a default static route that points to R1-ISP's serial interface IP address. These procedures were explained in the Chapter 5 and 6 Skills Integration Challenges.

Task 3: Test the Network

Use ping, trace, web traffic, and the Inspect tool to trace packet flow in simulation mode, with HTTP, DNS, TCP, UDP, ICMP, and ARP viewable, to test your understanding of how the network is operating.

Task 4: Reflection

The two Layer 2 and Layer 1 technologies in this model are a serial connection (between the routers) and the Ethernet LANs (for the ISP server and with the S1-Central switch). Compare and contrast the serial connection with Ethernet. In a future course you will learn much more about switched Ethernet technologies.

CHAPTER 10

Planning and Cabling Networks

The Study Guide portion of this chapter uses a combination of multiple-choice, matching, fill-in-the-blank, and open-ended questions to test your knowledge of planning and cabling networks.

The Labs and Activities portion of this chapter includes all the online curriculum labs to further reinforce that you have mastered the practical, hands-on skills needed.

As you work through this chapter, use Chapter 10 in the Network Fundamentals CCNA Exploration online curriculum or use the corresponding Chapter 10 in the *Network Fundamentals CCNA Exploration Companion Guide* for assistance.

Study Guide

LANs: Making the Physical Connection

A networking professional needs to know how to select and interconnect the proper devices for a network. Routers, hubs, and switches are common network devices. As a networking professional, you need to be familiar with the different device selection factors, including cost, types, and speeds of different ports and interfaces, expandability, and manageability. It is essential that you have knowledge of the different media types and the distinct roles they play with the devices that they connect. In this chapter, you identify the cables needed to make successful LAN and WAN connections and learn how to use device management connections. The design of an IP addressing scheme is presented and then practiced with the help of concept questions and the hands-on labs.

Concept Questions

1. Compare and contrast the function of hubs and switches. Be as detailed as possible. Explain the advantage of one device over the other.

   _____

   _____

   _____

   _____

   _____

   _____

   _____

2. Explain how adaptability to new technologies can be taken into consideration when selecting devices for a LAN. How does this affect the cost calculations?

   _____

   _____

_____

_____

_____

_____

Multiple-Choice Questions

Choose the best possible answer for each of the following questions.

1. How can redundancy be provided in a switched network?

    a. By deploying one central switch with a high port density

    b. By using high-speed fiber-optic media

    c. By providing multiple interconnections between a number of switches

    d. By delpoying gigabit switches only

2. How do switches create collision domains?

    a. Each switch port creates a point-to-point dedicated connection to the devices connected to that port.

    b. Switches regenerate each bit of the frames they receive.

    c. By using a special cable type to connect to the devices on its ports.

    d. By allowing the interconnection of segments with different speeds.

Vocabulary Exercise: Completion

Fill in the blanks for the following statements.

1. Even though hubs can be interconnected, they remain in a single _____.

2. A swich is used to _____ a network into multiple collision domains.

3. A switch provides dedicated _____ on each port, which can increase LAN performance.

Device Interconnections

When planning the installation of LAN cabling, there are several physical areas to consider. Each area has its unique requirements and standards. A network administrator needs to be familiar with the different standards that define devices and cabling in these areas.

Concept Questions

1. Explain what will happen when you use a straight-through cable to connect your computer to the Fast Ethernet interface of a router.

    _____

    _____

    _____

    _____

2. Explain how the serial connection to a WAN service provider differs from the way the serial connections are set up for the curriculum labs.

_____

_____

_____

_____

_____

_____

_____

3. There are four physical areas to consider when planning the installation of LAN cabling. List these four areas and their main components.

_____

_____

_____

_____

_____

_____

_____

_____

_____

_____

Vocabulary Exercise: Completion

Fill in the blanks for the following statements that discuss features and issues related to different types of media.

1. The _____ standard specifies the maximum cable length in UTP installations.

2. _____ is the decrease in signal strength along an electrical or optical cable.

3. Signal attenuation and exposure to possible interference _____ with cable length.

4. _____ can be produced by electrical machines, lighting, and other communications devices, including computers and radio equipment.

5. UTP cabling uses _____ connectors.

Developing an Addressing Scheme

Developing an IP addressing scheme is one of the most important tasks that you will have to perform as a network professional. It is extremely important that you understand IP addressing. This knowledge is vital in designing, configuring, and troubleshooting networks.

Concept Questions

1. What devices do you need to consider when counting devices in your network that need IP addresses.

     _____

     _____

     _____

     _____

     _____

     _____

2. Why does each connection between routers count as a separate subnet if there are no hosts connected?

     _____

     _____

3. It is good practice to use IP addresses that fit a common pattern across all subnets. What are some common categories that you can use to allocate IP addresses? Explain why you should use address schemes that fit a common pattern across your network.

     _____

     _____

     _____

     _____

Vocabulary Exercise: Completion

Fill in the blanks for the following statements dealing with IP addressing and subnetting.

1. Network devices that require IP addresses for management purposes include _____ and _____.

2. Subnets divide _____ into a number of smaller domains.

3. Each subnet requires a router interface as the _____ for that subnet.

Multiple-Choice Questions

Choose the best possible answer(s) for the following questions.

1. Which addresses cannot be assigned to hosts? Choose all that apply.

    a. Management address

    b. Network address

    c. Broadcast address

    d. Gateway address

2. Which formula is used to calculate the number of hosts per network or subnet? Use *n* to represent the number of bits.

    a. $(2^{\wedge}n - 1)$

    b. $2^{\wedge}n$

    c. $(2^{\wedge}n - 2)$

    d. $(n - 2)$

3. What are advantages of dividing networks into subnets? Choose all that apply.

    a. Decreased costs

    b. Smaller broadcast domains

    c. Implementation of different levels of security

    d. Larger collision domains

Calculating the Subnets

Two different methods can be used for allocating addresses to an Internetwork. Variable-length subnet masking (VLSM) assigns the prefix and host bits to each network based on the number of hosts in that network. The non-VLSM approach uses the same prefix length and the same number of host bits for each subnet.

Concept Questions

1. If your network uses the address 172.16.0.0 and you need to create 64 subnets, what will be the subnet mask for your network?

_____

2. You have the following network requirements:

    Network 1 needs to support 32 host addresses.

    Network 2 needs to support 64 host addresses.

    Network 3 needs to support 2 host addresses.

    Network 4 needs to support 52 host addresses.

    Network 5 needs to support 128 host addresses.

    Which addressing method will allow you to design an IP addressing scheme without wasting any host addresses? How is the efficiency of this method achieved?

_____

_____

_____

_____

Device Interconnections

Cisco devices, routers, and switches have several different types of interfaces associated with them. These interfaces are also referred to as *ports*. It is important to understand the different types of interfaces and know the types of cable required to connect to the interfaces. LAN and WAN interfaces require different cabling and configuration.

Concept Question

List the four types of interfaces on Cisco routers and switches. Briefly describe the function of each of these interfaces.

_____

_____

_____

_____

_____

_____

_____

_____

Multiple-Choice Questions

Choose the best possible answers(s) for the following questions dealing with interface types.

1. What can Ethernet interfaces be used for? Choose all that apply.

    a. To connect the router to a terminal for configuration purposes

    b. To connect to LAN devices such as computers and switches

    c. To connect to other routers

    d. To connect the router to the DSU/CSU

2. Which interface is the primary interface for the initial configuration of a Cisco device such as a router or a switch?

    a. The Ethernet interface

    b. The Telnet interface

    c. The console interface

    d. The serial interface

3. What are serial interfaces used for? Choose all that apply.

    a. To establish a WAN connection

    b. To establish communication with a router via a console on a remote WAN

    c. To make a back-to-back connection between routers in the lab

    d. To connect to a terminating device such as a switch or a computer

Labs and Activities

Lab 10-1: How Many Networks? (10.3.2.2)

Upon completion of this lab, you will be able to do the following:

- Determine the number of subnets.

- Design an appropriate addressing scheme.

- Assign addresses and subnet mask pairs to device interfaces.

- Examine the use of the available network address space.

Scenario

In this lab, you have been given the network address 192.168.26.0/24 to subnet and provide the IP addressing for the networks shown in the topology diagrams. You must determine the number of networks needed then design an appropriate addressing scheme. Place the correct address and mask in the addressing table. In this example, the number of hosts is not important. You are only required to determine the number of subnets per topology example.

Task 1: Determine the Number of Subnets in Topology Diagram A

Use the topology in Figure 10-1 to answer the questions that follow.

Figure 10-1   Topology Diagram A

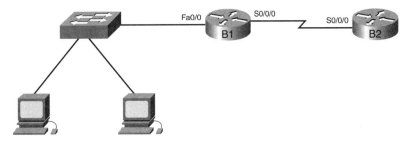

How many networks are shown in Figure 10-1? _____

How many bits should you allocate to create the required number of subnets? _____

How many usable host addresses did this give you? _____

What is the new subnet mask in decimal form? _____

How many subnets are available for future use? _____

Task 2: Record Subnet Information

Fill in Table 10-1 with the subnet information.

Table 10-1   Subnet Information

Subnet Number	Subnet Address	First Usable Host Address	Last Usable Host Address	Broadcast Address
0				
1				

Task 3: Determine the Number of Subnets in Topology Diagram B

Use the topology in Figure 10-2 to answer the questions that follow.

Figure 10-2   Topology Diagram B

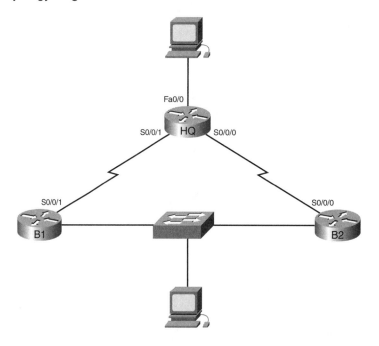

How many networks are there? _____

How many bits should you allocate to create the required number of subnets? _____

How many usable host addresses did this give you? _____

What is the new subnet mask in decimal form? _____

How many subnets are available for future use? _____

Task 4: Record Subnet Information

Fill in Table 10-2 with the subnet information. Use the subnet mask from Step 4.

Table 10-2   Subnet Information

Subnet Number	Subnet Address	First Usable Host Address	Last Usable Host Address	Broadcast Address
0				
1				
2				
3				

Task 5: Determine the Number of Subnets in Topology Diagram C

Use the topology in Figure 10-3 to answer the questions that follow.

Figure 10-3   Topology Diagram C

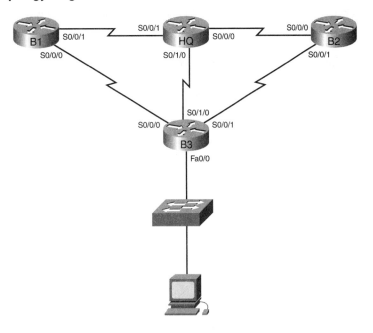

How many networks are there? _____

How many bits should you allocate to create the required number of subnets? _____

How many usable host addresses did this give you? _____

What is the new subnet mask in decimal form? _____

How many subnets are available for future use? _____

Task 6: Record Subnet Information

Fill in the Table 10-3 with the subnet information.

Table 10-3   Subnet Information

Subnet Number	Subnet Address	First Usable Host Address	Last Usable Host Address	Broadcast Address
0				
1				
2				
3				
4				
5				
6				
7				

Task 7: Determine the Number of Subnets in Topology Diagram D

Use the topology in Figure 10-4 to answer the questions that follow.

Figure 10-4   Topology Diagram D

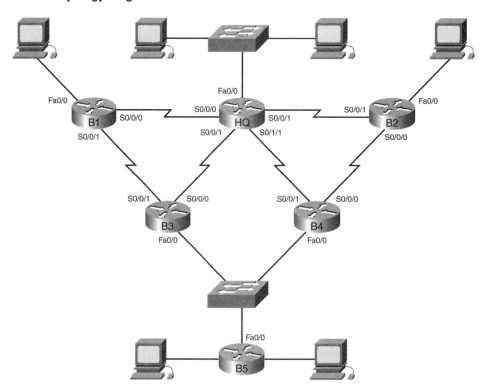

How many networks are there? _____

How many bits should you allocate to create the required number of subnets? _____

How many usable host addresses did this give you? _____

What is the new subnet mask in decimal form? _____

How many subnets are available for future use? _____

Task 8: Record Subnet Information

Fill in Table 10-4 with the subnet information.

Table 10-4   Subnet Information

Subnet Number	Subnet Address	First Usable Host Address	Last Usable Host Address	Broadcast Address
0				
1				
2				
3				
4				
5				
6				
7				
8				
9				
10				
11				
12				
13				
14				
15				

Task 9: Reflection

What information is needed when determining an appropriate addressing scheme for a network?

Lab 10-2: Creating a Small Lab Topology (10.6.1.1)

Upon completion of this lab, you will be able to do the following:

- Design the logical network.

- Configure the physical lab topology.

- Configure the logical LAN topology.

- Verify LAN connectivity.

Background

Table 10-5 shows the equipment and hardware requirements for this lab. Gather the necessary equipment and cables.

Table 10-5   Equipment and Hardware for Lab

Hardware	Quantity	Description
Cisco Router	1	Part of CCNA Lab bundle
Cisco Switch	1	Part of CCNA Lab bundle
Computer (host)	3	Lab computer
Cat5 better straight-through UTP cable	3	Connects Router 1 and computers Host1 and Host2 to Switch1
Cat5 crossover UTP cable	1	Connects computer Host1 to Router1

Scenario

In this lab, you create a small network that requires connecting network devices and configuring host computers for basic network connectivity, as shown in Figure 10-5. Subnet A and Subnet B are subnets that are currently needed. Subnet C and Subnet D are anticipated subnets, not yet connected to the network. Subnet zero will be used.

Figure 10-5   Topology for Lab 10-2

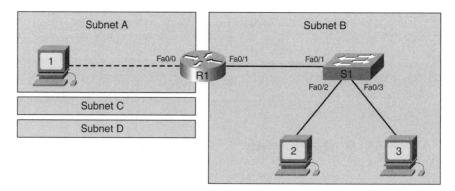

Note: The CD-ROM accompanying this book contains a subnet chart for the last IP address octet.

Task 1: Design the Logical Network

Given an IP address and mask of 172.20.0.0/24 (address / mask), design an IP addressing scheme that satisfies the requirements listed in Table 10-6.

Table 10-6   Subnet Requirements

Subnet	Number of Hosts
Subnet A	2
Subnet B	6
Subnet C	47
Subnet D	125

Host computers from each subnet will use the first available IP address in the address block. Router interfaces will use the last available IP address in the address block.

Step 1.   Design Subnet D address block.

Begin the logical network design by satisfying the requirement of Subnet D, which requires the largest block of IP addresses. Refer to the subnet chart on the CD-ROM, and pick the first address block that will support Subnet D.

Fill in Table 10-7 with IP address information for Subnet D.

Table 10-7   Subnet D IP Address Information

Network Address	Mask	First Host Address	Last Host Address	Broadcast

What is the bit mask?

Step 2.   Design Subnet D address block.

Satisfy the requirement for Subnet C, the next largest address block. Refer to the subnet chart on the CD-ROM, and pick the next available address block that will support Subnet C.

Fill in Table 10-8 with IP address information for Subnet C.

Table 10-8   Subnet C IP address information

Network Address	Mask	First Host Address	Last Host Address	Broadcast

What is the bit mask? _____

Step 3.   Design Subnet B address block.

Satisfy the requirement of Subnet B, the next largest IP address block. Refer to the subnet chart on the CD-ROM, and pick the next available address block that will support Subnet B.

Fill in Table 10-9 with IP address information for Subnet B.

Table 10-9   Subnet B IP Address Information

Network Address	Mask	First Host Address	Last Host Address	Broadcast

What is the bit mask?

_____

_____

Step 4.   Design Subnet A address block.

Satisfy the requirement of Subnet A. Refer to the subnet chart on the CD-ROM, and pick the next available address block that will support Subnet A.

Fill in Table 10-10 with IP address information for Subnet A.

Table 10-10   Subnet A IP Address Information

Network Address	Mask	First Host Address	Last Host Address	Broadcast

What is the bit mask?

_____

_____

Task 2: Configure the Physical Lab Topology

Step 1.   Physically connect devices.

Cable the network devices as shown in Figure 10-5.

What cable type is needed to connect Host 1 to Router 1, and why?

_____

What cable type is needed to connect Host 1, Host 2, and Router 1 to Switch 1, and why?

_____

_____

If not already enabled, turn power on to all devices.

Step 2.   Visually inspect network connections.

After cabling the network devices, take a moment to verify the connections. Attention to detail now will minimize the time required to troubleshoot network connectivity issues later. Ensure that all switch connections show green. Any switch connection that does not transition from amber to green should be investigated. Confirm that the power is applied to the connected device, the correct cable is used, and the correct cable is functional.

What type of cable connects Router1 interface Fa0/0 to Host 1? _____

What type of cable connects Router 1 interface Fa0/1 to Switch 1? _____

What type of cable connects Host 2 to Switch 1? _____

What type of cable connects Host 3 to Switch 1? _____

Is all equipment turned on? _____

Task 3: Configure the Logical Topology

Step 1.   Document logical network settings.

The host computer gateway IP address is used to send IP packets to other networks. Therefore, the gateway address is the IP address assigned to the router interface for that subnet.

From the IP address information recorded in Task 1, write down the IP address information for each computer in the tables that follow. In Table 10-11, enter the information for Host 1.

Table 10-11   Host 1

Address Type	Address
IP address	
IP mask	
Gateway address	

In Table 10-12, enter addressing information for Host 2.

Table 10-12   Host 2

Address Type	Address
IP address	
IP mask	
Gateway address	

In Table 10-13, enter addressing information for Host 3.

Table 10-13   Host 3

Address Type	Address
IP address	
IP mask	
Gateway address	

Step 2.   Configure the Host 1 computer.

On Host 1, click **Start** > **Control Panel** > **Network Connections**. Right-click the **Local Area Connection** device icon and choose **Properties**.

On the General tab, select **Internet Protocol (TCP/IP)**, and then click the **Properties** button.

Figure 10-6 shows Host 1 IP address and gateway settings. Manually enter the following information, recorded in the preceding Step 1:

- IP address: Host1 IP address

- Subnet mask: Host1 subnet mask

- Default gateway: Gateway IP address

Figure 10-6   Host 1 IP Addressing and Gateway Settings

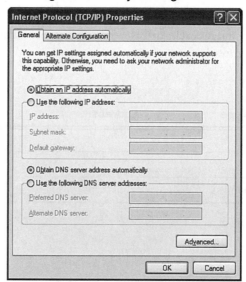

When finished, close the Internet Protocols (TCP/IP) Properties window by clicking **OK**. Close the Local Area Connection window. Depending on the Windows operating system, the computer might require a reboot for changes to be effective. Try to disable and then reenable the network interface card (NIC) by right-clicking the NIC in the Local Area Connection Properties window.

Step 3.   Configure Host 2 and Host 3 computers.

Repeat Step 2 for computers Host 2 and Host 3, using the IP address information for those computers. Remember that the default gateway address on the computers is the IP address of the Fast Ethernet interface of the router that the computers connect to via the switch.

Task 4: Verify Network Connectivity

Verify with your instructor that Router 1 has been configured. Otherwise, connectivity will be broken between LANs. Switch 1 should have a default configuration.

Network connectivity can be verified with the Windows **ping** command. Open a terminal window by clicking **Start > Run**. Type **cmd**, and then press **Enter**. If your computer's operating system is Windows XP SP2, disable the firewall (for your ping tests to work).

Use Table 10-14 to methodically verify and record connectivity with each network device. Take corrective action to establish connectivity if a test fails.

Table 10-14   Network Connectivity Test Results

From	To	IP Address	Ping Results
Host 1	Gateway (Router 1, Fa0/0)		
Host 1	Router 1, Fa0/1		
Host 1	Host 2		
Host 1	Host 3		
Host 2	Host 3		
Host 2	Gateway (Router 1, Fa0/1)		
Host 2	Router 1, Fa0/0		
Host 2	Host 1		
Host 3	Host 2		
Host 3	Gateway (Router 1, Fa0/1)		
Host 3	Router1, Fa0/0		
Host 3	Host 1		

Note any break in connectivity. When troubleshooting connectivity issues, the topology diagram shown in Figure 10-5 can prove extremely helpful.

In this scenario, how can you detect a malfunctioning gateway?

Task 5: Reflection

Review any physical or logical configuration problems encountered during this lab. Be sure that you have a thorough understanding of the procedures used to verify network connectivity.

This is a particularly important lab. In addition to practicing IP subnetting, you configured host computers with network addresses and tested them for connectivity.

It is best to practice host computer configuration and verification several times. This will reinforce the skills you learned in this lab and make you a better network technician.

Task 6: Challenge

Ask your instructor or another student to introduce one or two problems in your network when you aren't looking or are out of the lab room. Problems can be either physical (wrong UTP cable) or logical (wrong IP address or gateway). To fix the problems, follow these steps:

Step 1. Perform a good visual inspection. Look for green link lights on Switch 1.

Step 2. Use the table provided in Task 3 to identify failed connectivity. List the problems.

_____

Step 3. Write down your proposed solution(s).

_____

_____

Step 4. Test your solution. If the solution fixed the problem, document the solution. If the solution did not fix the problem, continue troubleshooting.

Task 7: Clean Up

Unless directed otherwise by the instructor, restore host computer network connectivity, and then turn off power to the host computers.

Carefully remove cables and return them neatly to their storage. Reconnect cables that were disconnected for this lab.

Remove anything that was brought into the lab, and leave the room ready for the next class.

Packet Tracer Companion: Creating a Small Topology (10.6.1.2)

You can now open the file LSG01-Lab10612.pka on the CD-ROM that accompanies this book to repeat this hands-on lab using Packet Tracer. However, keep in mind that Packet Tracer is not a substitute for a hands-on lab experience with real equipment. A summary of the instructions is provided within the Packet Tracer activity.

Lab 10-3: Establishing a Console Session with HyperTerminal (10.6.2.1)

Upon completion of this lab, you will be able to do the following:

- Connect a router and computer using a console cable.

- Configure HyperTerminal to establish a console session with a Cisco IOS router.

- Configure HyperTerminal to establish a console session with a Cisco IOS switch.

Background

HyperTerminal is a simple Windows-based terminal emulation program for serial communication that can be used to connect to the console port on Cisco IOS devices. A serial interface on a computer is connected to the Cisco device via a rollover cable. Using HyperTerminal is the most basic way to access a router for checking or changing its configuration. Another popular serial communication utility is TeraTerm Web. Instructions for TeraTerm Web use are contained in the section "Lab 10-3 (Alternative): Establishing a Console Session with TeraTerm" later in this chapter.

Scenario

Set up a network similar to the one in Figure 10-7. Any router that meets the interface requirements may be used. Possible routers include 800, 1600, 1700, 2500, 2600 routers, or a combination.

Figure 10-7   Establishing a Console Session with HyperTerminal

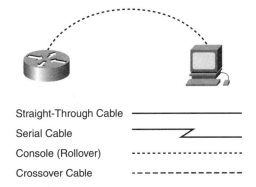

The following resources are required:

- Computer with a serial interface and HyperTerminal loaded

- Cisco router

- Console (rollover) cable for connecting the workstation to the router

Task 1: Connect a Router and Computer with a Console Cable

Step 1.   Set up the basic physical connection.

Connect the console (rollover) cable to the console port on the router. Connect the other cable end to the host computer with a DB-9 or DB-25 adapter to the COM 1 port.

Step 2.   Power on the devices.

If not already powered on, enable power to the computer and router.

Task 2: Configure HyperTerminal to Establish a Console Session with a Cisco IOS Router

Step 1.   Start the HyperTerminal application.

From the Windows taskbar, start the HyperTerminal program by clicking **Start** > **All Programs** > **Accessories** > **Communications** > **HyperTerminal**.

Step 2.   Configure HyperTerminal.

Figure 10-8 shows an example of the opening HyperTerminal configuration window. At the Connection Description window, enter a session name in the Name field. Select an appropriate icon, or leave the default. Click **OK**. If you are accessing HyperTerminal for the first time, the program prompts for an area code/phone number. You need to fill in a number to be able to continue.

Figure 10-8   HyperTerminal Connection Description Window

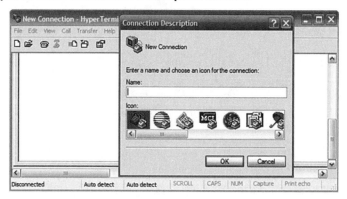

In the Connect To window shown in Figure 10-9, enter the appropriate connection type, COM 1, in the Connect using field. Click **OK**.

Figure 10-9   HyperTerminal Connection Type

In the COM 1 Properties box shown in Figure 10-10, change port settings to the values in Table 10-15.

Figure 10-10 HyperTerminal COM 1 Port Settings

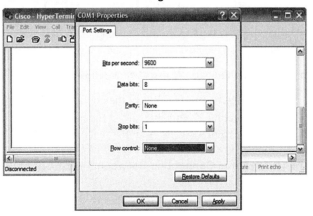

Table 10-15   HyperTerminal Port Settings

Settings	Value
Bits per second	9600
Data bits	8
Parity	None
Stop bits	1
Flow control	None

Click **OK**.

When the HyperTerminal session window comes up, press the **Enter** key. There should be a response from the router; this indicates that connection has been successfully completed. If there is no connection, troubleshoot as necessary. For example, verify that the router has power. Check the connection to the correct COM 1 port on the PC and the console port on the router. If there is still no connection, ask the instructor for assistance.

Step 3.   Close HyperTerminal.

When finished, close the HyperTerminal session. Click **File > Exit**. When asked whether to save the session, click **Yes**. Enter a name for the session.

Step 4.   Reconnect the HyperTerminal session.

Reopen the HyperTerminal session as described in Task 2, Step 1. This time, when the Connection Description window opens, click **Cancel**.

Click **File > Open**. Select the saved session, and then click **Open**. Use this technique to reconnect the HyperTerminal session to a Cisco device without reconfiguring a new session.

When finished, exit HyperTerminal.

Task 3: Configure HyperTerminal to Establish a Console Session with a Cisco IOS Switch

Serial connections between Cisco IOS routers and switches are similar. In this task, you make a serial connection between the host computer and a Cisco IOS switch.

Step 1.   Set up the basic physical connection.

See Figure 10-11. Connect the console (rollover) cable to the console port on the router. Connect the other cable end to the host computer with a DB-9 or DB-25 adapter to the COM 1 port.

Figure 10-11 Serial Connection Between a Host Computer and Cisco Switch

Step 2.   Power on the devices.

Use   If not already powered on, enable power to the computer and switch.

Step 3.   Start the HyperTerminal application.

From the Windows taskbar, start the HyperTerminal program by clicking **Start** > **Programs** > **Accessories** > **Communications** > **HyperTerminal**.

Step 4.   Configure HyperTerminal.

Use the procedure described in Task 2, Step 2, to configure HyperTerminal.

At the opening HyperTerminal Connection Description window, enter a session name in the Name field. Select an appropriate icon, or leave the default. Click **OK**.

In the Connect To window, enter the appropriate connection type, COM 1, in the Connect using field. Click **OK**.

In the COM 1 Properties window, change port settings to the values shown in Table 10-16.

Table 10-16   Port Settings

Settings	Value
Bits per second	9600
Data bits	8
Parity	None
Stop bits	1
Flow control	None

Click **OK**.

When the HyperTerminal session window comes up, press the **Enter** key. There should be a response from the switch; this indicates that connection has been successfully completed. If there is no connection, troubleshoot as necessary. For example, verify that the switch has power. Check the connection to the correct COM 1 port on the PC and the console port on the switch. If there is still no connection, ask the instructor for assistance.

Step 5.   Close HyperTerminal.

When finished, close the HyperTerminal session. Click **File > Exit**. When asked whether to save the session, click **No**.

Task 3: Reflection

This lab provided information for establishing a console connection to a Cisco IOS router and switch. Be sure to remember the correct HyperTerminal port settings. You will only be able to connect to the router if you are using the proper settings.

Task 4: Challenge

Draw the pin connections for the rollover cable and straight-through cable. Compare the differences, and be able to identify the different cable types.

Task 5: Clean Up

Unless directed otherwise by the instructor, turn off power to the host computer and router. Remove the rollover cable.

Remove anything that was brought into the lab, and leave the room ready for the next class.

Lab 10-3 (Alternative): Establishing a Console Session with TeraTerm

Upon completion of this lab, you will be able to do the following:

- Connect a router and computer using a console cable.

- Configure TeraTerm to establish a console session with the router.

Background

TeraTerm Web is another simple Windows-based terminal emulation program for serial communication that can be used to connect to the console port on Cisco IOS devices.

Scenario

Cable a network similar to Figure 10-12. Any router that meets the interface requirements may be used. Possible routers include 800, 1600, 1700, 2500, 2600 routers, or a combination.

Figure 10-12 Establishing a Console Session with TeraTerm

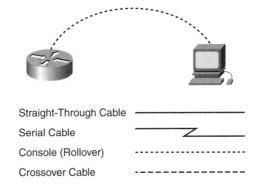

Straight-Through Cable	————————————
Serial Cable	——————⟋——
Console (Rollover)	------------------------
Crossover Cable	– – – – – – – – –

The following resources are required:

- Computer with a serial interface and TeraTerm Pro loaded

- Cisco router

- Console (rollover) cable for connecting the workstation to the router

Task 1: Connect a Router and Computer with a Console Cable

Step 1.   Set up the basic physical connection.

Ensure that power is turned off on the computer and Cisco router. Connect the console (rollover) cable to the console port on the router. Connect the other cable end to the PC with a DB-9 or DB-25 adapter to the COM 1 port.

Step 2.   Power on the devices.

Enable power to the computer and router.

Task 2: Configure TeraTerm Web to Establish a Console Session with the Router

Step 1.   Start TeraTerm Web application.

From the Windows taskbar, start the TeraTerm Web program by opening the TeraTerm Web folder, and starting the TeraTerm Web application, ttermpro.

Step 2.   Configure TeraTerm Web

Click **File > New Connection**. Refer to Figure 10-13. Select the appropriate serial COM port. Click **OK**.

Figure 10-13 TeraTerm Web Connection Configuration Window

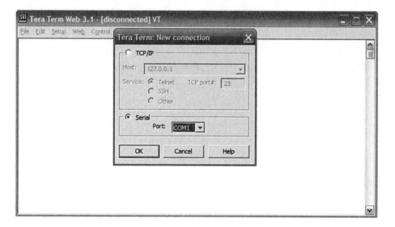

When the TeraTerm Web session window comes up, press the **Enter** key. There should be a response from the router; this indicates that the connection has been successfully completed. If there is no connection, troubleshoot as necessary. For example, verify that the router has power. Check the connection to the COM 1 port on the PC and the console port on the router. If there is still no connection, ask the instructor for assistance.

Step 3.   Close TeraTerm Web.

When finished, close the TeraTerm Web session. Click **File > Exit**. When asked whether to save the session, click **Yes**. Enter a name for the session.

Step 4.   Reconnect the TeraTerm Web session.

Reopen the TeraTerm Web session as described in Task 2, Step 1. This time, when the New Description window opens (see Figure 10-13), click **Cancel**.

Click **File > Open**. Select the saved session, and then click **Open**. Use this technique to reconnect the TeraTerm Web session to a Cisco device without reconfiguring a new session.

Task 3: Reflection

This lab provided information for establishing a console connection to a Cisco router. Cisco switches are accessed in the same way. Remember that you must use the correct serial port configurations to connect to the Cisco device via Minicom.

Task 4: Challenge

Draw the pin connections for the rollover cable and straight-through cable. Compare the differences, and be able to identify the different cable types.

Task 5: Clean Up

Unless directed otherwise by the instructor, turn off power to the host computer and router. Remove the rollover cable.

Remove anything that was brought into the lab, and leave the room ready for the next class.

Packet Tracer Companion: Establishing a Console Session with PT Terminal (10.6.2.2)

You can now open the file LSG01-Lab10622.pka on the CD-ROM that accompanies this book to repeat this hands-on lab using Packet Tracer. However, keep in mind that Packet Tracer is not a substitute for a hands-on lab experience with real equipment. A summary of the instructions is provided within the Packet Tracer activity.

Lab 10-4: Establishing a Console Session with Minicom (10.6.3.1)

Upon completion of this lab, you will be able to do the following:

- Connect a router and computer using a console cable.

- Configure Minicom to establish a console session with the router.

- Perform basic commands.

Background

Minicom is a text-based UNIX terminal emulation program, similar to the Windows HyperTerminal program. Minicom can be used for many purposes, such as controlling a modem or accessing a Cisco router through the serial console connection. The Linux or UNIX operating system is required.

Scenario

Set up a network similar to the one in Figure 10-14. Any router that meets the interface requirements may be used. Possible routers include 800, 1600, 1700, 2500, 2600 routers, or a combination.

Figure 10-14 Topology for Lab 10-4

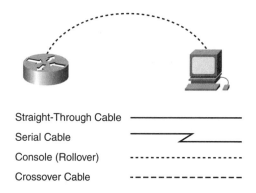

The following resources are required:

- Linux/UNIX computer with a serial interface and Minicom loaded

- Cisco router

- Console (rollover) cable for connecting the workstation to the router

Task 1: Connect a Router and Computer with a Console Cable

Step 1.   Set up the basic physical connection.

Ensure that power is turned off on the computer and Cisco router. Connect the console (rollover) cable to the console port on the router. Connect the other cable end to the PC with a DB-9 or DB-25 adapter to the COM 1 port.

Step 2.   Power on the devices.

Enable power to the computer and router.

Task 2: Configure Minicom to Establish a Console Session with the Router

Step 1.   Start the Minicom application in configuration mode.

Note: To configure Minicom, root access is required. From the Linux command prompt, to start Minicom, enter the **minicom** command with the **–s** option. This starts Minicom in configuration mode:

`[root]# minicom -s <ENTER>`

Step 2.   Configure Minicom for serial communications.

Figure 10-15 shows the main configuration window. To configure the serial port, scroll down the configuration list and select **Serial port setup**. Press **Enter**.

Figure 10-15 Main Configuration Window

Figure 10-16 shows the serial port configuration window. Use the letter by the field to change a setting. Table 10-17 shows the correct values.

Figure 10-16 Serial Port Configuration Window

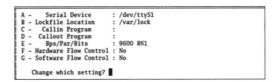

Table 10-17 Serial Port Settings

Option	Field	Value
A	Serial Device	Dev/ttyS0 for COM 1
		/dev/ttyS1 for COM 2
E	Bps/Par/Bits	Bps: 9600
		Par: None
		Bits: 8
		Stop bits: 1 (or, select option Q)
F	Hardware Flow Control	Toggle: No
G	Software Flow Control	Toggle: No

Return to the Configuration menu by pressing **Enter** or **Esc**.

In the window shown in Figure 10-17, select **Save setup as dfl** (default file). When Minicom is restarted, the default values will be reloaded.

Figure 10-17 Serial Port Configuration Window

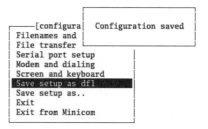

Step 3.   Close Minicom.

When finished, close the Minicom session. Select **Exit from Minicom**.

Step 4.   Restart the Minicom session, as follows:

```
[root]# minicom <ENTER>
```

When the session window starts, press the **Enter** key. There should be a response from the router; this indicates that a connection has been successfully completed. If there is no connection, troubleshoot as necessary. For example, verify that the router has power. Check the connection to the correct COM 1 port on the PC and the console port on the router.

Task 3: Perform Basic Commands

Minicom is a text-based, menu-driven, serial communication utility. Basic commands are not intuitive. For example, users communicate with remote devices within the terminal window. However, to control the utility, use **<Ctrl> A**. To get help, press **<Ctrl> A**, followed by **Z**.

Figure 10-18 shows a list of functions and corresponding keys. To quit Minicom, press **<Ctrl> A**, followed by either **Q** or **X**.

Figure 10-18 Minicom Command Summary Screen

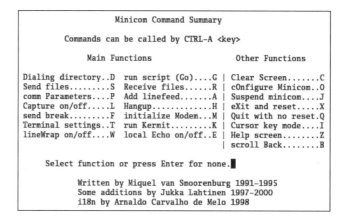

Task 4: Reflection

This lab provided information for establishing a console connection to a Cisco router using Minicom. Cisco switches are accessed in the same fashion.

Task 5: Clean Up

Unless directed otherwise by the instructor, turn off power to the host computer and router. Remove the rollover cable.

Remove anything that was brought into the lab, and leave the room ready for the next class.

Skills and Integration Challenge: Planning and Cabling Networks (10.7.1.3)

You can now open the file LSG01-PTSkills10.pka on the CD-ROM that accompanies this book to repeat this hands-on lab using Packet Tracer. However, keep in mind that Packet Tracer is not a substitute for a hands-on lab experience with real equipment. A summary of the instructions is provided within the activity.

Upon completion of this lab, you will be able to do the following:

- Build the network topology.

- Plan the IP addresses.

- Configure router and PC interfaces.

- Test the network.

Background

Table 10-18 shows the addressing for this lab.

Table 10-18   Addressing Table

Device	Interface	IP Address	Subnet Mask	Default Gateway
R1	Fa0/0	192.168.1.62	255.255.255.192	N/A
	S0/0/0	192.168.1.129	255.255.255.252	N/A
	S0/0/1	192.168.1.133	255.255.255.252	N/A
R2	Fa0/0	192.168.1.110	255.255.255.240	N/A
	Fa0/1	192.168.1.94	255.255.255.224	N/A
	S0/0/0	192.168.1.130	255.255.255.252	N/A
	S0/0/1	192.168.1.137	255.255.255.252	N/A
R3	Fa0/0	192.168.1.126	255.255.255.240	N/A
	S0/0/0	192.168.1.138	255.255.255.252	N/A
	S0/0/1	192.168.1.134	255.255.255.252	N/A
PC1-A	NIC	192.168.1.1	255.255.255.192	192.168.1.62
PC2-A	NIC	192.168.1.97	255.255.255.240	192.168.1.110
PC3-A	NIC	192.168.1.113	255.255.255.240	192.168.1.126
Eagle-Server	NIC	192.168.1.93	255.255.255.224	192.168.1.94

Practice your network building, planning, and configuration skills. Device names and routing have already been configured.

Task 1: Build the Network Topology

Use the following tables and the devices in the device pool to create the topology.

Table 10-19 shows the router information.

Table 10-19 Routers

Hostname	Interface	Connects To	Interfaces
R1	Fa0/0	SW-1	Fa0/1
R1	S0/0/0 (DCE)	R2	S0/0/0
R1	S0/0/1 (DCE)	R3	S0/0/1
R2	Fa0/0	SW-2A	Fa0/1
R2	S0/0/1 (DCE)	R3	S0/0/0
R2	Fa0/1	SW-2B	Fa0/1
R3	Fa0/0	SW-3	Fa0/1

Table 10-20 shows the switch information.

Table 10-20   Switches

Hostname	Interface	Connects To	Interfaces
SW-1	Fa0/2	PC-1A	FastEthernet
SW-2A	Fa0/2	PC-1B	FastEthernet
SW-2B	Fa0/2)	Eagle-Server	FastEthernet
SW-3	Fa0/2	PC-1C	FastEthernet

Task 2: Create and Assign an Addressing Scheme

You are asked to use the 192.168.1.0 /24 address space. Seven total networks are required; assign the networks in decreasing order of number of hosts required for efficient use of address space. Use Table 10-21 and Table 10-22 to create an effective addressing scheme.

Table 10-21   LAN

Hostname	Interface	Number of Hosts
R1	Fa0/0	60
R2	Fa0/0	10
	Fa0/1	30
R3	Fa0/0	7

Table 10-22 WAN

Hostname	Address to be Assigned	Number of Hosts
R1–R3	R1–First host address	2
R1–R3	R1–First host address	2
R2–R3	R2–First host address	2

Use the following rules to assign IP addresses:

- PCs will use the first host address in the subnet; the server will use the second to last host address in its subnet.

- All Fast Ethernet ports on a router will use the last host address of the assigned subnet.

- The R1–R2 link will use the first WAN subnet, the R1–R3 link will use the second WAN subnet, and the R2–R3 link will use the third WAN subnet. R1 and R2 DCE interfaces should have clock rates of 56000.

Task 3: Interface Configuration

Perform interface configuration of the R1, R2, and R3 routers, the PCs, and the server according to the preceding addressing scheme.

Task 4: Testing Connectivity

Make sure all PCs can ping their gateways, other PCs, and the server.

CHAPTER 11

Configuring and Testing Your Network

The Study Guide portion of this chapter uses a combination of matching, fill-in-the-blank, multiple-choice, and open-ended questions to test your knowledge of configuring and testing networks.

The Labs and Activities portion of this chapter includes all the online curriculum activities and labs to ensure you have mastered the practical, hands-on skills you need.

As you work through this chapter, use Chapter 11 in the Network Fundamentals CCNA Exploration online curriculum, or use the corresponding Chapter 11 in the *Network Fundamentals CCNA Exploration Companion Guide*, for assistance.

Study Guide

Configuring Cisco Devices: IOS Basics

Routers and switches need an operating system to function. The operating system on most Cisco devices is the Cisco IOS. It provides a number of network services, such as routing and switching, security, addressing, and quality of service. Understanding these functions and being able to access them is essential for network administrators and technicians.

Concept Questions

1. Describe the different access methods for Cisco devices. Discuss when and why you would use a certain method. What security concerns do you need to consider for the different access methods?

   _____

   _____

   _____

   _____

   _____

   _____

   _____

   _____

   _____

   _____

   _____

   _____

   _____

2. Compare and contrast the two main configuration files on Cisco devices in terms of function, location, and how they relate to each other.

_____

_____

_____

_____

_____

_____

_____

_____

_____

_____

_____

3. Describe the advantage of the hierarchical modal structure.

_____

_____

_____

_____

Vocabulary Exercise: Matching

In Table 11-1, match the device prompt on the left with the correct IOS configuration mode on the right.

Table 11-1   IOS Configuration Modes

Prompt	IOS Configuration Mode
a. Switch>	
b. Router#	
c. Router(config)#	
d. Switch(config-if)#	

Cisco IOS Command Exercises

Answer these questions based on the following command:

`Router#show ip interface brief`

1. What is the name of the command? _____

2. Does this command use arguments or keywords? _____

3. Where do the following commands get the information they display? Name the file if applicable and the storage location of this information. Possible locations are RAM, ROM, NVRAM, and flash.

show version: _____

show startup-config: _____

show running-config: _____

show flash: _____

Test Your Knowledge

Use Table 11-2 to test your knowledge of the command-line interface (CLI) shortcuts and hot keys.

Table 11-2   IOS Command-Line Help

Key	Function
Tab	
Ctrl-R	
Ctrl-Z	
Up arrow	
Down arrow	
Ctrl-D	
Ctrl-C	
Ctrl-Shift-6	
Backspace	
exit	

Applying a Basic Configuration Using Cisco IOS

All networking devices need a basic configuration to be functional. The most important initial configuration parameters include hostnames, passwords, and the IP addresses and descriptions on the interface. Hostnames are important for network documentation and remote access. Passwords establish basic security at the local level, and IP addresses are needed to establish connectivity with other devices on the network. Because configuration files are critical, the network administrator needs to exercise proper file management by saving changes to the configuration and by backing up configuration files.

Concept Questions

1. Explain why the hostname is an extremely important feature for networking devices. Be specific in your answer.

_____

_____

_____

_____

2. Briefly explain the purpose of banners, and explain why they should contain some type of warning message.

_____

_____

_____

_____

_____

3. Network configuration files are extremely important on a production network. There should always be backup copies of files to aid in disaster recovery. Therefore, proper file management is very important. Explain how good management of configuration files can be implemented.

_____

_____

_____

_____

_____

_____

Multiple-Choice Questions

Choose the best possible answer(s) for the following questions dealing with interface configuration network testing.

1. Which of the following interface commands allows you to enter interface configuration mode to configure a router's interface?

   a. Router(config)# **interface 0/1/0**

   b. Router# **interface s0**

   c. Router(config)# **interface s0/1/0**

   d. Router(config)> **interface s0/1/0**

2. Which of the following steps are required to configure an Ethernet interface? (Choose all that apply.)

   a. Enter global configuration mode.

   b. Enter interface configuration mode.

   c. Specify the interface address and subnet mask.

   d. Enable the interface.

3. The output of which of the following commands shows the interface description? (Choose all that apply.)

   a. **show IP interface brief**

   b. **show interfaces**

   c. **show running-configuration**

   d. **show interface description**

4. Why is the ping test also called testing the protocol stack?

   a. Because it tests all the layers of the OSI model.

   b. Because it tests connectivity at Layers 3, 2, and 1 of the OSI model.

   c. Because it uses a protocol stack to perform connectivity testing.

   d. Because the ping test tests all the layers of the TCP/IP model.

Vocabulary Exercise: Completion

Fill in the blanks in the following sentences.

1. Like other hosts, a switch needs a _____ address defined to communicate with hosts outside the local network.

2. One effective way to test network connectivity is to use the _____ command.

3. _____ defines the number of hops that the ping packet has remaining before it will be dropped.

Verifying Connectivity

A network needs full connectivity to converge. Testing network connectivity is a very important task. A network administrator needs to be familiar with the different testing utilities such as ping and traceroute and the different **show** commands. The output provided by the utilities and the **show** commands provides useful information for troubleshooting.

Test Your Knowledge

The ping utility yields useful indicators that can be used for troubleshooting. Describe the following indicators.

Exclamation mark (!): _____

Period (.): _____

_____

The letter U: _____

_____

Concept Question

Explain how the internal IP configuration on the local host can be tested.

_____

_____

_____

Labs and Activities

Lab 11-1: Network Latency Documentation with ping (11.4.3.3)

Upon completion of this lab, you will be able to

- Use the **ping** command to document network latency.

- Compute various statistics on the output of a ping capture.

- Measure delay effects from larger datagrams.

Background

To obtain realistic network latency statistics, this lab must be performed on a live network. Be sure to check with your instructor for any local security restrictions on using the **ping** command on the network.

The destination server computer must return ICMP echo replies; otherwise, delay cannot be computed. Some computers have this feature disabled through a firewall, and some private networks block transit ICMP echo datagrams. For this experiment to be interesting, a sufficiently distant destination should be chosen. Destinations on the same LAN or within a few hops may return an unrepresentative low latency. If you're patient, you can find a suitable destination.

The purpose of this lab is to measure and evaluate network latency over time, and during different periods of the day, to capture a representative sample of typical network activity. You will accomplish this by analyzing the return delay from a distant computer using the **ping** command.

You will perform statistical analysis of throughput delay with the assistance of a spreadsheet application such as Microsoft Excel. You will summarize return delay times, measured in milliseconds, by computing the average latency (mean). You will note the latency value at the center of the ordered range of latency points (median) and identify the most frequently occurring delay (mode).

You will also measure delay when the ICMP datagram size increases.

Scenario

In the topology diagram shown in Figure 11-1, the network cloud represents all the network devices and cabling between the student computer and the destination server computer. Normally these devices are the ones that introduce network latency. Network engineers routinely rely on networks outside of local administration for connectivity to external networks. Monitoring path latency provides some measure of administrative diligence, which may be used in decision-making when evaluating suitable applications for wide-area network (WAN) deployment.

Figure 11-1   Topology for Lab 11-1

This lab requires five days of testing. Three tests will be performed each day. Preferably, one test should be done in the early morning, one around midday, and one in the evening. The idea is to note and document latency differences that occur at different times of the day. When you're done, you will have 15 sets of data.

To understand the delay effects from larger datagrams, you will send and analyze increasingly larger ICMP datagrams.

Task 1: Use the ping Command to Document Network Latency

Step 1. Verify connectivity between the student computer and the destination server computer.

Open a terminal window by choosing **Start > Run**. Enter **cmd**, and then click **OK**. Attempt to ping a suitably distant destination, such as www.yahoo.com, as shown in Example 11-1.

Example 11-1   Ping Test

```
C:\> ping -n 1 www.yahoo.com
Pinging www.yahoo-ht3.akadns.net [209.191.93.52] with 32 bytes of data:
Reply from 209.191.93.52: bytes=32 time=304ms TTL=52
Ping statistics for 209.191.93.5:
Packets: Sent = 1, Received = 1, Lost = 0 (0% loss)
Approximate round trip times in milli-seconds:
Minimum = 304ms, Maximum = 304ms , Average = 304 ms
```

Use the **ping /?** command to answer the following questions:

What is the purpose of the **-n** option and argument **1**?

_____

What option and argument would change the default size to 100 bytes?

_____

Decide on a destination server computer, and write down the name:

_____

Use the **ping** command to verify connectivity with the destination, and write down the results:

Packets sent: _____

Packets received: _____

Packets lost: _____

_____

_____

If packets were lost, use another destination, and retest.

Step 2.   Perform a delay test.

Write down the command that sends 100 echo requests to the destination: _____

Use the **ping** command to send 100 echo requests to your destination. When you're finished, copy the replies into Notepad. Choose **Start > Programs > Accessories > Notepad**. Save the file using the name format *day-sample#*.txt, where *day* is the day the test was performed (1 through 5) and *sample#* is the sample period (1 through 3).

Alternatively, you can redirect output to a file by appending **>day-sample#.txt** to the end of the **ping** command. The command syntax is **ping** [*options*] **>day-sample#.txt**.

Note: The terminal remains blank until the command has finished.

Task 2: Compute Various Statistics on the Output of a ping Capture

Step 1.   Bring the text file into the Microsoft Excel spreadsheet application.

If it isn't already open, start Microsoft Excel. Choose **File > Open**. Click **Browse** to move to the directory that holds the text file. Highlight the filename and click **Open**. To format a text file for use within Excel, ensure that all numeric values are separated from text characters. In the Text Import wizard, Step 1, choose **Fixed Width**. In Step 2, shown in Figure 11-2, follow the instructions to separate numeric values from text values.

Figure 11-2   Excel Text Import Wizard

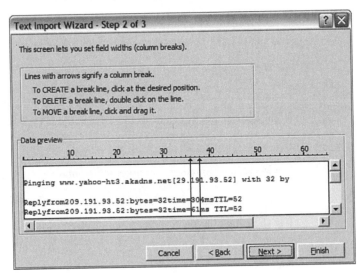

Step 2.   Compute the mean, median, and mode delay values.

When the input formatting is satisfactory, click **Finish**. If the spreadsheet has numbers in different fields, manually fix the numbers. After the spreadsheet has been opened, format the columns so that they are more readable. When you're done, you should have a spreadsheet that looks similar to Figure 11-3.

Figure 11-3 Partial Spreadsheet

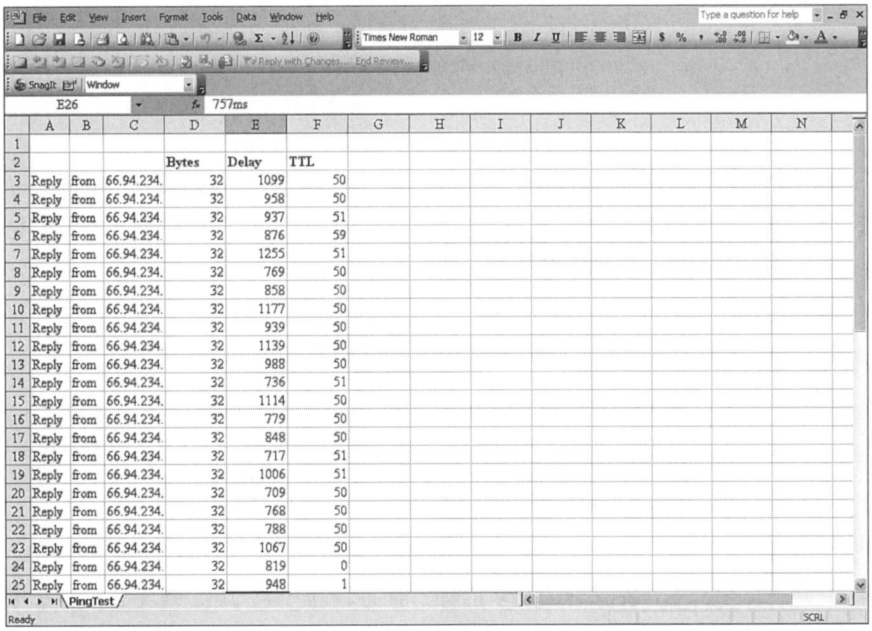

	A	B	C	D	E	F
1						
2				Bytes	Delay	TTL
3	Reply	from	66.94.234.	32	1099	50
4	Reply	from	66.94.234.	32	958	50
5	Reply	from	66.94.234.	32	937	51
6	Reply	from	66.94.234.	32	876	59
7	Reply	from	66.94.234.	32	1255	51
8	Reply	from	66.94.234.	32	769	50
9	Reply	from	66.94.234.	32	858	50
10	Reply	from	66.94.234.	32	1177	50
11	Reply	from	66.94.234.	32	939	50
12	Reply	from	66.94.234.	32	1139	50
13	Reply	from	66.94.234.	32	988	50
14	Reply	from	66.94.234.	32	736	51
15	Reply	from	66.94.234.	32	1114	50
16	Reply	from	66.94.234.	32	779	50
17	Reply	from	66.94.234.	32	848	50
18	Reply	from	66.94.234.	32	717	51
19	Reply	from	66.94.234.	32	1006	51
20	Reply	from	66.94.234.	32	709	50
21	Reply	from	66.94.234.	32	768	50
22	Reply	from	66.94.234.	32	788	50
23	Reply	from	66.94.234.	32	1067	50
24	Reply	from	66.94.234.	32	819	0
25	Reply	from	66.94.234.	32	948	1

Record the number of dropped packets in the column Dropped Packets. Dropped packets have a consistently large delay value.

Finally, the delay values must be ordered (sorted) when computing the median and mode values. You do this by choosing **Data > Sort**. Highlight all the data fields. Figure 11-4 shows a partial spreadsheet highlighted and the Data dialog box opened. If a header row was highlighted, click the Header row radio button. Select the column that contains the Delay values. In Figure 11-4 it is Column G. When you're finished, click **OK**.

Figure 11-4 Ordering on the Delay Column

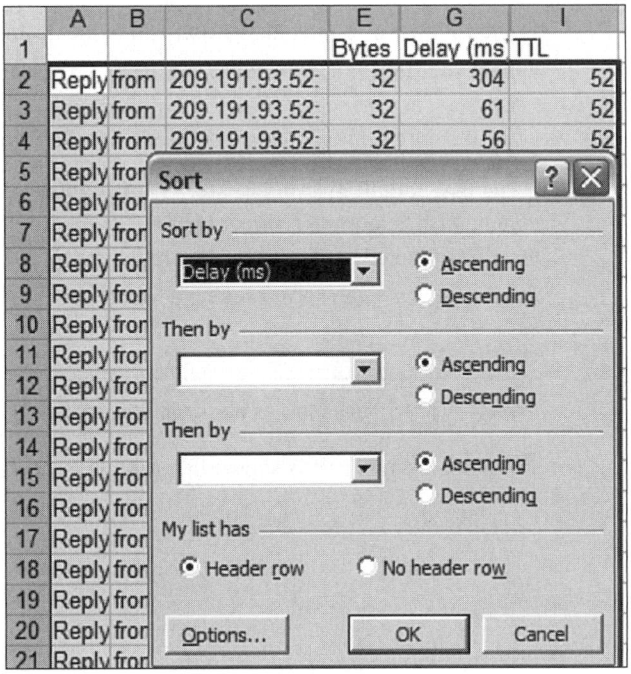

The formula used to compute the mean, or average, delay is the sum of the delays divided by the number of measurements. For this spreadsheet, this would equate to the formula in cell G102: =average(G2:G101). Perform a quick visual inspection to verify that your mean value is approximately the value shown. Record this number in your chart in the Mean column.

The formula used to compute the median delay, or the delay value in the center of the ordered range, is similar to the average formula. For the median value, the formula in cell G103 would be =median(G2:G101). Perform a quick visual inspection to verify that your median value is similar to what is shown midway in the data range. Record this number in your chart in the Median column.

The formula used to compute the modal delay, or the delay value that occurs the most frequently, is also similar. For the mode value, the formula in cell G104 would be =mode(G2:G101). Perform a quick visual inspection to verify that your mode value is the most frequently occurring value in the data range. Record this number in your chart in the Mode column. You may either save or discard the new spreadsheet file, but you should retain the data text file.

Task 3: Measure Delay Effects from Larger Datagrams

To determine if larger datagrams affect delay, you will send increasingly larger ICMP echo requests to the destination. In this analysis, 20 datagrams will be incremented by 100 bytes per ping request. You will create a spreadsheet with the reply results, as well as a chart that plots size versus delay.

Step 1.   Perform a variable-sized delay test.

The easiest way to accomplish this task is to use the Windows built-in **FOR** loop command. The syntax is

```
FOR /L %variable IN (start,step,end) DO command [command-parameters]
```

The set is a sequence of numbers from start to end, by step amount. So (1,1,5) would generate the sequence 1 2 3 4 5, and (5,–1,1) would generate the sequence (5 4 3 2 1).

In the following command, **destination** is the destination. Issue this command:

```
FOR /L %i IN (100,100,2000) DO ping -n 1 -l %i destination
```

Copy the output into Notepad, and save the file using the name variablesizedelay.txt.

To redirect output to a file, use the redirect append operator, **>>**, as shown in the following command. The normal redirect operator, **>**, overwrites the file each time the **ping** command is executed, and only the last reply is saved.

```
FOR /L %i IN (100,100,2000) DO ping -n 1 -l %i destination >> variable-
sizedelay.txt
```

Note: The terminal remains blank until the command has finished.

The output of one line is shown in Example 11-2. All 20 replies are arranged similarly.

Example 11-2   Variable-Size Delay Test

```
C:\> FOR /L %i IN (100,100,2000) DO ping -n 1 -l %i www.yahoo.com
>>variablesizedelay.txt
C:\> ping -n 1 -l 100
Pinging www.yahoo-ht3.akadns.net [209.191.93.52] with 100 bytes of data:
Reply from 209.191.93.52: bytes=100 time=383ms TTL=52
Ping statistics for 209.191.93.52:
Packets: Sent = 1, Received = 1, Lost = 0 (0% loss),
Approximate round trip times in milli-seconds:
Minimum = 383ms, Maximum = 383ms, Average = 383ms
```

Step 2.   Bring the text file into the Excel spreadsheet application.

Open the new text file in Excel, as shown in Figure 11-5.

Figure 11-5   Excel Text Import Wizard

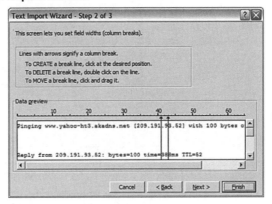

The difference between this file and the previous one is that the variable-size file has much more information than is really needed.

Step 3.   Format the spreadsheet.

Clean up and organize the spreadsheet data into two columns, Bytes and Delay. When you're finished, the spreadsheet should look similar to Figure 11-6.

Step 4.   Create a chart of the data.

Highlight the Delay column data and choose **Insert > Chart**. A number of charts can be used to display delay data. A chart should be clear, but there is room for individual creativity. The chart shown in Figure 11-7 is a stacked line chart.

When you're finished, save your spreadsheet and chart, and submit them to your instructor with the final delay analysis.

Can you make any assumptions about delay when larger datagrams are sent across a network?

Figure 11-6   Formatted Spreadsheet

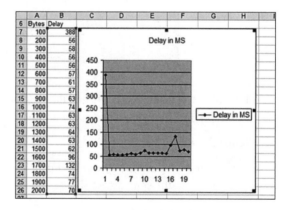

	A	B	C	D	E
6	Bytes	Delay			
7	100	388			
8	200	56			
9	300	58			
10	400	56			
11	500	56			
12	600	57			
13	700	61			
14	800	57			
15	900	63			
16	1000	74			
17	1100	63			
18	1200	63			
19	1300	64			
20	1400	63			
21	1500	62			
22	1600	96			
23	1700	132			
24	1800	74			
25	1900	77			
26	2000	70			

Figure 11-7   Plot of Delay Versus Datagram Size

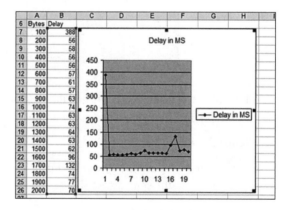

Task 4: Reflection

The **ping** command can provide important network latency information. Careful delay analysis over successive days and at different times of the day can alert the network engineer to changes in network performance. For example, network devices may become overwhelmed during certain times of the day, and network delay spikes. In this case, routine data transfers should be scheduled during off-peak times, when delay is less. Also, many users subscribe to peer-to-peer applications such as Kazaa and Napster. When these file-sharing applications are active, valuable bandwidth is diverted from critical business applications. If delays are caused by events within the organization, network analysis tools can be used to determine the source, and corrective action can be taken. When the source originates from external networks not under the control of the organization, try to work out the problem with the ISP first. If that does not work, subscribing with a different or additional Internet service provider (ISP) may prove beneficial.

Task 5: Challenge

If permitted, download a large file, and perform a separate delay test while the file is downloading. Write a one- or two-paragraph analysis that compares these delay results against a measurement made without the download.

Lab 11-2: Basic Cisco Device Configuration (11.5.1.1)

Learning Objectives

Upon completion of this lab, you will be able to

- Configure Cisco router global configuration settings.
- Configure Cisco router password access.
- Configure Cisco router interfaces.
- Save the router configuration file.
- Configure a Cisco switch.

Background

Figure 11-8 shows the topology for this lab.

Figure 11-8   Topology for Lab 11-2

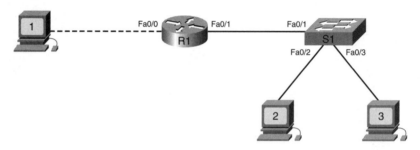

Gather the necessary equipment and cables. To configure the lab, make sure that the equipment listed in Table 11-3 is available.

Table 11-3   Equipment and Hardware Requirements

Hardware	Quantity	Description
Cisco router	1	Part of the CCNA Lab bundle
Cisco switch	1	Part of the CCNA Lab bundle
Computer (host)	3	Lab computer
Console (rollover) cable	3	Connects computer Host1 to the router console port
Crossover cable	1	Connects the computer to the router LAN interface FA0/0
Straight-through cable	3	Connects computer hosts to the switch and the switch to the router

Common configuration tasks include setting the hostname, access passwords, and message-of-the-day (MOTD) banner.

Interface configuration is extremely important. In addition to assigning a Layer 3 IP address, entering a description that describes the destination connection decreases troubleshooting time.

Configuration changes take effect immediately. The changes must be saved in NVRAM to be persistent across reboot. Configuration changes may also be saved offline in a text file for auditing or device replacement.

Cisco IOS switch configuration is similar to Cisco IOS router configuration.

Scenario

In this lab, you will configure common settings on a Cisco router and Cisco switch.

Given an IP address of 198.133.219.0/24, with 4 bits borrowed for subnets, fill in Table 11-4. (Hint: fill in the subnet number and then the host address. Address information is easy to compute with the subnet number filled in first.)

Maximum number of usable subnets (including the 0th subnet): _____

Number of usable hosts per subnet: _____

Table 11-4   Subnet Address Table

IP address:				Subnet mask:
#	Subnet	First host address	Last Host Address	Broadcast
0				
1				
2				
3				
4				
5				
6				
7				
8				
9				
10				
11				
12				
13				
14				
15				

Before proceeding, verify your addresses with the instructor. The instructor will assign subnetworks.

Task 1: Configure Cisco Router Global Configuration Settings

Step 1.   Physically connect the devices.

Figure 11-9 shows the cabling for this lab. Connect the console or rollover cable to the console port on the router. Connect the other end of the cable to the host computer using a DB-9 adapter to the COM 1 port. Connect the crossover cable between the host computer's network interface card (NIC) and Router interface Fa0/0. Connect a straight-through cable between the Router interface Fa0/1 and any of the switch's interfaces (1 through 24).

Ensure that power has been applied to the host computer, switch, and router.

Figure 11-9   Lab Cabling

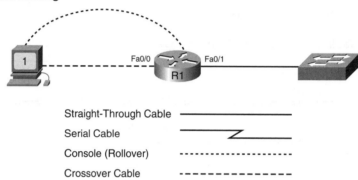

Configure HyperTerminal with the proper settings:

■ Name the connection description: Lab 11_5_1

■ Connect using: COM1 (or an appropriate COM port)

Configure the COM1 properties:

■ Bits per second: 9600

■ Data bits: 8

■ Parity: None

■ Stop bits: 1

■ Flow control: None

When the HyperTerminal session window comes up, press the **Enter** key until the router responds.

If the router terminal is in configuration mode, exit by entering **no**:

```
Would you like to enter the initial configuration dialog? [yes/no]: no

Press RETURN to get started!
Router>
```

In privileged EXEC command mode, the router attempts to translate any misspelled or unrecognized commands as a domain name. Because no domain server is configured, a delay occurs while the request times out. This can take from several seconds to several minutes. To terminate the domain name lookup process, press **Ctrl-Shift-6**, release, and then press **X**.

The following shows a user mistyping a command and the router attempting a domain name lookup:

```
Router>enabel
Translating "enabel"...domain server (255.255.255.255) %
```

Press **Ctrl-Shift-6**, release, and then press **X**. This results in the following:

```
Name lookup aborted
Router>
```

From user EXEC mode, enter privileged EXEC mode:

```
Router> enable
Router#
```

Verify a clean configuration file using the privileged EXEC command **show running-config**. If a configuration file was previously saved, it must be removed. Depending on the router's model and the IOS version, your configuration may look slightly different from a typical default router's configuration. However, it should have no configured passwords or IP addresses. If your router does not have a default configuration, ask the instructor to remove the configuration.

Step 3. Configure global configuration hostname settings.

What two commands may be used to leave privileged EXEC mode? _____

What shortcut command can you use to enter privileged EXEC mode? _____

Examine the different configuration modes that can be entered with the command **configure?**. Write down the list of configuration modes, and describe them:

_____

_____

_____

_____

_____

_____

From privileged EXEC mode, enter global configuration mode:

```
Router# configuration terminal
Router(config)#
```

What three methods may be used to leave global configuration mode and return to privileged EXEC mode?

What shortcut command can be used to enter global configuration mode?

Set the device hostname to Router1:

```
router(config)# hostname Router1
Router1(config)#
```

How can the hostname be removed?

Step 4.   Configure the MOTD banner.

In production networks, banner content may have a significant legal impact on the organization. For example, a court might interpret a friendly "Welcome" message as permission for an attacker to hack into the router. A banner should include information about authorization, penalties for unauthorized access, connection logging, and applicable local laws. The corporate security policy should cover all banner messages.

Create a suitable MOTD banner. Only system administrators of the ABC Company are authorized users. Unauthorized access will be prosecuted, and all connection information will be logged.

For example, suppose you are connected to an ABC network device. Access is granted to only current ABC system administrators with prior written approval. Unauthorized access is prohibited and will be prosecuted. All connections are continuously logged.

```
Router1(config)# banner ?
```

Examine the different banner modes that can be entered. Write down the list of banner modes, and describe them.

Choose a terminating character that will not be used in the message text, such as % (percent).

Configure the MOTD banner. The MOTD banner is displayed on all connections before the login prompt. Use the terminating character on a blank line to end the MOTD entry, as shown in Example 11-3.

Example 11-3   banner motd Output

```
Router1(config)# banner motd %
Enter TEXT message.  End with the character %'
***You are connected to an ABC network device. Access is granted to only
current
  ABC company system administrators with prior written approval. ***

*** Unauthorized access is prohibited, and will be prosecuted.

*** All connections are continuously logged. ***
%
Router1(config)#
```

What is the global configuration command to remove the MOTD banner?

_____

_____

_____

_____

_____

_____

_____

_____

_____

_____

Task 2: Configure Cisco Router Password Access

Access passwords are set for privileged EXEC mode and the user entry point such as console, aux, and virtual lines. The privileged EXEC mode password is the most critical password, because it controls access to configuration mode.

Step 1.   Configure the privileged EXEC password.

Cisco IOS supports two commands that set access to privileged EXEC mode. One command, **enable password**, contains no encryption or weak cryptography and should never be used if the **enable secret** command is available. The **enable secret** command uses a very secure MD5 cryptographic hash algorithm. Cisco says "As far as anyone at Cisco knows, it is impossible to recover an enable secret based on the contents of a configuration file (other than by obvious dictionary attacks)." Password security relies on the password algorithm and the password. In production environments, strong passwords should be used at all times. A strong password consists of at least nine characters of uppercase and lower-case letters, numbers, and symbols. In a lab environment, we will use weak passwords.

Set the privileged EXEC password to **class**:

```
Router1(config)# enable secret class
Router1(config)#
```

Step 2.   Configure the console password.

Set the console access password to **cisco**. The console password controls console access to the router.

```
Router1(config)# line console 0
Router1(config-line)# password cisco
Router1(config-line)# login
```

What is the command to remove the console password? _____

Step 3.   Configure the virtual line password.

Set the virtual line access password to **cisco**. The virtual line password controls Telnet access to the router. In early Cisco IOS versions, only five virtual lines could be set—0 through 4. In newer Cisco IOS versions, the number has been expanded. Unless a Telnet password is set, access on that virtual line is blocked.

```
Router1(config-line)# line vty 0 4
Router1(config-line)# password cisco
Router1(config-line)# login
```

There are three ways to exit line configuration mode. Fill in Table 11-5 with the correct answers.

Table 11-5   Ways to Exit Line Configuration Mode

Command	Effect
exit	
end	
Ctrl-Z	

Issue the command **exit**. What is the router prompt? What is the mode?

```
Router1(config-line)# exit
```

_____

_____

Issue the command **end**. What is the router prompt? What is the mode?

_____

Task 3: Configure Cisco Router Interfaces

All cabled interfaces should contain documentation about the connection. On newer Cisco IOS versions, the maximum description length is 240 characters.

Figure 11-10 shows a network topology in which a host computer is connected to Router 1, interface Fa0/0.

Figure 11-10 Network Topology

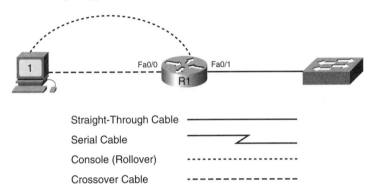

Straight-Through Cable

Serial Cable

Console (Rollover)

Crossover Cable

Write down your subnet number and mask: _____

_____

The first IP address will be used to configure the host computer LAN. Write down the first IP address:

_____

The last IP address will be used to configure the router fa0/0 interface. Write down the last IP address:

_____

Step 1.   Configure the router interface Fa0/0.

Write a short description for the connections on Router1:

Fa0/0 ->

_____

Apply the description on the router interface with the interface configuration command **description**, as shown in Example 11-4.

Example 11-4   Interface Configuration

```
Router1(config)# interface fa0/0
Router1(config-if)# description Connection to Host1 with crossover cable
Router1(config-if)# ip address address mask
Router1(config-if)# no shutdown
Router1(config-if)# end
Router1#
```

Look for the interface to become active:

```
*Mar 24 19:58:59.602: %LINEPROTO-5-UPDOWN: Line protocol on Interface
    FastEthernet0/0, changed state to up
```

Step 2.   Configure the router interface Fa0/1.

Write a short description for the connections on Router1:

Fa0/1 ->

Apply the description on the router interface with the interface configuration command **description**, as shown in Example 11-5.

Example 11-5   Interface Configuration

```
Router1(config)# interface fa0/1
Router1(config-if)# description Connection to switch with straight-
through cable
Router1(config-if)# ip address address mask
Router1(config-if)# no shutdown
Router1(config-if)# end
Router1#
```

Look for the interface to become active:

```
*Mar 24 19:58:59.602: %LINEPROTO-5-UPDOWN: Line protocol on Interface
    FastEthernet0/1, changed state to up
```

Step 3. Configure the host computer.

Configure the host computer for LAN connectivity. Recall that you access the LAN configuration window by choosing **Start > Control Panel > Network Connections**. Right-click the **LAN** icon, and choose **Properties**. Highlight the Internet Protocol field, and choose **Properties**. Fill in the following fields:

- IP Address: The first host address

- Subnet Mask: The subnet mask

- Default Gateway: The router's IP address

Click **OK**, and then click **Close**. Open a Windows command window, and verify network settings with the **ipconfig** command.

Step 4. Verify network connectivity.

Use the **ping** command to verify network connectivity with the router. If ping replies are not successful, troubleshoot the connection.

What Cisco IOS command can you use to verify the interface status?

_____

What Windows command can you use to verify host computer configuration? _____

What is the correct LAN cable between Host1 and Router1? _____

Task 4: Save the Router Configuration Files

Cisco IOS calls RAM configuration storage the running configuration, and it calls nonvolatile RAM (NVRAM) configuration storage the startup configuration. For configurations to survive rebooting or power restarts, the RAM configuration must be copied into NVRAM. This does not occur automatically. NVRAM must be manually updated after any changes are made.

Step 1.   Compare router RAM and NVRAM configurations.

Use the Cisco IOS **show** command to view RAM and NVRAM configurations. The configuration is displayed one screen at a time. A line containing — **more** — indicates that there is additional information to display. Table 11-6 describes acceptable key responses.

Table 11-6   Key Responses

Key	Description
Spacebar	Displays the next page
Enter	Displays the next line
Q	Quits
Ctrl-C	Quits

Write down one possible shortcut command that displays the contents of NVRAM:

_____

Use this command to show the contents of NVRAM. If the output of NVRAM is missing, it is because there is no saved configuration, as shown in Example 11-6.

Example 11-6   Missing NVRAM

```
Router1# show startup-config
startup-config is not present
Router1#
Display the contents of RAM.
Router1# show running-config
```

Use the output to answer the following questions:

How large is the configuration file?

_____

_____

What is the enable secret password?

_____

_____

_____

_____

_____

_____

_____

- Does your MOTD banner contain the information you entered earlier? _____

- Do your interface descriptions contain the information you entered earlier? _____

- Write down one possible shortcut command that will display the contents of RAM.

  _____

Step 2.   Save the RAM configuration to NVRAM.

> For a configuration to be used the next time the router is powered on or reloaded, it must be manually saved in NVRAM. Save the RAM configuration to NVRAM, as shown in Example 11-7.
>
> **Example 11-7   Saving the RAM Configuration**

```
Router1# copy running-config startup-config
Destination filename [startup-config]? <ENTER>
Building configuration...
[OK]
Router1#
```

Write down one possible shortcut command that will copy the RAM configuration to NVRAM.

_____

Review the contents of NVRAM, and verify that the configuration is the same as the configuration in RAM.

The contents should be the same.

Task 5: Configure a Cisco Switch

Cisco IOS switch configuration is similar to configuring a Cisco IOS router. The benefit of learning IOS commands is that they are similar to many different devices and IOS versions.

Step 1.   Connect the host to the switch.

Move the console, or rollover, cable to the console port on the switch. Ensure that power has been applied to the switch. In HyperTerminal, press **Enter** until the switch responds.

Step 2.   Configure the global configuration hostname setting.

Depending on the switch model and IOS version, your configuration may look slightly different from the typical default switch configuration. However, there should be no configured passwords. If your switch does not have a default configuration, ask the instructor to remove the configuration.

From user EXEC mode, enter global configuration mode:

```
Switch> en
Switch# config t
```

```
Switch(config)#
```

Set the device hostname to Switch1:

```
Switch(config)# hostname Switch1
Switch1(config)#
```

Step 3.   Configure the MOTD banner.

Create a suitable MOTD banner. Only system administrators of the ABC company are authorized users. Unauthorized access will be prosecuted, and all connection information will be logged.

Configure the MOTD banner:

```
Switch1(config)# banner motd %
```

The MOTD banner is displayed on all connections before the login prompt. Use the terminating character on a blank line to end the MOTD entry. For assistance, review the similar step for configuring a switch MOTD banner.

```
Switch1(config)# banner motd %
You are connected to an ABC network device. Access is granted to only
current ABC system administrators with prior written approval.

Unauthorized access is prohibited, and will be prosecuted.

All connections are continuously logged.%
```

Step 4.   Configure the privileged EXEC password.

Set the privileged EXEC password to **cisco**:

```
Switch1(config)# enable secret cisco
Switch1(config)#
```

Step 5.   Configure the console password.

Set the console access password to **class**:

```
Switch1(config)# line console 0
Switch1(config-line)# password class
Switch1(config-line)# login
```

Step 6.   Configure the virtual line password.

Set the virtual line access password to **class**. Sixteen virtual lines can be configured on a Cisco IOS switch, 0 through 15:

```
Switch1(config-line)# line vty 0 15
Switch1(config-line)# password class
Switch1(config-line)# login
```

Step 7.   Configure the interface description.

Figure 11-11 shows a network topology in which Router1 is connected to Switch1, interface Fa0/1. Switch1 interface Fa0/2 is connected to host computer 2, and interface Fa0/3 is connected to host computer 3.

Figure 11-11 Network Topology

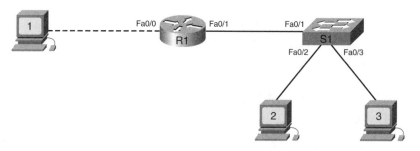

In Table 11-7, write a short description for the connections on Switch1.

Table 11-7   Interface Description

Switch1 Interface	Description
Fa0/1	
Fa0/2	
Fa0/3	

Apply the descriptions on the switch interface using the interface configuration command **description**, as shown in Example 11-8.

Example 11-8   Interface Description

```
Switch1(config)# interface fa0/1
Switch1(config-if)# description Connection to Router1
Switch1(config)# interface fa0/2
Switch1(config-if)# description Connection to host computer 2
Switch1(config)# interface fa0/3
Switch1(config-if)# description Connection to host computer 3
Switch1(config-if)# end
Switch1#
```

Step 8. Save the RAM configuration to NVRAM.

For a configuration to be used the next time the switch is powered on or reloaded, it must be manually saved in NVRAM. Save the RAM configuration to NVRAM as shown in Example 11-9.

Example 11-9   Saving the Configuration

```
Switch1# copy run start
Destination filename [startup-config]? <ENTER>
Building configuration...
[OK]
Switch1#
```

Review the contents of NVRAM, and verify that the configuration is the same as the configuration in RAM.

The contents should be the same.

Task 6: Reflection

The more you practice the commands, the faster you will become at configuring a Cisco IOS router and switch. It is perfectly acceptable to use notes at first to help configure a device, but an experienced network engineer does not need a cheat sheet to perform common configuration tasks. Table 11-8 lists the commands covered in this lab.

Table 11-8 Commands Covered in This Lab

Action	Command
Enter global configuration mode.	**configure terminal**
	Example:
	Router> **enable**
	Router# **configure terminal**
	Router(config)#
Specify the router's name.	**hostname** *name*
	Example:
	Router(config)# **hostname Router1**
	Router1(config)#
Specify an encrypted password to prevent unauthorized access to privileged EXEC mode.	**enable secret** *password*
	Example:
	Router(config)# **enable secret cisco**
	Router(config)#
Specify a password to prevent unauthorized access to the console.	**password** *password*
	login
	Example:
	Router(config)# **line con 0**
	Router(config-line)# **password class**
	Router(config-line)# **login**
	Router(config-line)#
	Specify a password to prevent unauthorized Telnet access.
Router vty lines: 0 4	**password** *password*
	login
	Example:
	Router(config)# **line vty 0 4**
	Router(config-line)# **password class**
	Router(config-line)# **login**
	Router(config-line)#

continues

Table 11-8   Commands Covered in This Lab   *continued*

Action	Command
Configure the MOTD banner.	**banner motd %**
	Example:
	Router(config)# **banner motd % banner text %**
	Router(config)#
	Configure an interface.
	Router: Interface is off by default
Switch: Interface is on by default	**interface type/port**
	Example:
	Router(config)# **interface fa0/0**
	Router(config-if)# **description** *description*
	Router(config-if)# **ip address** *address mask*
	Router(config-if)# **no shutdown**
	Router(config-if)#
Save the configuration to NVRAM.	**copy running-config startup-config**
	Example:
	Router# **copy running-config startup-config**
	Router#

Task 7: Challenge

It is often necessary, and always handy, to save the configuration file to an offline text file. One way to do so is to choose **Transfer > Capture Text** from HyperTerminal, as shown in Figure 11-12.

Figure 11-12 HyperTerminal Capture Menu

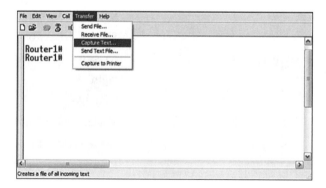

All communication between the host computer and router is saved to a file. The file can be edited and saved. It also can be copied and pasted into a router.

Step 1.   To start a capture, from HyperTerminal choose **Transfer > Capture Text**. Enter a path and filename, and click **Start**.

Step 2. Issue the privileged EXEC command **show running-config**, and press **Spacebar** until all the configuration has been displayed.

Step 3. Stop the capture. Choose **Transfer > Capture Text > Stop**.

Step 4. Open the text file and review the contents. Remove any lines that are not configuration commands, such as the — **more** — prompt. Manually correct any lines that were scrambled or places where several lines occupy the same line. After checking the configuration file, highlight the lines and choose **Edit > Copy** from Notepad. This places the configuration in host computer memory.

To load the configuration file, it is *always* a best practice to begin with a clean RAM configuration. Otherwise, stale configuration commands may survive a paste action and have unintended consequences.

Erase the NVRAM configuration file:

```
Router1# erase start
Erasing the nvram filesystem will remove all configuration files! Continue?
  [confirm] <ENTER>
[OK]
Erase of nvram: complete
```

Reload the router:

```
Router1# reload
Proceed with reload? [confirm] <ENTER>
```

When the router reboots, enter global configuration mode:

```
Router> en
Router# config t
Router(config)#
```

Right-click inside the HyperTerminal window and choose **Paste To Host**. The configuration is quickly loaded to the router. Watch closely for error messages. Each message must be investigated and corrected. After the reload is complete, manually enable the interfaces by issuing the **no shutdown** command in interface configuration mode.

Verify the configuration, and save to NVRAM.

Task 8: Clean Up

Before turning off power to the router and switch, remove the NVRAM configuration file from each device using the privileged EXEC command **erase startup-config**.

Delete any configuration files saved on the host computers.

Unless directed otherwise by the instructor, restore host computer network connectivity, and then turn off power to the host computers. Remove anything that was brought into the lab, and leave the room ready for the next class.

Packet Tracer Companion: Basic Cisco Device Configuration (11.5.1.2)

You can now open the file LSG1-Lab11512.pka on the CD-ROM that accompanies this book to repeat this hands-on lab using Packet Tracer. Remember, however, that Packet Tracer is not a substitute for a hands-on lab experience with real equipment. A summary of the instructions is provided within the activity.

Lab 11-3: Managing Device Configuration (11.5.2.1)

Upon completion of this lab, you will be able to

- Configure network connectivity.

- Use TFTP to save and restore a Cisco IOS configuration.

Background

Figure 11-13 shows the topology for this lab.

Figure 11-13 Topology for Lab 11-3

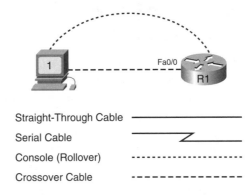

Table 11-9 lists the lab equipment and hardware requirements for this lab.

Table 11-9   Lab Equipment and Hardware Requirements

Hardware	Quantity	Description
Cisco router	1	Part of the CCNA Lab bundle
Computer (host)	1	Lab computer
Console (rollover) cable	1	Connects computer Host1 to the router console port
Crossover cable	1	Connects the Host1 NIC to Router1 Fa0/0

The host computer will be used as a TFTP server. This lab requires the use of SolarWinds TFTP server software. SolarWinds is a free TFTP application for Windows.

You may download a free copy of the SolarWinds TFTP server software from www.solarwinds.com/products/freetools/free_tftp_server.aspx or from any freeware or shareware website.

Scenario

In this lab, you will configure common settings on a Cisco router, save the configuration to a TFTP server, and then restore the configuration from a TFTP server.

You are given an IP address of 10.250.250.0/24 and additional 6 bits for subnets. Use the *last* valid subnet. Host1 should use the *first* valid host address, and Router1 should use the *last* valid host address.

Use Table 11-10 to record your addressing.

Table 11-10   IP Addressing

IP address: 10.250.250.0   Subnet mask: _____

Subnet	First Host Address	Last Host Address	Broadcast

Task 1: Configure Network Connectivity

Step 1.   Physically connect the devices.

Refer to Figure 11-13. Connect the console, or rollover, cable to the console port on the router. Connect the other cable end to the host computer with a DB-9 adapter to the COM 1 port. Ensure that power has been applied to both the host computer and the router.

Step 2.   Logically connect the devices.

Using the IP address information from the scenario, configure the Host1 computer with an IP address, subnet mask, and default gateway.

Step 3.   Connect the host computer to the router through HyperTerminal.

From the Widows taskbar, start the HyperTerminal program by choosing **Start > Programs > Accessories > Communications > HyperTerminal**.

When the HyperTerminal session window opens, press the **Enter** key until the router responds.

Step 4.   Configure Router1.

The configuration tasks for Router1 are as follows:

- Specify the router name: Router1

- Specify an encrypted privileged EXEC password: cisco

- Specify a console access password: class

- Specify a Telnet access password: class

- Configure the MOTD banner.

- Configure the Router1 interface Fa0/0:

    - Set the description.

    - Set the Layer 3 address.

    - Issue the **no shutdown** command.

Caution: Do not save the configuration in NVRAM. In this lab you practice transferring a configuration file to a router that does not have a configuration file in NVRAM.

Step 5.   Verify connectivity.

Verify connectivity between Host1 and Router1, as shown in Example 11-10.

Example 11-10 Verify Connectivity

```
Router1# ping 10.250.250.249
Type escape sequence to abort.
Sending 5, 100-byte ICMP Echos to 10.250.250.249, timeout is 2 seconds:
.!!!!
Success rate is 80 percent (4/5), round-trip min/avg/max = 1/1/1 ms
Router1#
```

Task 2: Use TFTP to Save and Restore a Cisco IOS Configuration

Step 1.   Install the SolarWinds TFTP application.

Double-click the SolarWinds TFTP application to begin the installation. Click **Next**. Agree to the license agreement, and accept the default settings. After SolarWinds has finished the installation, click **Finish**.

Step 2.   Start the TFTP server.

Figure 11-14 shows an active TFTP server window.

Figure 11-14 TFTP Server Window

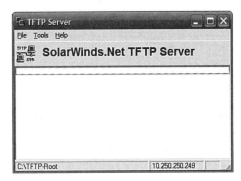

Start the TFTP server by choosing **Start > Programs > SolarWinds Free Tools > TFTP Server**.

Step 3.   Configure the TFTP server.

To configure the TFTP server, as shown in Figure 11-15, choose **File > Configure**. Verify the settings, as shown in Table 11-11.

Figure 11-15 Active TFTP Server Window

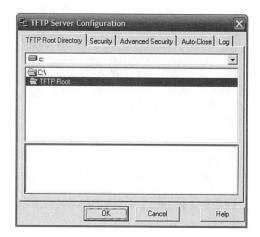

Table 11-11   TFTP Server Settings

Setting	Value
TFTP Root Directory	TFTP-Root
Security	Transmit and Receive Files
Advanced Security	10.250.250.250 To 10.250.250.250
Auto-Close	Never
Log	Enable Log Requests to the Following File. Leave the default file.

When you're finished, click **OK**.

Step 4.   Save the Router1 configuration to the TFTP server.

From HyperTerminal, begin a TFTP upload to the TFTP server, as shown in Example 11-11.

Example 11-11   Saving the Router Configuration to the TFTP Server

```
Router1#copy running-config tftp:
Address or name of remote host []? 10.250.250.249
Destination filename [router1-confg]? <ENTER>
!!
1081 bytes copied in 2.008 secs (538 bytes/sec)
Router1#
```

Verify a successful upload transfer. Open Log file c:\Program Files\SolarWinds\Free Tools\TFTP-Server.txt. The contents should be similar to the following:

3/25/2007 12:29 :Receiving router1-confg from (10.250.250.250)

3/25/2007 12:29 :Received router1-confg from (10.250.250.250), 1081 bytes

Verify the transferred file. Use Microsoft Word or WordPad to examine the contents of the file c:\TFTP-Root\router1-confg. The contents should be similar to the configuration shown in Example 11-12.

Example 11-12 Configuration File

```
!
version 12.4
service timestamps debug datetime msec
service timestamps log datetime msec
no service password-encryption
!
hostname Router1
!
boot-start-marker
boot-end-marker
!
enable secret 5 $1$D02B$AuX05n0HPT239yYRoQ0oE.
!
no aaa new-model
ip cef
!
interface FastEthernet0/0
 description connection to host1
 ip address 10.250.250.250 255.255.255.252
 duplex auto
 speed auto
!
interface FastEthernet0/1
 no ip address
 shutdown
 duplex auto
 speed auto
!
interface Serial0/1/0
 no ip address
 shutdown
 no fair-queue
!
interface Serial0/1/1
 no ip address
 shutdown
 clock rate 2000000
!
ip http server
no ip http secure-server
!
control-plane
!
banner motd
*** ABC COMPANY NETWORK DEVICE ****
*** Authorized access only *****
*** Logging is enabled ****
```

Example 11-12 Configuration File   *continued*

```
!
line con 0
 password class
 login
line aux 0
line vty 0 4
 password class
 login
!
scheduler allocate 20000 1000
End
```

Step 5.   Restore the Router1 configuration from the TFTP server.

Verify that NVRAM is clear, and then reboot Router1, as shown in Example 11-13.

Example 11-13 Verify Empty NVRAM

```
Router1# show startup-config
 startup-config is not present
Router1# reload
Proceed with reload? [confirm] <ENTER>
```

Connectivity must be established with the TFTP server. Router1 fa0/0 must be configured with an IP address, and the interface must be enabled, as shown in Example 11-14.

Example 11-14 Interface Configuration

```
Router> enable
Router# conf t
Enter configuration commands, one per line.  End with CNTL/Z.
Router(config)# interface fa0/0
Router(config-if)# ip address 10.250.250.250 255.255.255.252
Router(config-if)# no shutdown
Router(config-if)# exit

*Mar 25 16:43:03.095: %SYS-5-CONFIG_I: Configured from console by con-
sole
*Mar 25 16:43:04.967: %LINEPROTO-5-UPDOWN: Line protocol on Interface
  FastEthernet0/0, changed state to up
```

Configure the hostname of the router to TEST, as shown in Example 11-15.

Example 11-15 Hostname Configuration

```
Router(config-if)# exit
Router(config)# hostname TEST
Test(config-if)# end
TEST#
```

Verify connectivity using the **ping** command, as shown in Example 11-16.

Example 11-16 Ping Test

```
Test# ping 10.250.250.249
Type escape sequence to abort.
Sending 5, 100-byte ICMP Echos to 10.250.250.249, timeout is 2 seconds:
.!!!!
Success rate is 80 percent(4/5), round-trip min/avg/max = 1/1/1ms
Router#
```

Download the Router1 configuration file from the TFTP server, as shown in Example 11-17.

Example 11-17 File Transfer from the TFTP Server

```
Test# copy tftp startup-config
Address or name of remote host []? 10.250.250.249
Source filename []? router1-confg
Destination filename [startup-config]? <ENTER>
Accessing tftp://10.250.250.249/router1-confg...
Loading router1-confg from 10.250.250.249 (via FastEthernet0/0): !
[OK - 1081 bytes]

1081 bytes copied in 9.364 secs (115 bytes/sec)
Router1#
*Mar 25 16:55:26.375: %SYS-5-CONFIG_I: Configured from
  tftp://10.250.250.249/router1-confg by console
Router1#
```

View the configuration in NVRAM to verify an accurate transfer. The configuration should be the same as what was configured in Task 1, Step 4.

Reload the router. Select no at the prompt that says "Configuration has been modified."

The previous configuration should be restored, and the router's hostname should now be Router1.

Task 3: Reflection

TFTP is a fast, efficient way to save and load Cisco IOS configuration files.

Task 4: Challenge

Similar to uploading a configuration file, the IOS can also be stored offline for future use. To discover the IOS filename, issue the Cisco IOS command **show version**. The filename is highlighted in Example 11-18.

Example 11-18 IOS Filename in Flash

```
Router1# show version
Cisco IOS Software, 1841 Software (C1841-ADVIPSERVICESK9-M), Version
12.4(10b),
RELEASE SOFTWARE (fc3)
Technical Support: http://www.cisco.com/techsupport
Copyright (c) 1986-2007 by Cisco Systems, Inc.
Compiled Fri 19-Jan-07 15:15 by prod_rel_team
```

Example 11-18 IOS Filename in Flash *continued*

```
ROM: System Bootstrap, Version 12.4(13r)T, RELEASE SOFTWARE (fc1)


Router1 uptime is 17 minutes
System returned to ROM by reload at 16:47:54 UTC Sun Mar 25 2007
System image file is "flash:c1841-advipservicesk9-mz.124-10b.bin"


This product contains cryptographic features and is subject to United
States and local country laws governing import, export, transfer and
use. Delivery of Cisco cryptographic products does not imply third-party
authority to import, export, distribute or use encryption. Importers,
exporters, distributors and users are responsible for compliance with
U.S. and local country laws. By using this product you agree to comply
with applicable laws and regulations. If you are unable to comply with
U.S. and local laws, return this product immediately.
A summary of U.S. laws governing Cisco cryptographic products may be
found at:
http://www.cisco.com/wwl/export/crypto/tool/stqrg.html
If you require further assistance, contact Cisco by sending email to
  export@cisco.com.
Cisco 1841 (revision 6.0) with 174080K/22528K bytes of memory.
Processor board ID FHK110918KJ
2 Serial(sync/async) interfaces
DRAM configuration is 64 bits wide with parity disabled.
191K bytes of NVRAM.
62720K bytes of ATA CompactFlash (Read/Write)


Configuration register is 0x2102


Router1#
```

The commands to upload the IOS are similar to uploading the configuration file, as shown in Example 11-19.

Example 11-19 File Transfer to TFTP Server

```
Router1# copy flash tftp
Source filename []? c1841-advipservicesk9-mz.124-10b.bin
Address or name of remote host []? 10.250.250.249
Destination filename [c1841-advipservicesk9-mz.124-10b.bin]?
!!!!!!!!!!!!!!!!!!!!!!!!!!!!!!!!!!!!!!!!!!!!!!!!!!!!!!!!!!!!!!!!!!!!!!!!!!!!!!!!!!
!!!!!
22063220 bytes copied in 59.564 secs (370412 bytes/sec)
Router1#
```

Task 5: Clean Up

Before turning off power to the router, remove the NVRAM configuration file if it was loaded. Use the privileged EXEC command **erase startup-config**.

Delete any configuration files saved on the host computers.

Unless directed otherwise by the instructor, restore host computer network connectivity, and then turn off power to the host computers. Remove the SolarWinds TFTP server from the host computer. Choose **Start > Control Panel**. Click **Add or Remove Applications**. Choose **SolarWinds** and click **Remove**. Accept the defaults.

Remove anything that was brought into the lab, and leave the room ready for the next class.

Packet Tracer Companion: Managing Device Configuration (11.5.2.2)

You can now open the file LSG1-Lab11522.pka on the CD-ROM that accompanies this book to repeat this hands-on lab using Packet Tracer. Remember, however, that Packet Tracer is not a substitute for a hands-on lab experience with real equipment. A summary of the instructions is provided within the activity.

Lab 11-4: Configure Host Computers for IP Networking (11.5.3.1)

Upon completion of this lab, you will be able to

- Design the logical lab topology.

- Configure the physical lab topology.

- Configure the logical LAN topology.

- Verify LAN connectivity.

Background

Figure 11-16 shows the topology diagram for this lab.

Figure 11-16 Topology for Lab 11-4

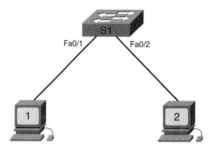

Gather the necessary equipment and cables. Table 11-12 lists the lab equipment and hardware requirements.

Table 11-12 Lab Equipment and Hardware Requirements

Hardware	Quantity	Description
Cisco router	1	Part of the CCNA Lab bundle
Cisco switch	1	Part of the CCNA Lab bundle
Computer (host)	2	Lab computer
Category 5 or better straight-through UTP cables	2	Connects computers Host1 and Host2 to Switch1

Scenario

In this lab you will create a small network that requires connecting network devices and configuring host computers for basic network connectivity.

Task 1: Design the Logical Lab Topology

Given an IP address of 192.168.254.0/24, and 5 bits used for subnets, fill in the following information:

Maximum number of usable subnets (including the 0th subnet): _____

Number of usable hosts per subnet: _____

Use Table 11-13 to record the addressing scheme.

Table 11-13   Addressing Table

IP address: 192.168.254.0		Subnet mask: _____	
Subnet	**First Host Address**	**Last Host Address**	**Broadcast**

continues

Table 11-13   Addressing Table   *continued*

IP address: 192.168.254.0		Subnet mask: _____	
Subnet	**First Host Address**	**Last Host Address**	**Broadcast**

Before proceeding, verify your addresses with the instructor. The instructor will assign one subnetwork per student or team.

Task 2: Configure the Physical Lab Topology

Step 1.   Physically connect the devices.

Cable the network devices as shown earlier in Figure 11-16.

Is a crossover cable needed to connect host computers to the switch? Why or why not?

_____

_____

If it's not already enabled, turn on power to all devices.

Step 2.   Visually inspect network connections.

After cabling the network devices, take a moment to verify the connections. Attention to detail now will minimize the time required to troubleshoot network connectivity issues later.

Task 3: Configure the Logical Topology

Step 1.   Document logical network settings.

Host computers will use the first two IP addresses in the subnetwork. Write down the IP address information for each device in Table 11-14.

Table 11-14   Logical Topology

Device	Subnetwork	IP Address	Mask
Host1			
Host2			

From the information given in Table 11-15, write down the IP network addressing for each computer.

Table 11-15   Host Addressing Table

Host1	
IP address	
IP mask	
Host2	
IP address	
IP mask	

Step 2.   Configure the Host1 computer.

On Computer1, choose **Start > Control Panel > Network Connections**. Right-click the **LAN** icon, and choose **Properties**. On the **General** tab, choose **Internet Protocol (TCP/IP)**, and then click the **Properties** button.

Refer to Figure 11-17 for Host1 IP address and gateway settings.

Figure 11-17 Host IP Address and Gateway Settings

When you're finished, click **OK**, and then click **Close**. The computer may require a reboot for changes to be effective.

Verify proper configuration of Host1 with the **ipconfig /all** command.

Record the output in Table 11-16.

Table 11-16   ipconfig Output

Setting	Value
Ethernet device	
Physical address	
IP address	
Subnet mask	
Default gateway	

Step 3.   Configure Host2.

Repeat Step 2 for Host2 using IP address information from Table 11-15, which you filled out in Step 1.

Verify proper configuration.

Record the output in Table 11-17.

Table 11-17   Host ipconfig Output

Setting	Value
Ethernet device	
Physical address	
IP address	
Subnet mask	
Default gateway	

Task 4: Verify Network Connectivity

Network connectivity can be verified with the Windows **ping** command.

Use Table 11-18 to methodically verify connectivity with each network device.

Table 11-18   Ping Results

From	To	IP Address	Ping Result
Host1	Host2		
Host2	Host1		

Take corrective action to establish connectivity if a test fails.

Note: If pings to host computers fail, temporarily disable the computer firewall, and retest. To disable a Windows firewall, choose **Start > Control Panel > Windows Firewall**, click **Off**, and then click **OK**.

Task 5: Reflection

Review any physical or logical configuration problems encountered during this lab. Make sure you have a thorough understanding of the procedures used to configure a Windows host computer.

Task 6: Challenge

Ask your instructor or another student to introduce one or two problems in your network when you aren't looking or are out of the lab room. Problems can be either physical (the wrong UTP cable) or logical (the wrong IP address). To fix the problems, perform a good visual inspection. Look for green link lights on Switch1.

Use Table 11-18 to identify failed connectivity. List the problems.

_____

_____

_____

_____

Write down your proposed solution(s).

_____

_____

_____

Test your solution. If the solution fixed the problem, document the solution. If the solution did not fix the problem, continue troubleshooting.

Task 7: Clean Up

Unless directed otherwise by the instructor, restore the host computer network connectivity, and then turn off power to the host computers. Remove anything that was brought into the lab, and leave the room ready for the next class.

Lab 11-5: Network Testing (11.5.4.1)

Upon completion of this lab, you will be able to

- Design the logical lab topology.
- Configure the physical lab topology.
- Configure the logical LAN topology.
- Verify LAN connectivity.

Background

Figure 11-18 shows the topology for this lab.

Figure 11-18 Topology for Lab 11-5

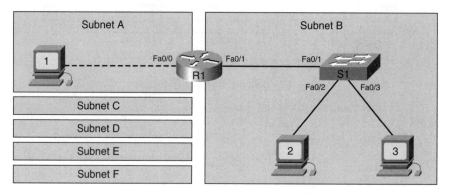

Gather the necessary equipment and cables. Table 11-19 lists the equipment and hardware requirements for this lab.

Table 11-19   Lab Equipment and Hardware Requirements

Hardware	Quantity	Description
Cisco router	1	Part of the CCNA Lab bundle
Cisco switch	1	Part of the CCNA Lab bundle
Computer (host)	3	Lab computer
Category 5 or better straight-through UTP cables	3	Connects Router1, Host2, and Host3 to Switch1
Category 5 crossover UTP cable	1	Connects Host1 to Router1
Console (rollover) cable	1	Connects Host1 to the Router1 console

Scenario

In this lab, you will create a small network that requires connecting network devices and configuring host computers for basic network connectivity. Subnet A and Subnet B are subnets that are currently needed. Subnet C, Subnet D, Subnet E, and Subnet F are anticipated subnets, not yet connected to the network. The 0th subnet will be used.

Task 1: Design the Logical Lab Topology

Given an IP address and mask of 172.20.0.0/24 (address/mask), design an IP addressing scheme that satisfies the requirements listed in Table 11-20.

Table 11-20   Addressing Requirements

Subnet	Number of Hosts
Subnet A	As shown in the topology diagram
Subnet B	Between 80 and 100
Subnet C	Between 40 and 52
Subnet D	Between 20 and 29
Subnet E	12
Subnet F	5

Note: Always start with the subnet that has the largest number of hosts, and work your way down. Therefore, you should start with Subnet B and finish with Subnet A.

Step 1.   Design the Subnet B address block.

Begin the logical network design by satisfying the requirements of Subnet B, which requires the largest block of IP addresses. Using binary numbers to create your subnet chart, pick the first address block that will support Subnet B.

Fill in Table 11-21 with the IP address information for Subnet B.

Table 11-21   Subnet B IP Address Information

Network Address	Mask	First Host Address	Last Host Address	Broadcast

Step 2.   Design the Subnet C address block.

Satisfy the requirements of Subnet C, the next-largest IP address block. Using binary numbers to create your subnet chart, pick the next available address block that will support Subnet C.

Fill in Table 11-22 with the IP address information for Subnet C.

Table 11-22   Subnet C IP Address Information

Network Address	Mask	First Host	Last Host	Broadcast

What is the bit mask?

Step 3.   Design the Subnet D address block.

Satisfy the requirements of Subnet D, the next-largest IP address block. Using binary numbers to create your subnet chart, pick the next available address block that will support Subnet D.

Fill in Table 11-23 with the Subnet D IP address information.

Table 11-23   Subnet D IP Address Information

Network Address	Mask	First Host Address	Last Host Address	Broadcast

What is the bit mask?

Step 4.   Design the Subnet E address block.

Satisfy the requirements of Subnet E, the next-largest IP address block. Using binary numbers to create your subnet chart, pick the next available address block that will support Subnet E.

Fill in Table 11-24 with the Subnet E IP address information.

Table 11-24   Subnet E IP Address Information

Network Address	Mask	First Host Address	Last Host Address	Broadcast

What is the bit mask?

Step 5.   Design the Subnet F address block.

Satisfy the requirements of Subnet F, the next-largest IP address block. Using binary numbers to create your subnet chart, pick the next available address block that will support Subnet F.

Fill in Table 11-25 with the Subnet F IP address information.

Table 11-25   Subnet F IP Address Information

Network Address	Mask	First Host Address	Last Host Address	Broadcast

What is the bit mask?

Step 6.   Design the Subnet A address block.

Satisfy the requirements of Subnet A, the smallest IP address block. Using binary numbers to create your subnet chart, pick the next available address block that will support Subnet A.

Fill in Table 11-26 with the Subnet A IP addressing table.

Table 11-26   Subnet A IP Addressing Table

Network Address	Mask	First Host Address	Last Host Address	Broadcast

What is the bit mask?

Task 2: Configure the Physical Lab Topology

Step 1.   Physically connect the lab devices.

Cable the network devices as shown earlier, in Figure 11-18. Pay special attention to the crossover cable required between Host1 and Router1.

If it's not already enabled, turn on power to all devices.

Step 2.   Visually inspect the network connections.

After cabling the network devices, take a moment to verify the connections. Attention to detail now will minimize the time required to troubleshoot Layer 1 connectivity issues later.

Task 3: Configure the Logical Topology

Step 1.   Document logical network settings.

On Subnet A, Host1 uses the first IP address in the subnet. Router1, interface Fa0/0, uses the last host address. On Subnet B, host computers use the first and second IP addresses in the subnet, respectively. Router1, interface Fa0/1, uses the last network host address.

To properly route Layer 2 frames between LAN devices, Switch1 does not require Layer 3 configuration. The IP address assigned to Switch1, interface VLAN 1, is used to establish Layer 3 connectivity between external devices and the switch. Without an IP address, upper-layer protocols such as Telnet and HTTP will not work. The default gateway address permits the switch to respond to protocol requests from devices on distant networks. For example, the IP gateway address extends Layer 3 connectivity beyond Subnet B. Switch1 uses the next-to-last host address.

Write down the IP address information for each device listed in Table 11-27.

Table 11-27   IP Address Information

Device	Subnet	IP Address	Mask	Gateway
Host1				
Router1-Fa0/0				
Host2				
Host3				
Switch1				
Router1-Fa0/1				

Step 2.   Configure host computers.

On each computer, in turn, choose **Start > Control Panel > Network Connections**. Right-click the **LAN** icon, and choose **Properties**. On the **General** tab, choose **Internet Protocol (TCP/IP)**, and then click the **Properties** button.

Verify that the Host1 Layer 3 IP address is on a different subnet than Host2 and Host3. Configure each host computer using the IP address information recorded in Step 1.

Verify proper configuration of each host computer with the **ipconfig** command, and fill in Table 11-28.

Table 11-28   Host Configuration

Device	IP Address	Mask	Default Gateway
Host1			
Host2			
Host3			

Step 3.   Configure Router1.

From the Windows taskbar, start the HyperTerminal program by choosing **Start > Programs > Accessories > Communications > HyperTerminal**. Configure HyperTerminal for access to Router1. Configuration for Router1 includes the following tasks:

- Specify the router name: Router1
- Specify an encrypted privileged EXEC password: cisco
- Specify a console access password: class
- Specify a Telnet access password: class
- Configure the MOTD banner.

- Configure Router1 interface Fa0/0:

  - Set the description.

  - Set the Layer 3 address.

  - Issue the **no shutdown** command.

- Configure Router1 interface Fa0/1:

  - Set the description.

  - Set the Layer 3 address.

  - Issue the **no shutdown** command.

Save the configuration in NVRAM.

What command do you use to display the contents of RAM? _____

Record the configuration specifications:

- Hostname: _____

- Enable secret password: _____

- Console access password: _____

- Telnet access password: _____

- MOTD banner: _____

What command do you use to display configuration information for interface Fa0/0?
_____

Record the configuration specifications:

- FastEthernet 0/0 status (up/down): _____

- Line protocol: _____

- MAC address: _____

What command do you use to display configuration information for interface Fa0/1?
_____

Record the configuration specifications:

- FastEthernet 0/0 status (up/down): _____

- Line protocol: _____

- MAC address: _____

What command do you use to display brief IP address information about each interface?
_____

Record the configuration specifications:

Interface	IP-Address	OK? Method Status	Protocol
FastEthernet0/0	_____	_____	_____
FastEthernet0/1	_____	_____	_____

Take corrective action with any problems, and retest.

Step 4.   Configure Switch1.

Move the console cable from Router1 to Switch1.

Press **Enter** until you receive a response.

Configuration for Switch1 includes the following:

- Specify a switch name: Switch1

- Specify an encrypted privileged EXEC password: cisco

- Specify a console access password: class

- Specify a Telnet access password: class

- Configure the MOTD banner.

- Configure Switch1 interface Fa0/1:

    - Set the description.

- Configure Switch1 interface Fa0/2:

    - Set the description.

- Configure Switch1 interface Fa0/3:

    - Set the description.

- Configure the management VLAN1 IP address:

    - Set the description.

    - Set the Layer 3 address.

    - Issue the **no shutdown** command.

- Configure the default IP gateway address.

What command do you use to display the contents of RAM? _____

Write the configuration specifications:

- Hostname: _____

- Enable secret password: _____

- Console access password: _____

- Telnet access password: _____

- MOTD banner: _____

- Interface VLAN 1: _____

- Default IP gateway address: _____

What command do you use to display configuration information for interface VLAN 1?

_____

- VLAN 1 status (up/down): _____

- Line protocol: _____

Task 4: Verify Network Connectivity

Step 1.   Use the **ping** command to verify network connectivity.

You can verify network connectivity using the **ping** command. It is very important that connectivity exist throughout the network. Corrective action must be taken if a failure occurs.

Use Table 11-29 to methodically verify connectivity with each network device.

Table 11-29   Connectivity Testing

From	To	IP Address	Ping Result
Host1	LocalHost (127.0.0.1)		
Host1	NIC IP address		
Host1	Gateway (Router1, Fa0/0)		
Host1	Router1, Fa0/1		
Host1	Switch1		
Host1	Host2		
Host1	Host3		
Host2	LocalHost (127.0.0.1)		
Host2	NIC IP address		
Host2	Host3		
Host2	Switch1		
Host2	Gateway (Router1, Fa0/1)		
Host2	Router1, Fa0/0		
Host2	Host1		
Host3	LocalHost (127.0.0.1)		
Host3	NIC IP address		
Host3	Host2		
Host3	Switch1		
Host3	Gateway (Router1, Fa0/1)		
Host3	Router1, Fa0/0		

Take corrective action to establish connectivity if a test fails.

Note: If pings to host computers fail, temporarily disable the computer firewall, and retest. To disable a Windows firewall, choose **Start > Control Panel > Windows Firewall**, click **Off**, and then click **OK**.

Step 2. Use the **tracert** command to verify local connectivity.

From Host1, issue the **tracert** command to Host2 and Host3.

Record the results:

- From Host1 to Host2: _____

- From Host1 to Host3: _____

Step 3. Verify Layer 2 connectivity.

If it's not already connected, move the console cable from Router1 to Switch1.

Press the **Enter** key until Switch1 responds.

Issue the command **show mac-address-table**. This command displays static (CPU) and dynamic, or learned, entries.

List the dynamic MAC addresses and their corresponding switch ports in Table 11-30.

Table 11-30   MAC Address Table

MAC Address	Switch Port

Verify that there are three dynamically learned MAC addresses—one each from Fa0/1, Fa0/2, and Fa0/3.

Task 5: Reflection

Review any physical or logical configuration problems encountered during this lab. Make sure you have a thorough understanding of the procedures used to verify network connectivity.

Task 6: Challenge

Ask your instructor or another student to introduce one or two problems in your network when you aren't looking or are out of the lab room. Problems can be either physical (the wrong UTP cable) or logical (the wrong IP address or gateway). To fix the problems, perform a good visual inspection. Look for green link lights on Switch1.

Use Table 11-18 to identify failed connectivity. List the problems.

_____

Write down your proposed solution(s).

_____

Test your solution. If the solution fixed the problem, document the solution. If the solution did not fix the problem, continue troubleshooting.

Task 7: Clean Up

Unless directed otherwise by the instructor, restore host computer network connectivity, and then turn off power to the host computers.

Before turning off power to the router and switch, remove the NVRAM configuration file from each device with the privileged EXEC command **erase startup-config**.

Carefully remove the cables, and return them neatly to their storage. Reconnect cables that were disconnected for this lab.

Remove anything that was brought into the lab, and leave the room ready for the next class.

Lab 11-6: Network Documentation with Utility Commands (11.5.5.1)

Upon completion of this lab, you will be able to

- Design the logical lab topology.

- Configure the physical lab topology.

- Design and configure the logical LAN topology.

- Verify LAN connectivity.

- Document the network.

Background

Figure 11-19 shows the topology for this lab.

Figure 11-19 Topology for Lab 11-6

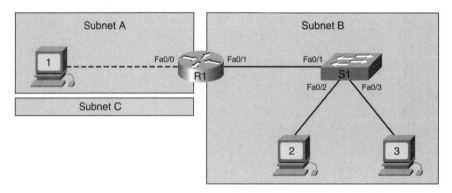

Gather the necessary equipment and cables. Table 11-31 lists the equipment and hardware requirements for this lab.

Table 11-31   Equipment and Hardware Requirements

Hardware	Quantity	Description
Cisco router	1	Part of the CCNA Lab bundle
Cisco switch	1	Part of the CCNA Lab bundle
Computer (host)	3	Lab computer
Category 5 or better straight-through UTP cables	3	Connects Router1, Host1, and Host2 to Switch1
Category 5 crossover UTP cable	1	Connects Host1 to Router1
Console (rollover) cable	1	Connects Host1 to the Router1 console

In this lab, router and host output will be copied from the devices and into Notepad for use in network documentation.

Scenario

Network documentation is a very important tool for the organization. A well-documented network enables network engineers to save significant time in troubleshooting and planning future growth.

In this lab you will create a small network that requires connecting network devices and configuring host computers for basic network connectivity. Subnet A and Subnet B are subnets that are currently needed. Subnet C is an anticipated subnet, not yet connected to the network. The 0th subnet will be used.

Task 1: Design the Logical Lab Topology

Given an IP address of 209.165.200.224/27 (address/mask), design an IP addressing scheme that satisfies the requirements listed in Table 11-32.

Table 11-32   IP Addressing Requirements

Subnet	Number of Hosts
Subnet A	2
Subnet B	Between 2 and 6
Subnet C	Between 10 and 12

Step 1.   Design the Subnet C address block.

Begin the logical network design by satisfying the requirements of Subnet C, the largest IP address block. Using binary numbers to create your subnet chart, pick the next available address block that will support Subnet C.

Fill in Table 11-33 with the IP address information for Subnet C.

Table 11-33   Subnet C IP Address Information

Network Address	Mask	First Host Address	Last Host Address	Broadcast

What is the bit mask?

Step 2.   Design the Subnet B address block.

Satisfy the requirements of Subnet B, the next-largest block of IP addresses. Using binary numbers to create your subnet chart, pick the first address block that will support Subnet B.

Fill in Table 11-34 with the IP address information for Subnet B.

Table 11-34   Subnet B IP Address Information

Network Address	Mask	First Host Address	Last Host Address	Broadcast

What is the bit mask?

Step 3.   Design the Subnet A address block.

Satisfy the requirements of Subnet A, the smallest IP address block. Using binary numbers to create your subnet chart, pick the next available address block that will support Subnet A.

Fill in Table 11-35 with the IP address information for Subnet A.

Table 11-35   Subnet A IP Address Information

Network Address	Mask	First Host Address	Last Host Address	Broadcast

What is the bit mask?

Task 2: Configure the Physical Lab Topology

Step 1.   Physically connect lab devices.

Cable the network devices as shown in Figure 11-19. Pay special attention to the crossover cable required between Host1 and Router1.

If it's not already enabled, turn on power to all devices.

Step 2.   Visually inspect the network connections.

After cabling the network devices, take a moment to verify the connections. Attention to detail now will minimize the time required to troubleshoot network connectivity issues later.

Task 3: Configure the Logical Topology

Step 1.   Document the logical network settings.

Host computers use the first two IP addresses in the subnetwork. The network router uses the last network host address. Write down the IP address information for each device in Table 11-36.

Table 11-36   IP Address Information

Device	Subnet	IP Address	Mask	Gateway
Router1 -FA0/0				—
Host1				
Router1 -FA0/1				—
Host2				
Host2				
Switch	—	—	—	—

Step 2. Configure the host computers.

On each computer in turn, choose **Start > Control Panel > Network Connections**. Highlight the Local Area Connection device icon, right-click, and choose **Properties**. Highlight **Internet Protocol (TCP/IP)**, and choose **Properties**.

Verify that the Host1 Layer 3 IP address is on a different subnetwork than Host2 and Host3. Configure each host computer using the IP address information recorded in Step 1.

Verify proper configuration of each host computer using the **ipconfig /all** command. Record your information in a separate document, and name it Documentation_Lab11-6.

Step 3. Configure Router1.

From the Windows taskbar, start the HyperTerminal program by choosing **Start > Programs > Accessories > Communications > HyperTerminal**. Configure HyperTerminal for access to Router1. These are the configuration tasks for Router1:

- Specify the router name: Router1

- Specify an encrypted privileged EXEC password: cisco

- Specify a console access password: class

- Specify a Telnet access password: class

- Configure the MOTD banner.

- Configure Router1 interface Fa0/0:

  - Set the description.

  - Set the Layer 3 address.

  - Issue the **no shutdown** command.

- Configure Router1 interface Fa0/1:

  - Set the description.

  - Set the Layer 3 address.

  - Issue the **no shutdown** command.

Specify the command you use to save the configuration in NVRAM: _____

Specify the command you use to display the contents of RAM: _____

Save the output of the configuration to your document named Documentation_Lab11-6.

Copy the output of the **show interface fa0/0** and **show interface fa0/1** commands into your document named Documentation_Lab11-6.

Copy the output of the **show ip interface brief** command to your document named Documentation_Lab11-6.

Step 4.   Configure Switch1.

Move the console cable from Router1 to Switch1. Press **Enter** until you receive a response. Configuration tasks for Switch1 are as follows:

- Specify the switch name: Switch1

- Specify an encrypted privileged EXEC password: cisco

- Specify a console access password: class

- Specify a Telnet access password: class

- Configure the MOTD banner.

- Configure Switch1 interface Fa0/1:

  - Set the description.

- Configure Switch1 interface Fa0/2:

  - Set the description.

- Configure Switch1 interface Fa0/3:

  - Set the description.

Specify the command you use to display the contents of RAM: _____

Copy the output of the configuration to your document named Documentation_Lab11-6.

Copy the output of the **show mac address-table** command to your document named Documentation_Lab11-6.

Task 4: Verify Network Connectivity

Step 1.   Use the **ping** command to verify network connectivity.

Network connectivity can be verified with the **ping** command. It is very important that connectivity exist throughout the network. Corrective action must be taken if a failure occurs.

Note: If pings to host computers fail, temporarily disable the computer firewall, and retest. To disable a Windows firewall, choose **Start > Control Panel > Windows Firewall**, click **OFF**, and click **OK**.

Use Table 11-37 to methodically verify connectivity with each network device. Take corrective action to establish connectivity if a test fails.

Table 11-37   Connectivity Testing

From	To	IP Address	Ping Result
Host1	LocalHost (127.0.0.1)		
Host1	NIC IP Address		
Host1	Gateway (Router1, Fa0/0		
Host1	Router1, Fa0/1		
Host1	Host2		
Host1	Host3		
Host2	LocalHost (127.0.0.1)		
Host2	NIC IP Address		
Host2	Host3		
Host2	Gateway (Router1, Fa0/1)		
Host2	Router1, Fa0/0		
Host2	Host1		
Host3	LocalHost (127.0.0.1)		
Host3	NIC IP address		
Host3	Host2		
Host3	Gateway (Router1, Fa0/1)		
Host3	Router1, Fa0/0		
Host3	Host1		

Step 2.   Use the **tracert** command to verify local connectivity.

In addition to connectivity testing, the **tracert** command may be used as a crude throughput tester for network baselining. That is, with minimal traffic, **tracert** results can be compared against periods of high traffic. Results can be used to justify equipment upgrades or new purchases.

From Host1, issue the **tracert** command to Router1, Host2, and Host3. Record the results in your document named Documentation_Lab11-6.

From Host2, issue the **tracert** command to Host3, Router1, and Host1. Record the results in your document named Documentation_Lab11-6.

From Host3, issue the **tracert** command to Host2, Router1, and Host1. Record the results in your document named Documentation_Lab11-6.

Task 5: Document the Network

With all the work performed so far, it would seem that there is nothing left to do. The network was physically and logically configured and verified, and command output was copied into tables.

The last step in network documentation is to organize your output. As you organize, think about what might be needed six months or a year from now. For example, answer the following questions in the documentation, perhaps in a cover letter:

- When was the network created?

- When was the network documented?

- Were any significant challenges overcome?

- Who performed the configuration? (Talent like this needs to be tracked.)

- Who wrote the documentation? (Talent like this needs to be tracked.)

Be sure to include the following information:

- A copy of the physical topology

- A copy of the logical topology

Prepare your documentation in a professional format, and submit it to your instructor.

Task 6: Reflection

Review any physical or logical configuration problems you encountered during this lab. Ensure that you understand the procedures used to verify network connectivity.

Task 7: Challenge

Ask your instructor or another student to introduce one or two problems in your network when you aren't looking or are out of the lab room. Problems can be either physical (cables moved on the switch) or logical (the wrong IP address or gateway).

Use your network documentation to troubleshoot and remedy the problems. Perform a good visual inspection. Look for green link lights on Switch1.

Use your network documentation to make sure your configurations are correct:

_____

_____

_____

_____

Write down your proposed solution(s):

_____

_____

_____

Test your solution. If the solution fixed the problem, document the solution. If the solution did not fix the problem, continue troubleshooting.

_____

_____

_____

_____

Task 8: Clean Up

Unless directed otherwise by the instructor, restore host computer network connectivity, then turn off power to the host computers.

Before turning off power to the router and switch, remove the NVRAM configuration file from each device using the privileged EXEC command **erase startup-config**.

Carefully remove the cables, and return them neatly to their storage. Reconnect cables that were disconnected for this lab.

Remove anything that was brought into the lab, and leave the room ready for the next class.

Lab 11-7: Case Study: Datagram Analysis with Wireshark (11.5.6.1)

Upon completion of this exercise, you will be able to demonstrate

- How a TCP segment is constructed, and explain the segment fields.

- How an IP packet is constructed, and explain the packet fields.

- How an Ethernet II frame is constructed, and explain the frame fields.

- The contents of an Address Resolution Protocol (ARP) Request and ARP Reply.

Background

This lab requires two captured packet files and Wireshark, a network protocol analyzer. Download the following files from Eagle Server, and install Wireshark on your computer if it is not already installed:

- eagle1_web_client.pcap (discussed)

- eagle1_web_server.pcap (reference only)

- wireshark.exe

Scenario

This exercise details the sequence of datagrams that are created and sent across a network between a web client, PC_Client, and a web server, eagle1.example.com. Understanding the process involved in sequentially placing packets on the network will help you logically troubleshoot network failures when connectivity breaks. For brevity and clarity, network packet noise has been omitted from the captures. Before executing a network protocol analyzer on a network that belongs to someone else, be sure to get permission in writing.

Figure 11-20 shows the topology for this lab.

Figure 11-20 Topology for Lab 11-7

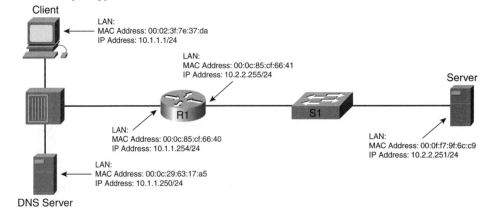

Client

LAN:
MAC Address: 00:02:3f:7e:37:da
IP Address: 10.1.1.1/24

LAN:
MAC Address: 00:0c:85:cf:66:41
IP Address: 10.2.2.255/24

Server

LAN:
MAC Address: 00:0c:85:cf:66:40
IP Address: 10.1.1.254/24

R1

S1

LAN:
MAC Address: 00:0f:f7:9f:6c:c9
IP Address: 10.2.2.251/24

LAN:
MAC Address: 00:0c:29:63:17:a5
IP Address: 10.1.1.250/24

DNS Server

Using Microsoft command-line tools, you can display IP configuration information and the contents of the ARP cache. Refer to Example 11-20.

Example 11-20 PC Client Initial Network State

```
C: > ipconfig / all
Windows IP Configuration
Ethernet adapter Local Area Connection:
     Connection-specific DNS Suffix  . :
     Description . . . . . . . . . . : Intel(R) PRO/1000 MT
Network Connection
     Physical Address. . . . . . . . : 00:02:3f:7e:37:da
     Dhcp Enabled. . . . . . . . . . : No
     IP Address. . . . . . . . . . . : 10.1.1.1
     Subnet Mask . . . . . . . . . . : 255.255.255.0
     Default Gateway . . . . . . . . : 10.1.1.254
     DNS Servers . . . . . . . . . . : 10.1.1.250
C: > arp -a
No ARP Entries Found
C: >
```

A web client is started, and the URL eagle1.example.com is entered, as shown in Figure 11-21. This begins the communication process to the web server, and it's where the captured packets start.

Figure 11-21 PC Client with Web Browser

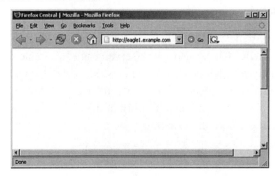

Task 1: Prepare the Lab

Step 1.   Start Wireshark on your computer.

Refer to Figure 11-22 for changes to the default output. Uncheck Main Toolbar, Filter Toolbar, and Packet Bytes. Verify that Packet List and Packet Details are checked. To ensure that there is no automatic translation in MAC addresses, uncheck Name Resolution for MAC Layer and Transport Layer.

Figure 11-22 Wireshark Default View Changes

Step 2.   Load the web client capture, eagle1_web_client.pcap.

A screen similar to Figure 11-23 appears. Various pull-down menus and submenus are available. There are also two separate data windows. The top Wireshark window lists all captured packets. The bottom window contains packet details. In the bottom window, each line that contains a plus sign next to it indicates that additional information is available.

Figure 11-23 Wireshark with eagle1_web_client.pcap

Task 2: Review the Process of Data Flowing Through the Network

Step 1.   Review transport layer operation.

When PC_Client builds the datagram for a connection with eagle1.example.com, the datagram travels down the various network layers. At each layer, important header information is added. Because this communication is from a web client, the transport layer protocol is

TCP. Consider the TCP segment shown in Figure 11-24. PC_Client generates an internal TCP port address—in this conversation, 1085—and knows the well-known web server port address, 80. Likewise, a sequence number has been internally generated. Data is included, provided by the application layer. Some information is unknown to PC_Client, so it must be discovered using other network protocols.

Figure 11-24 TCP Segment Field

TCP Segment

0	4	7	10		16		31
Source Port					Destination Port		
Sequence Number							
Acknowledgment Number							
Data Offset	Reserved	ECN	Control Bits		Window		
Checksum					Urgent Pointer		
Options and Padding							
Data							

There is no acknowledgment number. Before this segment can move to the network layer, the TCP three-way handshake must be performed.

Step 2.   Review network layer operation.

At the network layer, the IPv4 (IP) packet has several fields ready with information, as shown in Figure 11-25. For example, the packet version (IPv4) is known, as well as the source IP address.

Figure 11-25 IP Packet Fields

IP Packet

0	4	8	10	16		31
Version	IHL	TOS		Total Length		
Identification				Flags	Fragment Offset	
TTL		Protocol		Header Checksum		
Source IP Address						
Destination IP Address						
Data						

The destination for this packet is eagle1.example.com. The corresponding IP address must be discovered through Domain Name System (DNS). Until the upper-layer datagram is received, fields related to the upper-layer protocols are empty.

Step 3.   Review data link layer operation.

Before the datagram is placed on the physical medium, it must be encapsulated inside a frame, as shown in Figure 11-26. PC_Client knows the source MAC address, but it must discover the destination MAC address.

Figure 11-26 Ethernet II Frame Fields

Ethernet II Frame Format

Preamble	Destination Address	Source Address	Frame Type	Data	CRC
8 Octets	6 Octets	6 Octets	2 Octets	46–1500 Octets	4 Octets

Task 3: Analyze Captured Packets

Step 1.   Review the data flow sequence.

A review of missing information will be helpful in following the captured packet sequence:

- The TCP segment cannot be constructed because the acknowledgment field is blank. A TCP three-way handshake with eagle1.example.com must first be completed.

- The TCP three-way handshake cannot occur, because PC_Client does not know the IP address for eagle1.example.com. This is resolved with a DNS request from PC_Client to the DNS server.

- The DNS server cannot be queried, because the MAC address for the DNS server is unknown. The ARP protocol is broadcast on the LAN to discover the MAC address for the DNS server.

- The MAC address for eagle1.example.com is unknown. The ARP protocol is broadcast on the LAN to learn the destination MAC address for eagle1.example.com.

Step 2.   Examine the ARP request.

Refer to Wireshark's Packet List window, No. 1. The captured frame is an ARP Request. You can view the contents of the Ethernet II frame by clicking the checkbox in the second line of the Packet Details window. You can view the contents of the ARP Request by clicking the ARP Request line in the Packet Details window.

What is the source MAC address for the ARP Request? _____

What is the destination MAC address for the ARP Request? _____

What is the unknown IP address in the ARP Request? _____

What is the Ethernet II frame type? _____

Step 3.   Examine the ARP reply.

Refer to Wireshark's Packet List window, No. 2. The DNS server sent an ARP Reply.

What is the source MAC address for the ARP Reply? _____

What is the destination MAC address for the ARP Request? _____

What is the Ethernet II frame type? _____

What is the destination IP address in the ARP Reply? _____

Based on the observation of the ARP protocol, what can you infer about an ARP Request destination address and an ARP Reply destination address?

_____

_____

Why didn't the DNS server have to send an ARP Request for the PC_Client MAC address?

_____

_____

Step 4.   Examine the DNS query.

Refer to Wireshark's Packet List window, No. 3. PC_Client sent a DNS query to the DNS server. Using the Packet Details window, answer the following questions:

What is the Ethernet II frame type? _____

What is the transport layer protocol, and what is the destination port number?

_____

Step 5.   Examine the DNS query response.

Refer to Wireshark's Packet List window, No. 4. The DNS server sent a DNS query response to PC_Client. Using the Packet Details window, answer the following questions:

What is the Ethernet II frame type? _____

What is the transport layer protocol, and what is the destination port number?

_____

What is the IP address for eagle1.example.com? _____

One of your colleagues, a firewall administrator, asks you if you can think of any reason why all UDP packets should not be blocked from entering the internal network. What is your response?

_____

_____

_____

_____

Step 6.   Examine the ARP Request.

Refer to Wireshark's Packet List window, No. 5 and No. 6. PC_Client sent an ARP Request to IP address 10.1.1.254.

Is this IP address different from the IP address for eagle1.example.com? Explain.

_____

_____

Step 7.   Examine the TCP three-way handshake.

Refer to Wireshark's Packet List window, No. 7, 8, and 9. These captures contain the TCP three-way handshake between PC_Client and eagle1.example.com. Initially, only the TCP

SYN flag is set on the datagram sent from PC_Client, sequence number 0. eagle1.example.com responds with the TCP ACK and SYN flags set, along with an acknowledgment of 1 and a sequence of 0. In the Packet List window is an unexplained value, MSS=1460. MSS stands for maximum segment size. When a TCP segment is transported over IPv4, MSS is computed to be the maximum size of an IPv4 datagram minus 40 bytes. This value is sent during connection startup. This is also when TCP sliding windows are negotiated.

If the initial TCP sequence value from PC_Client is 0, why did eagle1.example respond with an acknowledgment of 1?

_____

_____

In eagle1.example.com, No. 8, what does the IP flag value of 0x04 mean?

_____

_____

_____

_____

When PC_Client completes the TCP three-way handshake, Wireshark's Packet List, No. 9, what TCP flag states are returned to eagle1.example.com?

Table 11-38 shows the TCP flag states.

Table 11-38   TCP Flag States

	Bit Position	Flag
1	0.	Congestion Window Reduced
2	.0.	ECN Echo
3	. .0. . . .	Urgent
4	. . .1. . .	ACK
5	. . . .0. .	PSH
6	. . . . .0.	SYN
7	0	FIN

Task 4: Complete the Final Analysis

Step 1.   Match the Wireshark output to the process.

It has taken a total of nine datagrams sent between PC_Client, DNS server, Gateway, and eagle1.example.com before PC_Client has sufficient information to send the original web client request to eagle1.example.com. This is shown in Wireshark's Packet List, No. 10, where PC_Client sent a web protocol GET request.

Fill in the correct Wireshark Packet List window number that satisfies each of the following missing entries:

- The TCP segment cannot be constructed because the acknowledgment field is blank. A TCP three-way handshake with eagle1.example.com must first be completed. _____

- The TCP three-way handshake cannot occur because PC_Client does not know the IP address for eagle1.example.com. This is resolved with a DNS request from PC_Client to the DNS server. _____

- The DNS server cannot be queried because the MAC address for the DNS server is unknown. The ARP protocol is broadcast on the LAN to discover the MAC address for the DNS server. _____

- The MAC address for the gateway to reach eagle1.example.com is unknown. The ARP protocol is broadcast on the LAN to learn the destination MAC address for the gateway. _____

Wireshark Packet List No. 11 is an acknowledgment from eagle1.example.com to the PC_Client GET request, Wireshark Packet List No. 10.

Wireshark Packet List No. 12, 13, and 15 are TCP segments from eagle1.example.com. Wireshark Packet List No. 14 and 16 are ACK datagrams from PC_Client.

To verify the ACK, highlight Wireshark Packet List No. 14. Next, scroll down to the bottom of the Detail List window, and expand the [SEQ/ACK analysis] frame. The ACK datagram for Wireshark Packet List No. 14 is a response to which datagram from eagle1.example.com? _____

The Wireshark Packet List No. 17 datagram is sent from PC_Client to eagle1.example.com. Review the information in the [SEQ/ACK analysis] frame. What is the purpose of this datagram? _____

_____

When PC_Client is finished, TCP ACK and FIN flags are sent, as shown in Wireshark Packet List No. 18. eagle1.example.com responds with a TCP ACK, and the TCP session is closed.

Step 2.   Use the Wireshark TCP stream.

Analyzing packet contents can be a daunting experience—time-consuming and error-prone. Wireshark includes an option that constructs the TCP stream in a separate window. To use this feature, first select a TCP datagram from the Wireshark Packet List. Next, from Wireshark, choose **Analyze > Follow TCP Stream**. A window similar to the one shown in Figure 11-27 appears.

Figure 11-27 Output of TCP Stream

Task 5: Conclusion

Using a network protocol analyzer can be an effective learning tool for understanding critical elements of network communication. As soon as the network administrator is familiar with communication protocols, the same protocol analyzer can become an effective troubleshooting tool when the network fails. For example, if a web browser could not connect to a web server, there could be multiple causes. A protocol analyzer shows unsuccessful ARP requests, unsuccessful DNS queries, and unacknowledged packets.

Task 6: Summary

In this exercise you have learned how a web client and web server communicate. Behind-the-scenes protocols such as DNS and ARP are used to fill in missing parts of IP packets and Ethernet frames, respectively. Before a TCP session can begin, the TCP three-way handshake must build a reliable path and supply both communicating ends with initial TCP header information. Finally, the TCP session is destroyed in an orderly manner, with the client issuing a TCP FIN flag.

Skills Integration Challenge: Configuring and Analyzing Networks (11.6.1.3)

Open file LSG01-PTSkills11.pka on the CD-ROM that accompanies this book to perform this exercise using Packet Tracer.

Upon completion of this activity, you will be able to

- Build, test, and configure the entire lab network.

- Integrate skills from throughout the course.

- Analyze the events involved in

    - Requesting a web page (DNS, ARP, HTTP, TCP, IP, Ethernet, HDLC)

    - Tracing the route to the web server (DNS, UDP, ARP, ICMP, IP, Ethernet, HDLC)

Background

Throughout this course, you have been developing network planning, building, configuring, and testing skills. You have also developed a conceptual understanding of networking protocols and device algorithms. Here is an opportunity to test yourself. See if you can complete this entire challenge (approximately 100 configurable components, although some are quite easy) in less than 30 minutes.

Figure 11-28 shows the topology for this lab.

Figure 11-28 Skills Integration Lab Topology

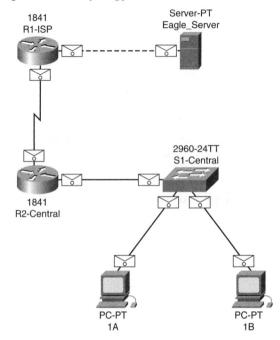

Task 1: Plan

Use the standard Exploration lab topology as you plan your IP addressing scheme:

- Two 1841 routers with WIC-2T interface cards, installed in the slot on the right—one named R1-ISP, which has a serial DCE WAN connection to R2-Central and an Fa0/0 LAN connection to Eagle_Server, and one named R2-Central, which has a serial DCE WAN connection to R1-ISP and an Fa0/0 LAN connection to S1-Central

- One 2960TT switch (S1-Central)

- Two PCs named 1A and 1B

- A server named Eagle_Server

Note that both the display names *and* hostnames for all devices must be configured exactly. In general, all strings (names, passwords, banners) should be entered exactly as specified in these instructions for the grading to work properly.

You have been given an IP address block of 192.168.3.0 /24. You must provide for existing networks as well as future growth.

Subnet assignments:

- First subnet, existing student LAN, up to 28 hosts (Fa0/0 on R2-Central, connected to Fa0/24 on S1-Central)

- Second subnet, future student LAN, up to 28 hosts (not yet implemented)

- Third subnet, existing ISP LAN, up to 14 hosts (Fa0/0 on R1-ISP)

- Fourth subnet, future ISP LAN, up to seven hosts (not yet implemented)

- Fifth subnet, existing WAN, point-to-point link (S0/0/0 on R1-ISP and S0/0/0 on R2-Central)

IP address assignments:

- For the server, configure the second-highest usable IP address on the ISP LAN subnet.

- For R1-ISP's Fa0/0 interface, configure the highest usable IP address on the ISP LAN subnet.

- For R1-ISP's S0/0/0 interface, configure the highest usable address on the existing WAN subnet.

- For R2-Central's S0/0/0 interface, use the lowest usable address on the existing WAN subnet.

- For R2-Central's Fa0/0 interface, use the highest usable address on the existing student LAN subnet, and connect it to the Fa0/24 interface on S1-Central.

- For hosts 1A and 1B, use the first two IP addresses (the two lowest usable addresses) on the existing student LAN subnet, and connect them to the Fa0/1 and Fa0/2 interfaces on S1-Central.

- For the switch management interface, use the second-highest usable address on the student subnet.

Use Table 11-39 to record your address information.

Table 11-39   Addressing Table

Device	Interface	IP Address	Subnet Mask	Default Gateway
R1-ISP	Fa0/0			—
	S0/0/0			—
R2-Central	Fa0/0			
	S0/0/0			
PC-1A	NIC			
PC-1B	NIC			
Eagle-Server	NIC			

Task 2: Build and Configure the Network

Build the network, taking care to make connections as specified. Configure both routers, the switch, the server, and the two PCs.

Configure the routers using the CLI to practice your skills. The router configuration must include "housekeeping" (display name, hostname, passwords, banner), interfaces (FastEthernet and serial), and routing (static route on R1-ISP, default route on R2-Central). The following login passwords should all be set to **cisco**: enable, console, and Telnet. The banners should say **This is lab router R1-ISP. Authorized access only.** and **This is lab router R2-Central. Authorized access only.**

The interfaces should be configured as specified in Table 11-39; use a clock rate of 64000 on the R1-ISP S0/0/0 interface. The static route on R1-ISP should point to the existing Student LAN subnet via R2-Central's serial interface IP address. The static route on R2-Central should be a default static route that points via R1-ISP's serial interface IP address. Whenever you configure a Cisco IOS device, be sure to save your configuration.

Hint: To configure static routes, use **ip route** global configuration mode. You can use the CLI help function to determine the command syntax.

On the switch, configure the display name, hostname, banner (**This is lab switch S1-Central. Authorized access only.**), login passwords for access (enable, console, and Telnet passwords all set to **cisco**), and management interface (int vlan1). Whenever you configure a Cisco IOS device, be sure to save your configuration.

For Hosts 1A and 1B, in addition to IP configuration, configure them to use DNS services. For the server, enable DNS services, use the domain name eagle-server.example.com, and enable HTTP services.

As you work, use "Check Results" to see what components still need to be configured. If you want more practice, use "Reset Activity" and retime yourself doing the entire configuration again.

Task 3: Test and Analyze

It is good practice to test connectivity through ping and Telnet, and to examine routing tables. As soon as you are convinced that your network is working, make sure you have saved your configurations on the Cisco IOS devices. Then power-cycle the devices and reset the network. In simulation mode, request a web page while making the following protocols visible in the event list: DNS, HTTP, Telnet, TCP, UDP, ICMP, ARP. Examine the packets as they are processed by the devices to study protocol behavior, especially how IP is involved in everything. Also note the algorithms used by hosts, switches, and routers. Explain the entire process to a peer. Power-cycle the devices to clear the network again and, also in simulation mode, issue a traceroute to the server from one of the PCs. Examine how the trace is built from ICMP echo requests. Again explain the entire process to a peer.

Task 4: Reflection

Relate the processes observed in Task 3 to the TCP/IP Protocol Graph. Your skills at modeling networks in Packet Tracer will serve you well in subsequent courses.

Notes

Notes

Notes

Notes

Notes

Notes

Notes

Notes

Notes

Notes

Notes

Notes